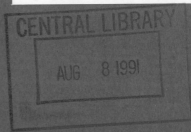

Psychoanalysis and Religion

Psychiatry and the Humanities, Volume 11

Assistant Editor
Gloria H. Parloff

Published under the auspices of the
Forum on Psychiatry and the Humanities,
The Washington School of Psychiatry

Psychoanalysis and Religion

Joseph H. Smith, M.D., *Editor*
Susan A. Handelman, Ph.D.,
Associate Editor

The Johns Hopkins University Press
Baltimore and London

The Johns Hopkins University Press, 701 West 40th Street
Baltimore, Maryland 21211
The Johns Hopkins Press, Ltd., London

The paper used in this publication meets the minimum
requirements of American National Standard for Information Sciences—Permanence of Paper for Printed
Library Materials, ANSI Z39.48–1984.

Library of Congress Cataloging-in-Publication Data

Psychoanalysis and religion / Joseph H. Smith, editor ; Susan A.
Handelman, associate editor.
     p.   cm. — (Psychiatry and the humanities ; v. 11)
  Includes bibliographical references.
  ISBN 0-8018-3895-9 (alk. paper)
  1. Psychoanalysis and religion. 2. Psychotherapy. I. Smith,
Joseph H., 1927– . II. Handelman, Susan A. III. Series.
RC321.P943 vol. 11
[BF175.4.R44]
616.89 s—dc20
[150.19′5]   89-45492
                                    CIP

Contributors

Don Browning
Alexander Campbell Professor of Religion and Psychological Studies,
Divinity School, University of Chicago

José Faur
Professor of Rabbinics, Jewish Theological Seminary of America,
1964–84; Research Professor, Sephardic Heritage Foundation, New
York City; Associate Fellow, Israel and Judaism Seminar, Columbia
University

Susan A. Handelman
Associate Professor of English and Jewish Studies, University of Maryland, College Park

Stanley A. Leavy
Clinical Professor of Psychiatry, Yale University, retired; Training and
Supervising Psychoanalyst, Western New England Institute for Psycho-
analysis, retired

William W. Meissner
Training and Supervising Analyst, Boston Psychoanalytic Institute;
University Professor of Psychoanalysis, Boston College

William J. Richardson
Professor of Philosophy, Boston College; practicing psychoanalyst

Graham M. Schweig
Director, Institute for Vaishnava Studies, American University

Joseph H. Smith
Chairman, Forum on Psychiatry and the Humanities, Washington School of Psychiatry; President, Washington Psychoanalytic Society, 1989–91; Supervising and Training Analyst, Washington Psychoanalytic Institute; Clinical Professor, Uniformed University of the Health Sciences

Robert Sokolowski
Professor of Philosophy, The Catholic University of America

Antoine Vergote
Professor of Philosophy, Catholic University of Louvain, Belgium

Edwin R. Wallace, IV
Professor and Acting Chairman, Department of Psychiatry and Health Behavior, Medical College of Georgia; Professor of Social Work, Graduate School, University of Georgia

Anne Shere Wallwork
Former lawyer; currently working on a novel

Ernest Wallwork
Associate Professor of Religion, Department of Religion, Syracuse University; Bioethicist, National Institutes of Health, Bethesda, Maryland; Candidate, Washington Psychoanalytic Institute

Merold Westphal
Professor, Department of Philosophy, Fordham University

Contents

Introduction

Joseph H. Smith and
Susan A. Handelman

T he idea of addressing the topic of psychoanalysis and religion originally arose in discussions with Hans Loewald. At the time, he hoped both to contribute to the volume and to write a book more thoroughly exploring and extending the thought he has devoted to the subject. He then envisioned a project that would

> be concerned with religious and moral dimensions of psychoanalysis. By *religious* I mean here that realm of human experience which is characterized by a sense of powers—impersonal or personal—underlying and transcending the limited scope of individual and societal life and of the strengths and weaknesses of personal and societal determination and control. These powers may be seen as benevolent, malevolent, or indifferent in regard to human concerns, but they are experiences as superior or all-encompassing and as beyond the full grasp of human understanding. *Morality* is meant here as referring to a self-understanding of man as being responsible, accountable, to himself or to other beings, or to superior powers, for what he is and what he does; it involves a sense of a future to anticipate and to aim at.
>
> Religious and moral dimensions of psychoanalysis . . . [can] be explored in respect to three aspects of that discipline: psychoanalysis as a theory of the human mind and personality, as a body of knowledge of unconscious mental processes, and as an investigative-interpretative and therapeutic procedure. Freud and other analysts have presented psychoanalytic interpretations or explanations of religious and moral phenomena and beliefs in terms of unconscious sources and motivations that account for them. Rather than following that line of study, I . . . [recommend exploration of] those basic and often tacit assumptions of psychoanalysis and of the action of psychoanalytic therapy

which I consider as inherently religious and moral, in the senses out-
lined above. In other words, my dominant theme . . . [would] not be the
psychoanalysis of religion and morality, but the exploration of certain a
priori assumptions that stamp or give life to the psychoanalytic enterprise; not what psychoanalysis contributes to the understanding of religion and morality, but what religion and morality as domains of human
experience may contribute to understanding psychoanalysis. [Loewald,
personal communication]

In his Weigert Lecture, which introduces the volume, Robert Sokolowski engages pertinent passages throughout Loewald's published
work, including particularly those gathered in *Psychoanalysis and the
History of the Individual* (Loewald 1978). The number of other contributors who also rely on Loewald's thought as context for their own
studies in psychoanalysis and religion attests to the widespread respect for Loewald's attunement to the wisdom in each.

In a reading of Loewald that also draws extensively on the principles of Edmund Husserl's phenomenology, Sokolowski joins the
issue of religion and psychoanalysis by asking how the psychoanalyst
can be related to the religious beliefs of his patient. "The interaction,"
he writes, "between therapist and patient is not a mere occasion that
lets the question be raised, something that could be discarded when
the two elements, religion and psychoanalysis, come to the center of
our discussion. The situation in which this problem arises is part of the
phenomenology of the problem and part of a possible resolution."

Of course, for a philosopher to ask how the psychoanalyst can be
related to the religious beliefs of his patient is to assert already that the
philosopher can be related to the interaction of analyst and patient.
Sokolowski structures both of these relations (and others) in terms of
the characteristic of higher-level mentation that permits many persons
to possess the same meaning. No matter how private one's "own appropriation of a meaning may be, the core meaning, the sense, can be
achieved by many." It is this which "permits agreement, but it also permits disagreement and confusion; people may think they are each formulating the same sense when in fact they are not."

Even when the core meaning is the same, there can be several perspectives, each formally different from the other, from which the same
meaning can be possessed. "There can be several formally different
voices that can each state one and the same sense." If the analysand be
taken as $voice_0$, then the "ordinary interlocutor with that person
would count as $voice_1$, which speaks from $perspective_1$. An ordinary
observer of the conversation . . . , a third party who simply watches
and listens, would count as $voice_2$. The analyst is $voice_3$, spoken from

perspective₃. Finally we can distinguish voice and perspective₄; this is . . . the voice and perspective of the philosopher. His stance is to reflect on the voices and perspectives of all the others."

In reflecting upon the interaction between patient and analyst, the philosopher examines the interaction "formally as a process of manifestation; he does not serve as a superior analyst who might give the original analyst tips on improving his technique. The philosophical perspective is to analyze the process of disclosure as such, and to consider the participants formally as agents and datives of manifestation."

We here detail Sokolowski's way of framing the issue not merely as a way of introducing his own article but in order to commend that framework for reading the entire volume. Sokolowski proceeds to a clarification of the various voices and their perspectives and specifically to question what voice the analyst uses when quoting and discussing religious beliefs. The importance of that clarification is foreshadowed in his final introductory paragraph:

> There is nothing to prevent one and the same person from working in more than one of these perspectives; the analyst may become a simple interlocutor for a moment ("Will you be able to take the subway home?"), or he can reflect philosophically on what he is doing as an analyst. But although the same person may speak in different voices, he should be careful not to blend and confuse what he says in one voice with what he says in another. A distorting fusion of horizons would result and perplexing ambiguities would follow; such overlaps provide the soil for category mistakes.

Virtually all the articles gathered here declare, explicitly or implicitly, that unless a thinker can conceive of God as real or, at a minimum, conceive that another can nondefensively conceive of God as real, he or she is significantly barred from understanding religious texts or religious belief. Psychoanalysts, by and large, are to be counted on the positive or negative side of the minimum provision of that declaration. Smith's effort is to affirm the positive response by marshaling reasons for believing that religious belief and practice can be nondefensive.

Stanley Leavy's topic is reality—"Reality in Religion and Psychoanalysis." He defines religion as "the recognition by a community of a real being or of beings transcending sense experience, with whom the members of the community exist in a mutual relationship." He proceeds to formulate a concept of reality that includes religious experience.

Although several other authors refer to or have been influenced by

Lacan, the contributions by William Richardson and Antoine Vergote are explicitly readings of or include commentaries on Lacan's thought. Having been asked to address the theme of "Lacan and Theological Discourse," Richardson forthwith rejects the assignment but, by the end of the article, leaves us bemused as to whether he has sidestepped the topic or, like Lacan, chosen indirectness, diversion, and allusion as means of access to it.

Paul Claudel, one of Lacan's authors of preference, was one of the most self-consciously religious of writers. "I am told," Richardson writes, "the well-known satirical journal, *Le Canard Enchainé,* once ran an editorial that carried the title 'I believe in Paul Claudel' and was signed 'God'." In a disquisition on Claudel's *The Hostage* Richardson moves back and forth between his own and Lacan's reading. In the process he succinctly explicates Lacan's understanding of desire, ethics, and the tragic view of life; illustrates metaphor, metonymy, and the Symbolic, the Imaginary, and the Real; and accounts for the symbolic order in terms of the Law, the Law of the Father, or the Name-of-the-Father. The main focus, though, is on the Real—the unspeakable and unrepresentable. "If God,"Richardson writes, "is to be encountered in the Lacanian paradigm, it is not in terms of the symbolic order. . . . His thought, however, permits us to ask whether the God whom Claudel worships is not to be found in the Real, the dimension of ineffable, unimaginable mystery."

Vergote gives this volume's most explicit critique of the positions of Freud, Jung, and Lacan on psychoanalysis and religion. His thesis is that all three fall short of a proper neutrality in both theory and practice. He believes that psychoanalysis can learn something from religion and also that psychoanalysis can clarify religious insight in a way that has practical value. Fundamental themes—desire, the meaning of the father figure, law, and guilt—characterize both religion and psychoanalysis. Vergote is also the only writer herein to discuss psychoanalytic work with neurotically disordered religious belief such as religious conflicts in megalomania and religious guilt neurosis. His ultimately stated stance on neutrality is that "psychoanalysis as science observes only psychic reality—neither the presence nor the absence of God. In this psychic reality it also recognizes the operable references to a divine reality. Concerning that reality it can only maintain silence, in its theory as well as in its practice."

William Meissner here addresses "The Role of Transitional Conceptualization in Religious Thought." His first two paragraphs describe the religious perspective and psychoanalytic neutrality repeatedly emphasized throughout this volume. The third paragraph surveys the all-too-frequent falling away from neutrality, and the fourth introduces his intention to extend Winnicott's formulations as a conceptual bridge over the "chasm between religious and psychoanalytic thinking."

Although his bridging efforts could be a point of tension with the thought of Leavy, it should be noted that in his appeal to a transitional model, Meissner is not limiting himself literally to Winnicott's transitional objects. He is instead reaching for a process of thinking and conceptualization that can be applied analogously to more evolved aspects of religious thinking. In more general terms, his intention is to "expand the implications of transitional phenomena to embrace more mature and adult forms of creative and cultural expression."

If Meissner's article evokes disagreement it will likely be not so much with his project and solution as with his statement of the problem. He sees Freud as having "set his face against illusion of all kinds." We believe, on the other hand, that what Freud sought to counter were only those illusions that he saw as infantile or defensive. His response to art, his respect for the value of play (as in the Fort! Da! game of *Beyond the Pleasure Principle*), his acknowledgment of relatively conflict-free "specially perfect" moments when id, ego, and superego all work together, his love of humor, the method of free association, and everything he did to establish the importance of primary-process functioning would incline one to think that his response to religion was based on his belief that religion is infantile and defensive and not simply an instance of illusion.

Rather than artistic creation being the "one exception to disparagement of illusion," it seems more likely that religion was the major exception to his respect for illusion. Who, after all, discovered in dreams, symptoms, and psychosis the royal road to the unconscious? Perhaps the mistake was Freud's association of religion with symptoms rather than with capacities for nondefensive regression in the service of a fuller life, which he clearly took artistic creation to be.

Of course, as Sokolowski here reminds us, the departure from Freud toward a more sympathetic psychoanalytic understanding of religion—the intent of Meissner and all other contributors to this volume—still involves a translation into psychoanalytic terms that the believing soul might not recognize as an understanding of his faith. Psychoanalytic inquiry is entitled to study all dimensions of life. However, the product can only be psychoanalytic understanding—understanding in psychoanalytic terms. In Meissner's phrasing, "The psychoanalytic perspective is not at all concerned with the truth or falsity of the belief; it is concerned with the understanding of the meaning of the belief in the context of individual psychic reality and in reference to the individual's sense of personal identity, selfhood, and the ultimate meaning, purpose, and belonging of his existence." This is to say that an ideal psychoanalytic understanding of an analysand's religious belief does not differ from the ideal psychoanalytic understanding of any aspect of the analysand's life.

The point about truth or falsity of belief in Meissner's conclusion is clearly elaborated in the opening pages of Merold Westphal's "Paranoia and Piety: Reflections on the Schreber Case," as is also the issue of objective and subjective truth. With the Schreber case as text, Westphal's purpose is to show how religious ideas can also function in ordinary people as a defense against guilt by legitimizing what would otherwise be immoral. While, with Ricoeur, welcoming psychoanalytic iconoclasm as a method for the destruction of idols, Westphal's task is to show how this destruction is not without remainder. "To show the logical possibility of religion in the service of nonrepressive honesty," Westphal writes, "is a task as easy as it is theoretical. To show the real possibility of such religion (by showing its actuality) is a task as difficult as it is practical."

Don Browning addresses the question of what kind of enterprise a psychoanalytically oriented psychology of religion would be. With the *Confessions* as text for reflecting on St. Augustine's life, he first reviews a body of literature composed of psychoanalytic and psychoanalytically oriented religious studies heavily slanted, apparently, toward the question of what Augustine's problem was. Was it oedipal or, more fundamentally, a problem of self-cohesion?

For Monica, Augustine's mother, good Christian that she no doubt was, the father as intervening third term to the mother/child relationship—the "name of the father" as metaphor for the paternal function (see Richardson and Vergote herein)—was virtually foreclosed from her way of being in the world. Augustine's conversion—the culmination, from a psychoanalytic point of view, of his struggle to transcend the narcissistic maternal enclosure—was mediated "by a long line of affirming Christian men whose faith allowed him to experience God's love as free, spontaneous, and gracious." The movement in Browning's paper is from the question of the nature of Augustine's problem toward the question of the nature of his achievement. It is a movement that parallels that of the *Confessions* itself. There the writer began "as a harried, middle-aged bishop. But as he moves . . . into the final and more peaceful theological sections . . . he feels 'apprehended' and 'gathered up' by God . . . 'no longer distracted' but able to concentrate anew on his 'heavenly calling'."

Anne and Ernest Wallwork appraise the history and current status of the antagonism between psychoanalysis and religion. They stress that Freud's position was that illusions may be valued where they "are recognized as such" (*S.E.* 21:80) and assert that Freud's *Wissenschaft,* comparable to the Greek "philosophia," is considerably richer than the English word "science." It is their contention that Freud's outlook was close to what has been called "positive secularism," a position that "retains a sense of mystery yet to be explored as a part of secularism, as opposed to 'negative secularism,' which denies the existence of any such mysteries."

"Sparks from God" by Graham Schweig explicates the structure of symbol. All the authors in this book rely on the concept of symbolization. Schweig's account of symbolization presents a core sense of meaning contained in the other contributions. He does not focus on particular religious symbols, nor does he offer a general typology of symbols. He instead analyzes symbolic being and experience—symbol as a dimension of human reality that encompasses its usage in both psychoanalysis and religious studies.

Edwin Wallace presents a history of the interaction between psychiatry/psychoanalysis and religion in America. This includes the early minister/physician collaborations that led to the now-burgeoning clinical pastoral movement and to a host of secular-religious psychotherapeutic endeavors such as Alcoholics Anonymous. His call is for a public philosophy of psychiatry—an understanding of its proper focus and the ways in which it should relate to broader aspects of social and cultural action.

José Faur's contribution comes as a lively disturber of the peace of the other articles, all bound together in ecumenical resistance to Freudian reductionistic interpretation of *all* religion. In contrast to Smith's assumption that any religion that has become established must in some way work and allow for both nondefensive and defensive participation by members of a community of believers, Faur suggests that Christianity as a religion of the son heightens oedipal strife and inhibits its resolution. Not only that, the repressed rage thus fomented may often have been enacted in the form of using Jews as scapegoats. Whereas the Greek heritage is usually contrasted with the Judeo-Christian heritage of the West, Faur interprets Christianity, through Paul, as the embodiment of the Greek—and perhaps the worst of the Greek—heritage.

Faur's historical account of the persecution of the Jews in the name of Christianity stands as a reminder of those passages throughout the volume that point toward the possibilities for defensive or demonic deployment of *any* religion. It should be noted, however, that his contribution, a late arrival for this collection, is not here answered by a Christian commentary. The latter, we assume, would consider Faur's radical association of Paul and Christianity with Greek arrogance as running roughshod over the differences between Greek and Christian (including Pauline) thought. As for the arrogance, Christians would no doubt argue that if Oedipus became his father in slaying him, as Faur asserts, in Christianity the father became the son.

From a psychoanalytic point of view, Faur's way of contrasting Judaism and Christianity in the context of oedipal issues is marred by his assumption that oedipal guilt arises primarily as a response to the rage evoked by the tyranny of the father. The implication is that with a benevolent father, intensity of oedipal strife—and perhaps the oedipal complex altogether—could be averted. That utopian implication of oedipal peace in Judaism as contrasted with Christianity is precisely opposite to the commentary on Jews and Egyptians in the Philippson Bible that Freud read as a child. Philippson there wrote, "all Egypt calmly allowed itself to be subjugated to its king while in Jacob's small family his blessing inspired boundless confusion, rebellion against the father, and wild passion" (Philippson Bible, 208, as cited in McGrath 1986, 50).

The matter could be psychoanalytically contextualized this way: the phylogenetic movement from fixity of instinctual control to language and freedom was the movement to the possibility of good and evil entering the world. There is at least some analogy, we would suggest, in the movement from the absolute authority of the father toward the possibilities for compliance *or* defiance, love *or* hate. This is to say that the coming to be of the possibility for failure of oedipal resolution is at the same time the appearance of the possibility for resolution of the oedipal complex; when internalization has proceeded to the point of allowing for relative autonomy, the oedipal complex and choices or options pertaining thereto ensue.

From the point of view of the clinician, all the essays assembled here can be taken as addressed to the issue of psychoanalytic listening. How the analyst hears accounts of the analysand's religious belief and practice provides but one instance, one test, of the meaning, use, and efficacy of the neutrality and abstinence that characterize all psychoanalytic listening.

The aim of neutrality is to give a hearing to all dimensions—id, ego, and superego—of the subject's response to the particular reality being encountered: a hearing, that is, in terms of the analysand's psychic reality. The aim of psychoanalytic abstinence is to bar the gratification of wishes that could short-circuit the accomplishment of such a full hearing. Abstinence thus bars the enactment of a multitude of wishes that might arise in either analyst or analysand. So far as they constitute specific constraints on the analyst, the aims of both neutrality and abstinence converge to bar any inclination the analyst might have to impose his or her own opinions and values on the analysand. Neutrality and abstinence are thus two modes of listening, but two modes of listening that combine to silently call upon the analysand to choose his or her own way on the basis of maximum clarity. The work of analysis, work in which both analyst and analysand join, is to facilitate the dynamic and structural change that allows for clarity. Choices on the basis of that clarity—not just at the end of an analysis but throughout—are those of the analysand alone.

It might be thought that the believing analysand provides a special test of neutrality because in the typical instance the interchange would be with a nonbelieving analyst. It could be argued, however, that an even more intricate test would be the case of an analyst and analysand who were both believers; perhaps, in terms of noting defensive identifications or subtle breaching of neutrality, the closer their religious belief and practice, the more intricate the test.

The responsible practice of abstinence and neutrality requires that the constant striving for the ideal be tempered by an owning that the achievement of the ideal aims of each is impossible. That is not only because the gratification of some wishes—on rare occasions even major wishes—can enhance more than detract from the ultimate achievement of clarity; nor is it only because there can be both defensive and nondefensive identification of analysand with analyst or analyst with analysand. It is also because the analytic process engages a person capable of permitting the evolution of a transference neurosis with a person capable of permitting attunement to the first in the form of a pertinent countertransference neurosis. The transference neurosis is the coming alive in the relationship with the analyst of the significant issues in the life of the analysand together with the characteristic defenses against danger associated with those issues. It is the subject of the overt verbal interchange.

Analysis of the countertransference neurosis is the ongoing silent task of the analyst alone. The latter involves the self-analysis and re-analysis of core elements of the analyst's history and subjecthood as these are evoked in the appraoch to core issues in the life of the analysand. What distinguishes analysis from wild analysis is an informed striving for the neutrality and abstinence that promote change and clarity by virtue of resolution of the transference and countertransference neuroses that have been permitted to evolve.

To touch even this briefly on the complexity of meaning of neutrality and abstinence is perhaps a sufficient basis for asserting that the constraints on the analyst's basic position are the same with either a believing or a nonbelieving analysand. Analysis begins with the chief complaint as stated by the analysand. The transference and countertransference neuroses evolve in the process of clarifying and elaborating the meaning and history of the problem or problems that brought the person to treatment. Regarding religious belief, neutrality requires keeping an open mind toward the question of the defensive or nondefensive or potentially defensive or nondefensive dimensions of such belief. "Defensive" and "nondefensive," it should be noted, are technical terms. In response to danger that has evoked anxiety, the various mechanisms of defense distance that danger by means of unconsciously initiated distortion of inner or outer reality. "Nondefensive" thus refers to the capacity in situations of either safety or threat to approach an object of desire or face an object of danger in relative clarity—with minimum distortion by reason of defense. Any defense can be a part of either pathological or nonpathological behavior. Nondefensive behavior is never pathological. Psychopathology occurs in situations of such extreme or ongoing danger that defense dominates to the point of seriously compromising capacities for love, work, or play.

Whether an analysand's religious belief or the lack thereof is central in the chief complaint or becomes central in the transference neurosis would depend on a number of variables, such as the degree of defensiveness involved in the analysand's belief, agnosticism, or atheism. Analysis aims for change that enchances clarity, bringing to light the defensive aspects of one's way of being. But most of what is defensive or nondefensive cannot be judged in advance by either the analysand or the analyst. That only comes to light as the dangers defended against are approached in the transference/countertransference recapitulation of significant experience.

Of course, everything hinges on the fact that there is no fixed reality (inner or outer) that would lend itself to uniform interpretation. Defenses, then, are not simply distortions of a reality waiting to be known. They are instead defensively motivated interpretations or constructions of inner and outer worlds—worlds always already established only by virtue of language, by virtue of interpretation. Who, then, but the analysand could be called upon to take responsibility for the ultimate decision as to what is defensive and what nondefensive?

This deciding is not ideally a one-time act. It is instead an ongoing readiness to be open to the question of meaning and motive at every level. If such openness characterizes the ideal analysand *and* the ideal penitent (see Westphal), should it not also characterize the ideal analyst?

How does the individual recapitulate construction of the linguistically established and culturally mediated world? Perhaps such construction of one's self and world could be said to begin with faith as negation. Freud's statement that unconscious processes know no negation is a way of stating that the one thing unconsciously negated is negation itself. The "no" of loss, boundaries, and finitude, initially intimated by absence of the object, is negated. In the identity of perception the image of the object is taken to *be* the object. A first step in coming to terms with the absence of the object is accomplished in the move from the identity of perception to the identity of thought in which image and object are differentiated. Coming to terms with loss beyond the loss of any particular object—with loss as such, loss to the second power—involves coming to terms with the unconscious processes of "the other scene," otherness within, where affirmation of the object begins by negation of the object's absence.

The unconscious negation of absence must be taken, that is, as the first step, via denial, in acknowledging absence. Since primitively there is no self/object, no inner/outer differentiation, the negation institutes the owning not only of the absence of the object but also of an absence or otherness within. Negating absence of the (pre)object as a danger and of absence within is primal repression. It is also negative acknowledgment of absence, which thus institutes not only self/object differentiation but also inner dividedness. This way of approaching one's finitude renders the line between ego and Other, inner and outer, now and then, fundamentally problematic.

Negation of absence and limit institutes boundary formation and the owning of temporal dimensions but, ideally, in a way that allows for nondefensive return at certain moments to the timeless "moments of eternity" of which Loewald (1978, 65) writes. At this level, the "problem with boundaries" is not in the first instance a reference to psychotic, borderline, or neurotic deficit or defense but simply the way things are. At the level of psychopathology "boundary problems" may actually cover and defend against the fundamental problem with boundaries. The general idea of the same covering the "same" is illustrated by the borderline young woman with hysterical features who said in all seriousness, "I was pretending to be frightened but really I was frightened." Generally, the device is frequently a form of distancing danger by means of subtle and not so subtle splitting, most commonly seen in the depression and masochism that cover mourning—pain or perversity that cover the pain of actual loss.

Failure to achieve the identity of thought, failure to achieve boundaries, failure to acknowledge absence, failure of differentiation of image and object or wish and gratification, are manifestations of psychosis. The nearness to psychosis and also the distance from psychosis of trust, faith, and love are that in the latter an element of truth in the original negation of absence comes to be known. The object whose absence was originally negated is nevertheless there. This is to say that at the center of every delusion there is a kernel of faith and that in the faith of even the sanest and saintliest of believers, there is a kernel of delusion.

"The difference," Barbara Johnson writes, "between difference and sameness can barely be said. It is as small and as vast as the difference between 'like' and 'as'" (1987, 178). *Like* and *as* usually convey similarity/simile—difference from identity. However, *like* and even more likely *as* can also connote identity. To say truly, "I am being like I really am" is not simile. But identity of the self always falls short of self-sameness. The subject, Ricoeur stresses (1970, 420 and repeatedly elsewhere), is never identical with itself. "Just as I am" is not simile, but neither is it ever pure self-sameness devoid of difference. This view of difference and sameness between faith and delusion is not a statement referring only to believers and the deluded. In the Kierkegaardian tradition, identifying defensive moves and their motives in the context of inner dividedness is the ongoing task of each person. Psychoanalysis or religion can clarify questions, but neither provides answers that can be rightly substituted for those of the individual alone. In this regard, the basic position of the ideal analyst or the ideal parent or the ideal religious mediator is one of respectful reserve. Where the practice of analysis (or of psychoanalytically oriented psychotherapy) and of religion approach each other has little to do with the specific precepts, beliefs, or myths of any particular school of psychoanalysis or of any particular religion. The closeness is between the analytic and the religious attitudes. Both, or at least what we take to be the best of both, are marked by a respectful reserve and a charged waiting for the analysand or the religious seeker to assume his or her own destiny in ways that will come partly as a surprise not only to the analysand or seeker but also to the analyst or the religious mediator.

References

Freud, Sigmund. *The Standard Edition of the Complete Psychological Works of Sigmund Freud.* Edited and translated by James Strachey. 24 vols. London: Hogarth Press, 1953–74. *Civilization and Its Discontents* (1930), vol. 21.

Johnson, Barbara. *A World of Difference.* Baltimore: Johns Hopkins University Press, 1987.

Loewald, Hans. *Psychoanalysis and the History of the Individual.* New Haven: Yale University Press, 1978.

McGrath, William J. *Freud's Discovery of Psychoanalysis: The Politics of Hysteria.* Ithaca: Cornell University Press, 1986.

Ricoeur, Paul. *Freud and Philosophy: An Essay on Interpretation.* New Haven: Yale University Press, 1970.

Psychoanalysis and Religion

1   Religion and Psychoanalysis: Some Phenomenological Contributions

Robert Sokolowski

How is the relationship between psychoanalysis and religion to be examined? It might seem that the best approach would be to study what each of them has to say about the human condition. We might compare religion and psychoanalysis as two theories about the human estate, two competing claims to truth. But there would be something abstract about treating them in this way. Psychoanalysis is a special kind of science and art, and religion comprises a way of life as well as a set of beliefs of a special kind. In many ways the two are incommensurate. I propose therefore to join the issue of religion and psychoanalysis in a more concrete way by asking how the psychoanalyst can be related to the religious beliefs of his patient. The issue of psychoanalysis and religion arises in its sharpest form in the interaction between analyst and patient, and some dimensions of this interaction may be relevant to the issue itself. The interaction between therapist and patient is not a mere occasion that lets the question be raised, something that could be discarded when the two elements, religion and psychoanalysis, come to the center of our discussion. The situation in which this problem arises is part of the phenomenology of the problem and part of a possible resolution.

I will examine the relationship between religion and psychoanalysis by commenting on the work of Hans W. Loewald, who has provided both an authoritative interpretation of the writings of Freud and a favorable view of the place of religion in psychoanalytic theory (Loewald 1978, 1980). My essay will discuss two topics: first, how the analyst can be related to the opinions of his patient, and how the patient can be related to the opinions of the analyst—in other words, how analyst

1

and patient can quote one another—and, second, how the object of religious dispositions and beliefs, how "the divine," is to be understood. A third part will be devoted to bringing these two themes together. In developing these issues I will draw extensively on the principles of Edmund Husserl's phenomenology.

I

Loewald mentions two features of psychoanalysis as a science. The first is that the essence of psychoanalysis is interpretation. Its task is to interpret whatever the patient makes known to the analyst and whatever can be deduced from what the patient makes known; its task is to interpret such things in terms of personal motivation (1980, 103). A second feature of psychoanalysis is that the patient, the "object" of the science, is also able to enter into the investigative process: "there is no other field of scientific activity where the order of organizing potential is the same in the 'object' and the 'investigator'." Loewald goes on to describe psychoanalysis as "calling forth . . . the investigator in the one investigated" (could Oedipus himself be described by a better phrase?). The object of study in psychoanalysis is not just a target; the object is called upon to express a self-understanding and hence to interpret himself and his behavior, to enter into interactions with the analyst, into transference relationships, and eventually to reinterpret himself and his actions in the light of what the analyst has said and done. Loewald, in "On the Therapeutic Action of Psychoanalysis," says, "If an [analyst's] interpretation of unconscious meaning is timely, the words by which this meaning is expressed are recognizable to the patient as expressions of what he experiences" (1980, 238). The words spoken by the analyst "organize for him [the patient] what was previously less organized and thus give him the distance from himself that enables him to understand, to see, to put into words and to 'handle' what was previously not visible, understandable, speakable, tangible" (238–39). The patient is able to assimilate "the organizing understanding which the analyst provides" (239). Patient and analyst must interpret each other. This dialogical process, which has been described as such by Stanley Leavy (1980), is based upon the ability of the patient and the analyst to quote each other. Even to begin the process, the analyst must be able to understand, and hence to quote, what the analysand says, and the patient, in order to bring the process to its end, must be able to share in the understanding of the analyst. The interpretative nature of psychoanalysis thus depends on the possibility of quotations.

A further refinement is necessary. "Possibility" can be taken in many senses. In one sense, we could investigate those conditions that render an individual psychologically capable of quoting someone else: we might ask whether this or that person has the detachment to cite someone else fairly, whether he has the acumen and linguistic resources to do so, whether this or that quotation is accurate, and the like. This sort of study of quotation presupposes that quotation as such is possible. It presupposes the ontology of quotation. Our discussion will move into the more philosophical issue of the ontology of quotation. We will examine how quotation as such occurs, how it differentiates itself from other modes of thought, awareness, and being, and how it occurs in the special context of the psychoanalytic relationship. The study of psychoanalytic quotation will shed light on the special form of intentionality at work in psychoanalysis.

One of the characteristics of higher-level mentation is that it permits many persons to possess the same meaning. No matter how private our own appropriation of a meaning may be, the core of the meaning, the sense, can be achieved by many. That is what permits agreement, but it also permits disagreement and confusion; people may think they are each formulating the same sense when in fact they are not. The publicness of meaning was recognized in antiquity and was forcefully restated in our time by Edmund Husserl in the critique of psychologism that he made, in 1900, in his *Logical Investigations* (1970, 90–224). Sameness of sense is made thematic in quotation, when we restate as the same what someone else says or thinks, and restate it precisely as having been stated or thought by that other person.

Although the core of meaning between quoted and quoter can be the same, there can be several perspectives, each formally different from the other, from which we can possess the one meaning. There can be several formally different voices that can each state one and the same sense. Let us consider the patient, the analysand, as the fundamental voice, as $voice_0$; then an ordinary interlocutor with that person would count as $voice_1$, which speaks from $perspective_1$. An ordinary observer of the conversation between the person and his interlocutor, a third party who simply watches and listens, would count as $voice_2$. The analyst is $voice_3$, spoken from $perspective_3$. Finally we can distinguish $voice_4$ and $perspective_4$; this is what we could call the voice and perspective of the philosopher. His stance is to reflect on the voices and perspectives of all the others, and also to think of the world and the things in it as they show up in the perspectives of all the others, as they are spoken about and disclosed by all the other voices. Of special importance for our concerns is the fact that the philosopher also reflects upon the interaction between patient and analyst, and he examines this interaction formally as a process of manifestation; he does not serve as a superior analyst who might give the original analyst tips on improving his technique. The philosophical perspective is to analyze the process of disclosure as such, and to consider the participants formally as agents and datives of manifestation. The present essay is done from perspective$_4$ and is written and read in voice$_4$.

There is nothing to prevent one and the same person from working in more than one of these perspectives; the analyst may become a simple interlocutor for a moment ("Will you be able to take the subway home?"), or he can reflect philosophically on what he is doing as an analyst. But although the same person may speak in different voices, he should be careful not to blend and confuse what he says in one voice with what he says in another. A distorting fusion of horizons would result and perplexing ambiguities would follow; such overlaps provide the soil for category mistakes.

Before we determine more fully the nature of the psychoanalytical voice, let us amplify somewhat voice$_0$, the voice of the analysand. This voice is by definition a fragmented one. Some of what it says is spoken by the person who has come for analysis, but some of what it says is spoken by voices that have become entangled with the voice of that person: the voice of his father or mother, for example, or his own childhood voice as responding to his father or mother. The mixing of voices yields incoherences of speech and action. Things are taken and stated by this person in ways that are not in keeping either with what they are or with what he is. The analysand comes to the analyst to gain the ability to untangle these voices: to become able to speak in his own voice and merely to quote the voices that ought not to be his own, to become free either to appropriate them as his own or to dissociate himself from them. In his present state he is so entangled with them that he cannot quote, appropriate, or deny them. He has no distance from them, no distance to the someone talking in him who really isn't he himself. The patient has not sufficiently grown out of the early stages in which there is not enough "I" to make a difference between what I say and what you or they say. The analyst helps voice$_0$ distinguish between his own appropriating voice, voice$_0^x$, and the voice he wishes either to confirm or negate, voice$_0^y$.

The task of the analyst is to help the analysand make these distinctions. The analyst can help him do so because he, the analyst, can hear levels of voices that the ordinary interlocutors and observers cannot hear; the analyst can hear these voices in the patient because he has heard them in himself through his own analysis, and because, through his training, he has acquired categories with which to name the many and various voices working through one speaker. He has disentangled voice^x and voice^y in himself and is free to hear similar voices in the patient and thus to help the patient to acquire his own voice. He can regress with the patient to lower levels of mentation, but can at the same time keep the higher levels intact and so, as Loewald often says, remain ahead of the patient much as the parent remains ahead of the child and helps the child to come to terms with the world (Loewald 1980, 93, 229–30).

Let us contrast the voice of the analyst, voice$_3$, with other voices we have distinguished. The voices of the ordinary interlocutor and of the observer, voice$_1$ and voice$_2$, both have their own point of view on the world. Things seem to them to be in a certain way. Both these voices will agree with voice$_0$ in some respects and disagree in others; when they disagree, they will take the propositions of voice$_0$ as mere opinions and as false ones. They will say that the person is simply wrong in what he says. The voice$_3$ of the analyst is different in that the analyst does not, as analyst and formally speaking, have an alternative view of the world. He works into and stays within the perspective$_0$ of voice$_0$; he takes seriously everything that is stated by the patient's voice and does not reject anything as merely a false opinion.

On the other hand, the analyst does not simply absorb the world of the patient; he sustains a special kind of detachment and exercises a special kind of quotation: not the kind exercised by voice$_1$ and voice$_2$, the kind that merely tests the opinion to see whether it is true or not, but a new kind, one that listens to what is said in order to find out who is speaking and to bring the presence and power and source of that voice to the attention of the patient. The analyst hears more than is said. What is said is treated as a clue to who is saying it. The analyst is to discover the truth in the falsity of what the patient says, he is to discover the past event that is being repeated even as the patient thinks he is involved only with what is going on now. And when the termination of analysis occurs, the patient should have come to distinguish his own voice from the others that had been speaking in him, but the analyst also changes from living within the perspective of the patient to being an ordinary interlocutor or observer, to speaking in voice$_1$ and in voice$_2$ in regard to the patient. Indeed, it is interesting to raise the question of when it is that the analyst shifts from voice$_3$ to voice$_1$; even during the time of analysis, the analyst cannot stop being someone who has his own view of how things are, someone who can say that what the analysand claims is not the case, someone who gradually "leads" the patient to himself and to the way things are.

In discussing the voices engaged in psychoanalysis, I have understated the affective dimension in this distinctive human relationship. Although psychoanalysis involves conversation and dialogue, its core lies in the transference that occurs between patient and analyst. This transference is substantially preverbal. The verbal dimension is essential to transference, but it lies on the surface. Transference is the reworking of affective attitudes and interactions that have been internalized by the patient; in analysis the patient is to reexternalize these interactions and attitudes, to direct them toward the analyst, who will respond in such a way as to help the patient to untangle appropriate and inappropriate feelings (Loewald 1980, 259–60, 309–11, 335). If in his early years the patient was, say, held in contempt by significant persons, and if he internalized this interaction and now holds himself in contempt, the transference allows him to reestablish the original interactions externally, to rework them and to make the crucial emotional distinctions, those that will allow him to react with appropriate feelings to new situations instead of blindly and persistently repeating the interactions of the past. The preverbal affective attitudes and interactions have to be reeducated; the analyst, the new object for the feelings, does not react in the way "the other person" used to act and react. The untangling that is done in regard to $voice_0$ is primarily an affective untangling; the $voice_0$ in question is a voice pervaded with affectivity. As Loewald puts it, "narrative is drawn into the context of transference dramatization, into the force-field of re-enactment" (1980, 366).

There is something like quotation, something analogous to verbal citation, in the transference relationship and in the analyst's reaction to it. The analyst has to "catch" and reflect a feeling in the way he feels, much as a listener must capture and return someone else's opinion in the words that he, the listener, uses. The patient, as time goes on, may become able to pick up the feeling at a distance himself, to feel the feeling as though quoted, then feel it as to be either appropriated or denied. Thus there is a preverbal, affective dialogue in psychoanalysis, and the verbal exchanges and quotations draw their substance from it. The affective exchanges set the stage for the "timely" verbal intervention; they establish when the moment to determine something by words has arrived, when the time for the appropriate intervention and distinction has come. The words are there for the affectivity.

I should make a refinement concerning the ontology of quotation, whether verbal or emotional. Because of certain philosophical pre-suppositions, but also because of natural inclination, we are very much tempted to think that when we quote someone else, we take over into our own awareness some sort of "mental representation" that exists in that person's psychic world. Loewald himself is aware of this mis-understanding regarding "mental contents" and he criticizes it; he writes, "I also question the by now common equation of self and self-representation, or of object and object representation, due to con-fused thinking in regard to the term 'mental representation'" (1980, 351). When we say we think this or that, what we mean is that we believe the world shows up in a certain way; when we quote someone else, we state that the world appears to him in such and such a way, and we may either agree or disagree with that proposal. Even when we emotionally "quote" others, when we feel what they feel, as felt by them, we do not merely perceive one of their feelings or sympathize with their mental states; rather, we let certain things appear to us as charged emotionally, but as being so charged for the other persons. What people are trying to get at when they speak of mental contents or mental representations is not some sort of mental thing, but the way things and persons in the world seem to be. Thus when the ana-lyst quotes the patient, he is not trying to discover what mental con-tents the patient has but trying to discover how the world appears to the patient, how the patient believes the world to be. Thinking is al-ways articulation of some part of the world, thinking is always "out-side"; even feeling is always a presentation of something worldly; and quotation is articulation of part of the world as it is proposed or articu-lated or felt by someone else. Quotation is an articulation to the sec-ond degree; it is not a peek inside, not a peek at someone's mental screen (Sokolowski 1979).

If the analyst's ordinary voice$_1$ is always in the background when he engages his professional voice$_3$ in analysis, the opposite is also true: when the analyst becomes involved in ordinary transactions, his pro-fessional voice$_3$ and perspective$_3$ cannot be expected to disappear al-together. Hans-Georg Gadamer (1971) has commented about this in his debate with Habermas. Gadamer criticizes the attempt to intro-duce a new sort of art and science similar to psychoanalysis, an "eman-cipating reflection" (257), that would try to remove impediments to public communication and free society from ideological constraints. He claims that ordinary public discourse has its own hermeneutic in-tegrity and that claims made in it should be answered on their own terms. Suppose there is a political disagreement and one of the speakers heatedly, even angrily, presents an argument for a particular course of action; this person has a right to be answered with political arguments, not with a psychological analysis of the causes of his anger (260). To blindside the speaker, to turn from the terms of the argument to an analysis of his voice$_1$ (in effect, to turn his voice$_1$ into a voice$_0$), is to destroy the integrity of public discussion; the intrusion of psychoanalytical expertise is "an upsetting factor," a *Störungsfaktor* in normal social exchanges (259). Gadamer admits that the technical ability of the analyst is bound to assert itself; even in ordinary conversations, the analyst will notice certain things. Speaking in voice$_1$ to an analyst is like writing a letter to a graphologist; you are "delivered over to him" even if you do not intend to address his analytical ability (259). But both the analyst and the graphologist must respect the content of the normal message and respond to it on its own terms. When they notice what is hidden to everyone else, they themselves must not become blind to what everyone else sees, the manifest content of what is being stated.

This brings us to the case of religion and the way quotations can take place in regard to religious language. What voice does the analyst use when quoting and discussing religious belief? And what is the content of religious expression?

II

The third chapter of Loewald's book *Psychoanalysis and the History of the Individual* is entitled, "Comments on Religious Experience." Loewald begins this chapter by reminding us of Freud's negative view of religion. Freud thought that religion was "an illusion to be given up as we are able to overcome our childish needs for all-powerful parents" (Loewald 1978, 57). Freud's interpretation of religion was challenged by his friend Romain Rolland, who claimed that the experiential root of religion was an underlying feeling of being at one with the entire world. Freud said that he himself did not experience this sensation, which Rolland called an "oceanic feeling" or a "sensation of eternity," but he claimed that if it was experienced by some people, it might well be explained psychoanalytically as derived from the primary narcissistic stage in which the child has not yet developed ego boundaries between himself and his mother and between himself and the world (59–60, 68). But Freud, says Loewald, "did not pursue his basic hunches, and under the weight of his authority religion in psychoanalysis has been largely considered a sign of man's mental immaturity" (57).

Loewald's own view, rather tentatively developed, is that religion may express not an immature regression, but a wholesome recognition of archaic mentation. He asserts that secondary processes should always be kept in touch with the primary processes that underlie them, at the risk of falling into "the madness of unbridled rationality" (56), and religion may be the expression of the archaic levels of psychic life that remain continuously present in us, no matter how easily we may overlook them. The point is not to allow primary processes to drown the secondary, but to keep access to the wellsprings of the primary process open even during the mature activation of secondary processes; the creative language found, among other places, in authentic religious expression may serve to express the moment at which "the density of the primary process gives way to the discursiveness and articulation of secondary process" (1980, 203). Secondary processes, says Loewald, are not a static state into which we enter, but activities that must be kept continuously alive, activities that must constantly draw nourishment from the primary process: "the range and richness of human life is directly proportional to the mutual responsiveness between these various mental phases and levels" (1978, 61). Freud tended to think of religion as dependent upon a need for an all-powerful, "enormously exalted" father who would protect the believer, but on his own admission he could not account for the belief in maternal divinities that seems to have preceded belief in paternal gods (1978, 57; 1980, 8–9).

After observing that Freud spoke particularly of the boundaries between ego and the outer world, Loewald introduces the "equal if not more basic differentiation" in the development of mental life, "that of temporal modes" (1978, 61). The differentiation of past, present, and future is as basic as—perhaps even more basic than—the distinction between internal and external, and certainly both distinctions arise in function of each other. The importance of the temporal modes is emphasized in many passages in Loewald's work (1980, 43–52, 138–47, 149–73). His own treatment of religion, in the chapter we are examining, is developed largely in terms of temporality and eternity.

Loewald says that the idea of eternity should not be confused with that of everlasting duration, which is time projected indefinitely; rather, "in the experience of eternity, time is abolished" (1978, 63). Temporality accompanies secondary forms of mentation, but a glimpse of primary forms would involve the de-articulation of present, past, and future, in an extreme condensation. "The primary process in pure form is, I believe, extant in the experience of eternity" (65). Loewald describes instances in which we might catch such glimpses, moments in which time seems to be surpassed or undercut; in such cases "the secondary, rational form of mentation loses its weight. It is over-shadowed or pervaded by the timelessness of the unconscious or pri-mary process" (67). We try to express, in secondary-process catego-ries, these experiences in which we touch the timelessness of the id, and then we speak, for example, of everlasting life after death (67). Loewald insists that such experiences are not simply illusions but "bring us in touch with levels of our being" (69). He observes that psychoanalysis can help formulate a positive sense for the experience of eternity and for the religious expressions to which it leads. This would be of great benefit because, he claims, religious experiences are "aspects of unconscious mentation . . . that in much of modern civi-lization are more deeply repressed than 'sexuality' is today" (74). He calls for a "genuine appropriation" of the forces at work behind the expressions found in religious traditions.

In response to Loewald's interpretation of religious experience, one might be inclined at first to object that he postulates religion as directed only inwardly, only toward the psychic primary process, whereas religious belief is concerned not only with the psychic but with the worldly as well. But such an objection would not be effective, because Loewald claims that primary process is not "internal" as op-posed to "external." On this most basic level, inner and outer have not yet been differentiated. In the primary process there is neither an ego nor objects, no inside as opposed to outside; there is only the matrix within which boundaries are to be drawn (1980, 127–29, 167, 185). There is nothing in Loewald's interpretation that would deny the pos-sibility of cosmological divinities.

The primitive unconscious does possess features that are attributed to the gods in pagan religions. It is all-encompassing, and it contains powers that we will forever be unable to master. These powers, fur-thermore, are not just a spectacle before us; they are causes of our human condition. Somehow or other we come to be because of them, and we remain permanently under their influence. It is not inappropri-ate for us to respect these causes of our being in a way analogous to the manner in which those who believed in the Homeric gods might have respected the forces that were thought to have brought the hu-man estate, and the world of that human estate, into being. Loewald makes a successful attempt to remythologize the chthonian gods.

It seems to me, however, that in his difference with Freud, in his criticism of Freud's tendency to take religion as the wish for and the fear of an all-powerful father, Loewald neglects the role of the forces that were personified and reverenced as the olympian gods. It would be difficult to consider Apollo, the god of music, law, prophecy, order, and pattern, as an expression of the id. Apollo is supposed to tame the dark gods of the underworld. That which arises as other to the primary unconscious is also one of the causes of our being, and it is equally unmasterable by our own deliberate efforts. It is true that the estab- lishment of boundaries, and subsequently the establishment of orders and patterns, are achievements that we ourselves must carry out; but the very *possibility* that such things can be at all is not our achieve- ment. As possibilities they transcend our own powers, and they are as "divine" to us as are the dark and chaotic forces. We can appropriate only what is already given as capable of being appropriated.

Loewald's interpretation of the meaning of religion, together with the modification I have introduced, allows an analyst to translate the religious beliefs of a patient into the expression of certain basic and irreducible levels of being. Loewald's interpretation allows the analyst to consider religious beliefs not as delusions but as the expression of something both real and important. It becomes possible for the analyst to "quote" the patient and to quote him with assent, but only after the belief of the patient has been translated into categories that are famil- iar and acceptable to the analyst, categories that express something positive in psychoanalytic theory. The quotation has to be mediated through a translation, and it is possible that the patient will not recog- nize the translation as valid. He might think that the translation says something other than the belief he wishes to express.

Such a concern about the accuracy of translation would be less likely to occur if the patient's idea of the divine were that of a god who is part of the world, as the divine was, say, for the Greek and Roman poets and philosophers. For these thinkers, the gods are and must be part of what is. The gods are the best, most powerful, the most impor- tant and most independent, the encompassing parts, the parts that somehow order all the rest, but they could not be except as part of the whole. Loewald's interpretation of the divine might give another name to such divinities, and it might locate the gods in another kind of part of the whole, but it would not really transform the divine into another kind of being. The translation would not be very different from calling Thor by the name of Jupiter.

The problem of the accuracy of religious translations becomes more urgent, however, in the case of a patient who believes in the God revealed in biblical religion, the God who created the world and is not merely a part within it. In this sense of the divine, the world is understood as existing not under the sway of ineluctable forces, not just there and fated to be as it is, but as existing through the freedom of the creator. The believer—in this case the patient—also understands himself to have been created, to have been chosen to be. His relationship to God is not taken to be like his relationship to his primary unconscious, nor like his relationship to the ordered patterns that transform the unconscious into secondary forms of mentation.

The Bible, and the religious traditions stemming from the Bible, present not only a recommendation about what our attitudes and behavior should be; they also present something to be understood about the nature of things, about the world, about being. Distinctions are made, and the primary distinction concerns how the divine or the ultimate is to be understood. In biblical religion, the divine or the ultimate is not simply a principle of order or an originating force that is part of the world; it is understood to be distinct from the world, to be creator of the world. The word "creator" has a very exact sense in these traditions; it does not mean merely a "maker" or merely one who brings order into chaos or light into darkness. The creator is understood as being so distinct from everything other to himself that he could have been (or could be) even if the world had not been. Such an understanding is required for the full freedom and generosity of creation; only someone who does not need to give and who does not gain from giving can be so completely generous as the creator is understood to be. And as a correlative to this independence and generosity, the world itself is understood not as simply being there but as having been given being by the creator; and the believer is understood not only as the outcome of natural forces, evolution, and parental generation but also as having been freely given being by God. In this biblical understanding, there is something like freedom and generosity at work in the very being of the created whole.

The biblical understanding of God as creator does not arise for the patient as a gradual transformation of his own personal experience. It is presented to him by a religious tradition as a possibility of belief. That tradition itself is understood to be more than just a human achievement, whether individual or social; it is understood to have involved revelation as its specifying element, no matter how much the revelation may have been embedded in the structures of human psychic development. The "translation" of the patient's beliefs, therefore, must not lose this understanding of God as other not only to the patient and his unconscious but other to the whole created world as well, and as capable of being, in undiminished goodness and greatness, even if there were no world.

In his essay entitled "Internalization and the Superego," Loewald briefly mentions Christianity as "initiating the greatest intensification of internalization in Western civilization" (1980, 260). He says that the death of Christ represents for the believer the radical loss of "the ultimate love object, which the believer loses as an external object and regains by identification with Him as an ego ideal." This occurs, Loewald says, in accord with the psychic processes of loss, mourning, and internalization. He calls this event "the death of God as incarnated in Christ." His remarks are provocative and point the way toward further reflection on psychoanalysis and Christian belief, but I think some refinement needs to be made. The term "the death of God" is misleading, because in Christian belief the Godhead did not die when Christ died. Christ the man died, and this person who died was God, but his divinity did not die. God, as the ultimate object of love, did not die, is not lost, and is not to be mourned. (Loewald's remarks show the contemporary relevance of the definitions of the Council of Chalcedon, which in A.D. 451 declared that the two natures of Christ, the divine and the human, retain their integrity in the Incarnation, and that the attributes of each nature as such do not become attributes of the other as such; the Godhead as such does not become mortal and does not die, no more than the humanity of Christ becomes eternal or omnipotent.)

I think that the set of relationships and transformations Loewald is getting at in his remark about the death of Christ are better determined in terms of creation than in terms of redemption. The believer, in his understanding of creation, holds that the entire world, himself included, might not have been, and God would still be in undiminished goodness and perfection. Both the believer and the world are held to exist through God's unnecessitated choice. The "loss" that is envisioned in this belief is the possible nonbeing of everything except God, not the loss of God. God is understood as that which could not die or be lost in this way. This belief is an understanding of how the world and the things in it can be; it is an intellectual comprehension. It is not presented as one of the affective object-relations the patient has developed during his life. The patient in question may, of course, cathect these objects in ways that are not in keeping with what they are understood to be, just as a particular patient may cathect, say, food in ways that are not in keeping with what food is as nourishment (as in the case of persons suffering from anorexia). A distortion brought about in a patient's appreciation of an object may be important in the treatment of the patient, but it does not destroy the sense that the object has as it is understood apart from that appropriation. In the case of the biblical understanding of God, the sense is determined by its expression in the Bible itself and in the ecclesial, theological, and spiritual tradition that stems from what is narrated in the Scriptures.

The biblical understanding of God, like all understandings of objects to which we can be related, indicates a pattern of behavior. It implies as a response biblical morality and virtues, such as faith, hope, and charity in the Christian biblical tradition. It also implies a biblical self-understanding on the part of the believer. If a person thinks he has been created by God, that he is known by God, and, in the Christian tradition, that he has been redeemed by the incarnate God, he will see his life and his relations to others in a distinctive light and will feel obliged to act in an appropriate way.

The biblical understanding of God goes beyond the senses of the divine expressed in both the chthonian and the olympian gods, since the biblical God is not part of the world; nevertheless the biblical understanding does bear some resemblance to these two senses and it could therefore be misinterpreted as one of them. Like the chthonian gods, the biblical God is understood to be an ultimate origin for everything that is subsequently determined, and like the olympians, he is understood to be a final end or completion of the things that are. Because of these resemblances, and because similarity is often taken for sameness, a writer like Loewald could misinterpret the biblical God in terms more appropriate to a worldly divinity. But the way the creator is an origin and an end is radically different from the way the pagan deities are understood to be sources and causes (Sokolowski 1982).

Loewald criticizes psychoanalytic theory for its tendency "to understand the very organization of the psychic apparatus in terms of defense" (1980, 27) and for its tendency to see "the relationship between organism and environment, between individual and reality . . . as basically antagonistic" (28). He says that psychoanalytic theory has been influenced by modern social estrangements and complexities, and that it has "taken for granted the neurotically distorted experience of reality" (30) that he finds so widespread in contemporary life. Loewald thinks that Freud's misinterpretation of religion as an obsessional neurosis might stem from this modern social context and this overemphasis on defensive reactions (30). He suggests that ego development should not be interpreted primarily in terms of warding off intrusive stimuli and trying to restore a stable state; it should be seen more positively as growth into higher levels of integration achieved through ever greater synthetic functions of the ego. "The ego is an agency which organizes," (44) and new achievements can mean "a gain in its organization and functioning" (74). He says, "With further and higher ego organization, far from getting closer to a state of rest, there is more life" (74; see 176–77, 234).

The biblical understanding of God, together with the self-understanding it proposes for the believer and the form of activity it implies for him, can be interpreted as an opportunity for greater expansion and integration. It can be taken to open a new possibility for development of the ego, even for certain kinds of renunciation, mourning, and internalization. Whether or not it can truly be interpreted in such a positive way depends on two things: on its own intrinsic intelligibility, and on the effect it has on human lives. Thus there are two questions that can be put to the biblical understanding. One is philosophico-theological: Is this an intelligible understanding and not an incoherence? The other is psychological: Has this understanding been lived by persons who are not neurotic, and has it motivated distinctive patterns of behavior, or is it somehow essentially a neurotic or defensive projection?

III

By way of conclusion, I will make only one point concerning the way psychoanalysis might approach these two questions.

As we have seen in the citation from Gadamer, both the handwriting expert and the psychoanalyst, when they enter into public discourse, must resist the temptation to overlook the face value of a message and to see primarily what the message reveals about the speaker. This temptation has been especially hard to resist because of the kind of natural science that was introduced by Francis Bacon, Galileo, Descartes, and Newton, and because of the kind of voice that was associated with this science. The modern scientific tradition considers the rigorous mathematical method of science as the only way of truly describing the world; everything else we are aware of becomes taken as a subjective projection, a mere appearance, a secondary quality. A distinction is then introduced between a physical "outside" and a psychic "inside," between an "outer world" and an "inner world." The only voice with the authority to speak truthfully about the outer world is the voice$_s$ of the one who can master the scientific method. This voice$_s$ tells the hard truth about the way things are; the other, nonscientific voices just tell us how things seem.

In this scientific tradition, it becomes plausible for the expert in psychoanalytic method to assume that he has the truth about the psyche and that he can hope to unlock the secret of all its projections, that he might be able to explain why things seem to us as they do, while leaving to the physicist the task of telling the truth about the external world. The Cartesian physicist, moreover, quotes the ordinary opinions of other speakers only with suspicion, taking them as *mere* opinions (Descartes 1955, 144–49), and the analyst may be inclined to do the same. This is the wrong kind of distance to take toward the statements of others; it is a misleading objectivity, one that emerges from the context set by the unfortunate dichotomy between inner world and outer world, a dichotomy related to what Loewald referred to as "confused thinking in regard to the term, 'mental representation'."

To adjust this context and to dissolve this dichotomy, one would need to show how the voice$_s$ behind scientific method is established and how it is related to the other voices I have talked about in this paper. I will not pursue this discussion now; I will only remark that natural science itself no longer speaks only of things like force and energy but has begun to employ such concepts as "signal," "representation," "information," "computation," "code," and "program," concepts that are now seen to straddle the natural and the psychic (Holenstein 1987), and that natural science has become acutely aware of the role of the observer even in physics; the strong dichotomy between nature and psyche seems to be giving way to a more flexible relationship between the two. As these developments continue, and as they have more and more impact on our general self-understanding, they will provide a less constricting context for determining the place of the psychoanalytical voice$_3$, which, as Loewald has so often stated, is a voice of conversational exchange, not simply of detached observation.

Notes

This essay was the Thirteenth Edith Weigert Lecture, sponsored by the Forum on Psychiatry and the Humanities, Washington School of Psychiatry, October 30, 1988.

I would like to thank Thomas Prufer and Joseph H. Smith for their help in writing this essay.

References

Decartes, René. *Meditations on First Philosophy,* 1:144–49. In *The Philosophical Works of Descartes.* Translated by Elizabeth Haldane and G. R. T. Ross. New York: Dover Publications, 1955.

Gadamer, Hans-Georg. "Replik zu Hermeneutik und Ideologiekritik. 1971." In *Gesammelte Werke,* 2:251–75. Tubingen: J. C. B. Mohr, 1986.

Holenstein, Elmar. "Maschinelles Wissen und menschliches Bewusstsein." *Studia Philosophica* 46 (1987):145–63.

Husserl, Edmund. *Logical Investigations.* Translated by John N. Findlay. New York: Humanities Press, 1970.

Leavy, Stanley A. *The Psychoanalytic Dialogue.* New Haven: Yale University Press, 1980.

Loewald, Hans W. *Psychoanalysis and the History of the Individual.* New Haven: Yale University Press, 1978.

———. *Papers on Psychoanalysis.* New Haven: Yale University Press, 1980.

Sokolowski, Robert. "Making Distinctions." *Review of Metaphysics* 32 (1979): 687–714.

———. *The God of Faith and Reason. Foundations of Christian Theology.* Notre Dame: University of Notre Dame Press, 1982.

2   On Psychoanalysis and the Question of Nondefensive Religion

Joseph H. Smith

> *Any attempt to speak without speaking any particular language is not more hopeless than the attempt to have a religion that shall be no religion in particular. . . . Thus every living and healthy religion has a marked idiosyncrasy. Its power consists in its special and surprising message and in the bias which that revelation gives to life. The vistas it opens and the mysteries it propounds are another world to live in; and another world to live in—whether we expect ever to pass wholly over into it or not—is what we mean by having a religion.*
> —Santayana, *Reason in Religion*

My purpose is to marshal reasons for believing that religious experience can be, in psychoanalytic terms, nondefensive. By religious experience here I mean belief, engagement, and participation in a particular religion and not simply an objectively sympathetic appreciation of elements that might be essential to a variety of religions.[1] Religious persons might well be offended by the radical modesty of aiming to show only that religious experience can be nondefensive. From the point of view of many of my analytic colleagues, however, it is an aim that could be seen as radically immodest. Indeed, I will be satisfied if my argument effectively challenges the widespread assumption among the brothers and sisters of my particular discipline that belief and participation in a particular religion are inherently defensive.

My attempts to persuade will touch on belief and delusion, belief and illusion, on Lacan's concept of "the Other," and on the thought of Julia Kristeva. I will also discuss the position of the analyst in relation to the analysand's faith. Those elements, along with defining statements regarding defensive and nondefensive behavior, will provide the framework for tracing the fate of the infantile in mature experience. Finally, I will briefly review the history and evolution of religious belief in individual development beginning with what Freud called identification with the father of personal prehistory and the ego ideal formed by that identification.

Belief and Delusion

Folie à deux is mad love not totally restricted to the partners being defensively (narcissistically) engaged with only the primitive mother of each. They each have broken out of their original (and pathologically extended) narcissistic enclosure to the extent that a shared set of beliefs has been established. In terms of going in the direction one needs to go—toward subjecthood and being with others in a world— the love between the two signified by their shared world is of more significance than the specific content of how that world is conceptualized, even though the conceptualization itself be defensive in the extreme—that is, delusional.

When beliefs are shared something of momentous significance has occurred, by comparison with which the literal truth or nontruth of the beliefs fades into relative inconsequentiality. The iconoclast will experience his or her attack to be on the literal untruth of the beliefs. The subjects of attack will, quite rightly, experience the attack to be on a way of being in the world the community has established.

Psychoanalysts at work with patients are not iconoclasts. Even with the individual psychotic no frontal attack is launched against faulty perceiving and thinking. Instead, one tries, partly as the mother, ultimately as the intervening father, to meet the patient where she or he is. With luck, sometimes, some capacity to share, some capacity to return such love, is evoked.

If a man tells us, to move from *folie à deux* to *folie à Dieu* and ordinary religious experience, that his neighbor only yesterday ascended directly to heaven, we do not hesitate to judge him psychotic. However, as Hartmann wrote (1964, 260), if a man tells us that Elijah did, even though we may be as far from believing the literal truth of the latter as we are the former, we do not so judge him.

There could be reasons for believing that a person tells us such a religiously sanctioned belief at a particular time or in a particular way for defensive purposes—for example, in an attempt to provocatively distance an analyst assumed to be a nonbeliever. In that case, we might be led to address such purposes. We do not, however, take the beliefs themselves to be delusions.

Again, the content of the belief is not so important as the meaning of the belief in the life of the person and in the life of the community of which that person is a member. The plane of reference of such beliefs is another scene—a scene other than the everyday commonsensical or the scientifically calculable world of objects. It is the scene of the individual's basic way of being in the world and of belonging with others in a community. It is more the reference of poetry and myth than of science—except for the science of psychoanalysis. That psychoanalysis does attend this other scene together with its way of attending is, no doubt, the reason that renders its status as science problematic.

Kristeva, Lacan, and the Other

While insisting that the position of the psychoanalyst is ultimately paternal and intervening rather than maternal and nurturing (Kristeva 1983, 6), Julia Kristeva emphasizes throughout her work the significance of the primitive, preverbal, symbiotic experience over which the mother presides and from which the subject emerges by virtue, in large part, of the father's (or the analyst's) intervention.

In *In the Beginning Was Love: Psychoanalysis and Faith* (Kristeva 1987b) all that was implicit on love and faith in *Tales of Love* (Kristeva 1987a) is, to the extent the subject matter allows, brought to explicitness. It is a rewrite of *The Future of an Illusion,* but this time by a woman analyst attuned to issues of early development, particularly narcissism (the story line of *Tales of Love*), the "general and lasting" effects of primary identifications (Freud, *S. E.* 19:31), symbiosis, the "essential alienation that conditions our access to language" (Kristeva 1987b, 41), and to language as that which both allows for and undermines whatever unity the human subject can achieve.

Although clinical description occupies very little of this brief book, there is enough both here and in her other translated work[2] to see a very sensitive, knowledgeable, and experienced clinician. Kristeva does not simply "apply" psychoanalytic theory to religion. "Every question," she writes, "no matter how intellectual its content, reflects suffering" (1987b, xiii). In the question of psychoanalysis and faith, she suspects, "may lurk the suffering of religion as well as of rationalism" (xiii). She thus heeds the question in the same way she heeds her analysands.

This position allows Kristeva to enlarge what is often taken as Freud's essentially oedipal father/son understanding of religion. She associates an understanding of the human source of religious experience with the most primitive levels of the formation of the self. From that source, although she herself stops just short of going so far, her thought follows a path that leads to associating mature religious experience with the most advanced human potentiality of coming to be as a subject in relation to others in the light of language, law, and the name of the father—in relation, that is, to what Lacan called "the Other."

Her differences from Lacan stem from the greater emphasis she gives to drives and affects—what she calls "the semiotic"—as opposed to the monolithic Lacanian emphasis on language and "the Symbolic." Hers is an emphasis wrought by showing that it is the mother who first occupies the place of the Other, interaction with the mother that shapes instinctual and affective experience, the mother who inaugurates the infant into language, and the mother who mediates the place of the Other to the father.

At least that is one way of phrasing it. But to dispel a bit of the mystery immediately, since the subject here is psychoanalysis and faith, just as Being (that which allows any entity, any being with a small "b," to be) is not God in Heidegger, the Other (that which allows a linguistically structured world in which my own and the other's otherness can be) is not God in Lacan.[3] In general, the way those who believe in the Other and those who believe in God talk to (or past) each other is that when the former say "Other" the latter hear "God," and when the latter say "God" the former hear "Other." Each believes that the other is talking about a reality he knows not of. Vergote (1969, 1983; Vergote and Tamayo 1981), for instance, does not hesitate to assume that the ultimate referent of Lacan's (and Kristeva's) Other is, in the West, the God of Abraham, Isaac, and Jacob. Lacan, on the other hand, writes of "one face of the Other, the God face" (1982, 147). Similarly, Kristeva, in an otherwise intensely sympathetic study of various "soldiers of God" in *Tales of Love,* does not hesitate to assume that the real meaning of God in her subjects of study is, unknown to them, Lacan's and her own understanding of the Other. The Other, as concept, partly derives from Lacan's meditation on Heidegger's Being, but it derives also from Lacan's thought on language and from his strictly psychoanalytic understanding—considerably extended since by Loewald, Kristeva, and, in their own very different ways, by Kohut and Kernberg—of the place of narcissism in human development, beginning with the narcissistic inattention, until Freud, to "the other scene."

The other scene is the scene of unconscious processes. When Freud realized that repressing forces can be just as unconscious as the dynamically repressed (*S. E.* 14:192–93), he shifted away from a topographical toward a structural model and (with some subsequent lapses) dropped the noun-rendering "the" from "the unconscious" in favor of simply "unconscious" as adjectival (Smith 1978). This did not suit Lacan. While accepting (and then some) the enlarged field of unconscious processes, he held on to the "the" not only in "the unconscious" and "the other scene," but also in his own "the Other."

Lacan's contribution was to locate the Freudian account of individual development and family dynamics within the larger arena of language and the cultural and symbolic order. The other scene is not constituted by that which is dynamically repressed. The other scene is always already there in the form of unconscious responses to the impressions of life and the linguistic, cultural, and symbolic orders that anticipate, shape, and determine individual destiny, largely in ways that, as Piaget (1973) argued in the case of the cognitive unconscious, are unconscious though not repressed.

Although the Other, contrary to what the "the" might suggest, is not an object and thus not an object of identification, the "the" carries over from and reveals "the Other" as a concept deriving partly from Freud's notion that the crucial primitive identification is with "the father . . . [of] personal prehistory" (*S. E.* 19:31). The father of personal prehistory is also not an object[4] but the notion of fatherhood and a beyond of the mother/infant symbiosis that has been mediated to the child by the mother. To the extent that it can be taken as an identification, the "father" of personal prehistory is the mother's nonnarcissistic way of being in the world beyond that of only herself and her child. The latter ideally, but not necessarily, includes her love for and acknowledgment of the actual father as the first significant other of the mother/infant unit. The child locates himself not only in relation to the father but also in the world (the world as constituted by language) through an initial identification with the mother's nonnarcissistic way of being—her way of being engaged with the infant in the name of the father[5] whether or not any actual father is on the scene.

Narcissism, before it can turn defensive, is an achievement. It is a higher unity accomplished by mourning the lack of union with the mother, in whatever primitive way an infant can, and identifying with her way of being in the name of the father. The mother mediates to the child language and the symbolic order and in so doing mediates the place of the Other to the father. But prior to mediating the place of the Other to the father, the mother has already made manifest to the child a maternally mediated world-as-love that will always remain as a sustaining dimension in the field of the Other, or of any male Divinity.

I assume that for a nonbeliever like Lacan to retain the "the" in "the Other" is to acknowledge the mediation of the Other by the actual mother and father. Perhaps for that reason there is a universal tendency to personify or anthropomorphize the Other. In any event, it is important to bear in mind that "the Other," "the Symbolic Father," and "the name of the father," though heavily laden with religious connotation and symbolization, have nothing to do with Lacan's being a theist (he was not) or advocating theism (he did not). His borrowing from that source, I take it, means that he was able to see more nondefensive aspects of religious belief and practice than most psychoanalysts or philosophers, the corollary of which was that he was able to see more defensiveness in much atheism than most. He was inclined to see, for example, the easy acceptance of Nietzsche's "God is dead" as a palliative for castration anxiety (Lacan 1978, 27). Similarly, Kristeva (1987b, 26) argues that atheism can be the product of repression rather than renunciation.

Belief and Analytic Abstinence

In Lacan's view, psychoanalysis is "neither for nor against any particular religion" (1977, 316). But the evidence is that his attitude toward religion was more to listen for that which might enlarge psychoanalytic understanding than to assume that psychoanalysis had more to offer than to receive. However, it is a mistake to follow Freud's assumption that these are alternate possibilities. In "applying" psychoanalysis to any arena, just as in "applying" psychoanalysis in the treatment of an individual, it is only in listening to and learning from the other that psychoanalytic concepts can be altered or newly formed. Such listening, that is, not only allows for better psychoanalytic understanding of the person or arena studied but also allows for psychoanalysis itself to change.

In such study there is no offering that does not also imply a receiving. One listens and, at best, learns. The interpretation given on the basis of that learning is the sign of change or potential change in both the interpreter and the subject interpreted. In Kristeva's words, "Each analysis modifies—or should modify—at least some of the beliefs about psychodynamics that I held before hearing what the analysand had to say" (1987b, 51). Lacan, similarly, wrote of the analyst's "ignorance of each subject who comes to him for analysis, of an ever renewed ignorance that prevents anyone becoming a 'case'" (1977, 322).

The analyst's commitment either to religious belief or to atheism should be in abeyance in his or her actual work with an analysand.

Lacan believed that the analyst can seriously consider the question "What does the Other want of me? . . . precisely because there is nothing doctrinal about our office. We are answerable to no ultimate truth" (1977, 316). Such abstinence is a means of being as open as possible to learning from the analysand about aspects of experience that the analyst perhaps heretofore knew not of. This is not to say that the analyst should be reticent to interpret what he can clearly see to be defensive uses of religion. But that judgment should be based on peremptoriness, lack of ego syntonicity, and/or other comparable evidence revealed in the transference/countertransference recapitulation of the patient's experience and not on a preconceived position the analyst has taken on the validity or nonvalidity of religious experience.

No matter the problematic status of what Freud could have meant by "analogue" (LaCapra 1987, 248–50), is there not, between an analogue and an identity, a remainder of difference of the utmost significance? It is one thing to consider religious experience the cultural analogue of neurotic, or psychotic, or infantile experience. It is quite another to judge in advance that religion is neurotic, psychotic, or infantile. The former stance allows the analyst both to learn from another's religious experience and to offer a deeper understanding of the human origins of that experience.

What is a cultural analogue? What change of function is wrought when certain solutions of the private struggles of men and women become established in the cultural order as a body of belief and practice? Does the culturally sanctioned sublime derive from private sublimation in such fashion that both can be or become nondefensive?

As with Freud, and also as with Kristeva, it is easier for most of us to stay with these questions in the realms of art and literature than in the realm of religion. The majority of analysts, along with Kristeva, would believe that an analysis would be less than complete if it did not "lead to renunciation of faith with clear understanding" (Kristeva 1987b, 26).

Kristeva sees faith as pathological merger. Primary identification with the father of personal prehistory models a subsequent "'semiotic' leap toward the other" (1987b, 26). This semiotic leap could be (if it is not regression in the service of achieving some higher level of integration and organization) the level at which religion is the analogue of psychotic experience. It would be difficult for most of us not to think that at least that part of religion should be renounced in a successful analysis. But what if the crucial test of analytic neutrality is precisely at this point? What if, from an analytic point of view, the core validity of religious experience is the return and replaying of the very first steps toward becoming a subject? Who is to say that faith is defensive fusion rather than the product of nondefensive regression and the continuing potentiality for regression in the service of one's being, based on an achieved separateness? Ricoeur (1970, 230) insists that psychoanalysis must go as far as it can in clarifying the sources and meaning of religious experience, but the ultimate move regarding faith or nonfaith is that of the analysand.

There is probably warrant for assuming that any set of practices and beliefs enduringly sanctioned by a cultural order in some way works as the nondefensive product of sublimation that is then presented to individuals of that culture as the sketches of a possible solution to universal private struggles. This *could* be true even though no single individual makes use of those practices and beliefs in purely nondefensive fashion and even though the same set of beliefs and practices *can* lend themselves to the utmost defensive or even demonic deployment by individuals or groups.

An only *possible* solution would imply that nothing in the cultural (or parental) presentation of religion would guarantee either its nondefensive or its defensive use. Again, the judgment, often not an easy one in any event, regarding defensive or nondefensive use is to be made in the individual case. For it to be based on a preconceived position about the beliefs, rather than on their meaning and use in an individual life, would amount to its being not a judgment but a bias and thus the same kind of defensiveness in the analyst that one tends to attribute to the blind believer.

I assume that in primal repression whatever is turned away from is marked by that turning and remains as a danger or a loss to be eventually faced or mourned (Smith 1976a). Turning away structures the human subject from the start as a being marked by a lack and always already unconsciously resisting an unconscious call to reckon with that which is no longer or not yet or incapable of being consciously known. The conflict between the call and resisting the call is forever renewed in each instance of turning away. Each instance of effective mourning not only establishes a separateness from an other but also acknowledges the original and abiding conflict, splitting, or dividedness of the self instituted by primal repression.

Defense

If we take *defensive* to describe a response to dangers involving flight or fight in the form of self-originating, peremptory, unconscious modes of distorting inner and outer reality, and *nondefensive* to describe efforts to know as fully as possible an object of desire or of danger as a basis for approaching the one or facing the other, then either science or religion (or anything else) could be defensively or nondefensively deployed (Smith 1983). I shall attempt to outline here in purely psychoanalytic terms what might be seen as the origins of the possibility for nondefensive religious experience.

Although the dominant elements of maternality and the symbolic mother may be nurturance and unconditional love, and those of paternality and the symbolic father intervention, upholding the law, and mediating the child's entrance into a world that language discloses, actual mothers and actual fathers participate at all these levels. Nurturance and unconditional love are also attributes of the father. Intervention in the infant's implicit assumption of oneness with the mother, upholding the law, helping the child to face dangers, and mediating the child's achievement of separateness and entry into language and thus a world are constant aspects of actual mothering. Within a community of believers in the Judeo-Christian world, all of these parental functions are ultimately experienced as attributes of God. The believer sees this as God's attributes being mediated to the child via the parents. The nonbeliever sees God as a symbol constructed as a consequence of the child's (and the child's family and community) having internalized these aspects of the relationship with parents.

It is often no easy matter for either the subject or a participant observer to judge whether an item or pattern of behavior is defensive or nondefensive. If I feel called upon to face one danger am I thereby, unconsciously, avoiding another, perhaps more pressing danger? If I deny one danger, might I not, in even the unconscious activity of turning away from it, be denying another, unknown but more crucial threat? If I feel called upon to approach an object of desire, might I not in so doing forsake another that, at another level, I am even more urgently called upon to approach? If I believe I am doing the right thing, must I still ask myself whether I do so more for defensive than nondefensive reasons? If so, would that render the "right" thing, for me, in some way "wrong"? And would these be honest questions of a subject striving for greater clarity, or an obsessional defense against any move whatsoever?

Not to ask such questions would be to live one's life forgoing clarity. But, in order to move, to love, to be, one cannot obsessively await answers that are certain. One ultimately moves not on the basis of certainty but on the basis of faith, more or less blind, depending upon one's capacity for clarity. The religious person happily accepts this faith as a gift of grace. The nonreligious person also moves on faith, often no less blindly for having to insert reasons as rationalization. One could even wonder whether what is meant by the question of faith is not the presence or absence of faith but the presence or absence of the capability of confessing it. In this sense, the faith of both the religious and the nonreligious is anchored in the primitive experience of one's needs being met, no matter how inchoately those needs are imagined.

The Fate of the Infantile

In the infant, internalization is instituted by the repeated experience of the mother's absence at a moment of need. If the infant, without boundaries, without language, without temporal dimensions, without being able to think "she was present, she will be present," is limited to either/or primitive responses, which would be closer to the truth, "My mother is always with me" or "My mother has utterly abandoned me"? The cry "says" the latter, the internal image of the mother the former, but it is the former that tends to be confirmed by the repeated experience of the mother's caring response.

Such confirmation, with good-enough mothering, is tempered through repeated experiences of absence, internalization, and thus individuation away from the assumption of being forever merged with the mother, into a faith that one's cry will be heard, one's need met, one's hope fulfilled, one's prayer answered. The early instillation of such faith, though subject to further tempering, can subsequently be eclipsed in various ways but probably never fully extinguished. It has its source in being loved and is also the source of one's ability to love. And if I understand Tillich correctly, to love is what he means by "participation in the eternal" (1967, 2:67). As was said to the woman at Jacob's well, "Every one who drinks of this water will thirst again, but whoever drinks of the water that I shall give him will never thirst; the water that I shall give him will become in him a spring of water welling up to eternal life" (John 4:13–14); and (in 1 John 4:16), "God is love, and he who abides in love abides in God, and God abides in him."

I take Ricoeur, in his comment about psychoanalysis and the possibilities of faith or nonfaith (1970, 230), to mean that psychoanalysis ought to accomplish some prerequisite for that decision, a prerequisite that the ordinary believer has to accomplish on his own. Love as participation in the eternal would not be simply a replay of what Lacan wrote of as the infant's demand for unconditional love. That would be transference as resistance against the necessary recognition of one's specific lot, lack, and limit. Such a demand for love is primarily refusal to accept the empty-handedness with which one enters the world and the lack and dividedness that mark the subject as subject. For Lacan, what is meant by the tempering of the infant's trust that is the presupposition of participation in the eternal is that the analysand should see beyond the "signification that is essential to the advent of the subject . . . to [the] signifier—to [the] irreducible, traumatic, non-meaning—[to which] he is, as a subject, subjected" (1978, 251). To that he added, "In so far as the primary signifier is pure nonsense, it becomes the bearer of the infinitization of the value of the subject," and he further wrote of "the mediation of this infinity of the subject with the finiteness of desire" (1978, 252).

I will not even attempt here to unpack these enigmatic statements, and their implication regarding Lacan's thought on freedom as the acceptance of necessity, beyond noting that the first one cited is an ultimate formulation of experiencing one's thrownness into the world.

Primarily I am here simply playing together psychoanalytic and scriptural refrains to hear what there is to be heard. The only pertinent confession I have to make is that I harbor a constant temptation to wonder whether at least some believing souls might not have traversed the terrain of thrownness and achieved clearer insight about it than is accomplished in the ordinary analysis.

When Voltaire, on his deathbed, was approached by priests pleading that he finally repent his sins and renounce the devil, his response is said to have been, "Now is no time to be making enemies."[6] When I say that I am tempted to think believing souls might have a clearer grasp of the significance of some aspects of human existence, I don't mean just in case there *is* a God. Obviously, if God does exist, those among us who are nonbelievers have, to say the least, rather missed the boat. What I mean, even on the assumption that He does not, is that belief in God, in some instances (Smith 1983, 26), may signify a more valid congruency with the father of personal prehistory and a more mature complement of the ego ideal than what is currently regarded as sophisticated philosophic, psychoanalytic, or scientific understanding. Considering the men and women who have believed and do believe, it is unlikely that a relationship with God is an invariable indicator of having inadequately mourned one's parents.

To suggest that what is perhaps most important in religious experience crucially pertains to the most primitive stages of the self entering the world is not to say, with Freud, that religion is essentially infantile or that the future of infantilism is extinguishment. To put it in the extreme, Freud saw religion as either defense or defect, as either defensive infantilism or infantilism as the sign of thwarted maturation.[7] But mature understanding, mature love, mature hope do not appear on the basis of extinguished infantilism but emerge as the capacity for non-defensive access to the most primitive levels—the capacity at certain moments to be as a child or even as an infant. Such maturity is the aim of both religion and psychoanalysis.

Of course, religion *can* serve as defense or signify defect. But the world was not waiting for psychoanalysis to demonstrate that. Each religious individual, just like any other individual, has always been called upon to wrestle with defense and reckon with the possibility of defect. On that issue, Westphal (1987, 18) reminds us of Jeremiah and advises reading Kierkegaard, who wrote, "Seriousness consists precisely in having the honest suspicion of thyself, treating thyself as a suspicious character, as a capitalist treats an insolvent person" (Kierkegaard 1944, 68, as cited in Westphal 1987, 18).

What Freud did was to specify with greater clarity the meanings of defense and the sources of defect, at the same time showing the ultimate difficulty of drawing a definite line between the two. The whole gist of Tillich's and Ricoeur's writing on psychoanalysis and religion is that psychoanalytic iconoclasm can reveal the naïve and defensive idolization of religious practice and belief and thus allow for the achievement of a "second naïveté" and a more mature religion.[8]

It was Freud's belief that both art and religion are illusions, illusion acknowledged in the case of art and illusion unacknowledged in the case of religion. He was able to ponder the truth of illusion but not what he perceived to be illusion construed as truth. The former involved the creative inventiveness of play, the latter, to his mind, the static, infantile fixity of delusion.[9]

Arguably, this extreme contrast may have been a bias according to which he was more willing to see the individual and cultural value of the sublimatory working through of childhood issues than he was those of infancy. The consequence, according to Ricoeur, is that any adequate Freudian understanding of religious experience can only be found by transposing his thought on art into the religious realm.

I would only add that between the lines of Freud's severe rejection of religion (and not always just between the lines [*S. E.* 21:74]), there is an even more ardent rejection of those who would deprive religion of its essence by rendering it more "rational" and thus *less* infantile. This could be taken as his impatience with any attempt to hold onto something that should, with maturity and the courage to face life and death without false consolation, be thrown out kit and caboodle. However, when he chastises religious modernists by writing, "One would like to mix among the ranks of the believers in order to meet these philosophers, who think they can rescue the God of religion by replacing him by an impersonal, shadowy and abstract principle, and to address them with the warning words: 'Thou shalt not take the name of the Lord thy God in vain'" (*S. E.* 21:74), one could be led to another interpretation. Could it be that he harbored a covert aspiration to find a psychoanalytic validity of religious experience that would make his own work on art, and certainly that of modern rationalizers of religion, seem like child's play? Was he not attempting some such thing in *Totem and Taboo* and *Moses and Monotheism*?

Perhaps the either/or, all-or-none tendency of infantile response is also evoked in the thinker who attempts to trace the ultimate fate of the infantile in a mature individual or culture. Freud's overt rejection of the validity of religious experience might suggest such a possibility. But actually Freud is subject to two related and seemingly contradictory accusations. One is that he saw religion as nothing but infantile. The other is that (as in areas other than religion also) he almost totally ignored the infantile and preoedipal roots of religion in favor of a primarily oedipal interpretation.

In *Civilization and Its Discontents* he wrote, "In my *Future of an Illusion* [1927] I was concerned much less with the deepest sources of the religious feeling than with what the common man understands by his religion" (*S. E.* 21:74). However, in the following I will argue that, in his overall work, Freud's greatest contribution to understanding the deepest human sources of religious experience was his rigorous delineation of its infantile roots and its connection with the paternal function. The justification of his writing in oedipal terms is that it is only there—in the replaying at a higher, linguistically based, triadic level—that the events leading to early mother/infant differentiation come to light. It is not just that the paternal function comes sharply into focus in the oedipal era; it is also that oedipal renunciation interprets, sheds light on, the role of the paternal function in the renunciation of symbiosis. The oedipal level interprets infantilism.

I do not mean to suggest that religion derives only from infantile experience and not also from the oedipal crisis and the replaying of that crisis in adolescence and later periods of life. I mean only that the oedipal crisis is already a replaying of the crisis of early individuation and the advent of language. Any religion that sought to base itself exclusively in an oedipal beginning could only be a watered-down religion, which, as Freud knew (*S. E.* 21:54), would be of no interest.

Ricoeur (1969, 152; 1970, 342, 364) argues that in any symbolic series, subsequent levels interpret prior ones, but the symbolic efficacy of all later levels derives from their most primitive form. The greatest flaw in Freud's interpretation of religion is not his contention that religion is infantile but his conviction that it is nothing but infantile. For him, the story of religion is not the story of stages in life's way, or of sublimation, or of mature forms of infantile experience. It is instead the ahistorical story of infantilism and neurosis prolonged.

I do not doubt Freud's courage to face life and death without false consolation. But what, in Freud, would true consolation have been? Was this only courage or was it courage admixed with the kind of denied nostalgia for a lost prior consolation that leads some persons to resist all future consolations? Religion aside, what is going on in a man's engagement with a work of art when he stops to remind himself that art is illusion? Is that not already saying what he specifically wrote of religion, "Its consolations deserve no trust" (*S. E.* 22:168)?

But, of course that would be the writing Freud and not Freud in San Pietro in Vincoli allowing Michelangelo's *Moses* to work on him. I find Peter Gay's (1987) insistence that we should take Freud at his word regarding his atheism convincing. This leaves me at quite a distance, certainly, from the thesis of Vitz's *Sigmund Freud's Christian Unconscious* (1988). However, I assume from Freud's writing on religion that, as in the case of art, the nonwriting Freud, perhaps unlike Gay and other modernists, was able to put himself in the shoes of both the Jewish and Christian believer, and allow their faith to work on him.

As for consolations, I have no doubt that a mother picking up a crying infant or a two-year-old with a skinned knee, the early identification with the mother's trust in her world, the early identification with the father of personal prehistory, were, for Freud, valid consolations and not just magical rites in any pejorative sense. But what would be the form of oedipal, adolescent, and later consolation?

Well, courage itself is consolation. But how does courage become established? That it becomes established through the experience of facing danger and withstanding adversity still leaves the question of how one achieves and maintains the capacity to do so.

Of course, underlying the consolation of anything that is its own reward (like courage, love, honesty, humor, scientific truth, art, all other products of sublimation that constitute the cultural order, and the cultural order as such) is trust that had its beginnings as one dimension of love. Without love/trust the capacity to face danger in noncounterphobic fashion is hampered in the extreme, and even when severe adversity is endured, which it surely is by those without love, it more heightens defense than augments courage. In fact, being without love is the ultimate adversity in life and gives death itself its sting. Love—not love instead of recognition, but love as recognition of and by the specific other—Freud would have agreed, is the ultimate consolation.

As for maturity, the question is, what does it mean to have put away childish things? Surely no one would argue that it means to put away love, but only childish modes of loving. However, it is more ambiguous than that since adult love includes the capacity to be as a child and to love as a child. An instance of the latter is the capacity to be as a child that is one component of the mother's attunement to her infant, as is also the openness of lovers to the multiple levels of each other.

Adults live in a world, in a cultural and symbolic order, that the child is only entering. They know much about the dangers that will challenge the child's future happiness, but they also harbor a faith in at least the possibility that those dangers can be traversed and that a measure of feeling at home in the world can be achieved. They have faith in the world, the world being the symbolic order in its cultural embodiment, which they experience as given in trust by God and/or forefathers. They also have hope that their child will be able to enter that world, to have faith in it, and to participate in the sense of being both sustained by it and called upon to sustain it.

Beyond threats to life itself, the chief danger to be traversed is that of the child's remaining mired in only narcissistic, self-centered modes of love and hate. For that reason, ethical teaching—teaching the child regard for others—begins early. Freud's dominant idea is that ethical teaching takes hold in the child because of desperate need for the parent's love and care. Ethical standards are imposed from without, though later internalized through the mourning consequent to repeated instances of guilt in which the parent's love is experienced as lost. This is the origin of the superego, the internal silent "voice" that, according to Freud and Heidegger (1962, 325–29), can only say "Guilty!" The child is called unto (Heidegger) or is forced into (Freud) obedience.

Imperative need unmet is the scene of rage, primitive guilt, identification with the bad, absent, witch-mother, an identification that tells the infant its own needs are the evil that disturbs paradise. To feel one's needs and peremptory wishes as evil is to feel one's self as evil and therefore dependent—desperately dependent—on one's mother for absolution. It is the scene of preoedipal primitive guilt (Smith 1986) that lies behind oedipal guilt. It is the scene that is covered by Freud's (S. E. 13:141–45) story of the guilty bonding together and renunciation of incest consequent to the murder of the primal father, a loveless bonding together to care for each other under the pressure of guilt, expedience, and necessity.

The Father of Personal Prehistory

But there is another story line in Freud regarding the origin and development of the capacity to care for others. It is the story of primitive trust, identification with the father of personal prehistory, the ego-ideal, sublimation, and unforced, freely given love. His statement that something in sexuality itself fosters sublimation ("something in the nature of the [sexual] function itself . . . urges us along other paths [into sublimations and libidinal displacements]" [S. E. 21:105–6; cf. S. E. 12:61]) can be taken as a claim that all love is sexual in the sense that sexuality leads one to the object, to an interest in the object, and, eventually, to knowing and loving the separate object in its own right.

Peremptory drivenness countered by peremptory no-saying is the mode of primitive id-superego interaction. However, not all infantile interaction with the object is a moment of peremptory need. At moments after awakening but before needs have mounted to a peremptory level and also after feeding but before falling asleep, the infant can take an unpressured interest in the mother's attributes and, eventually, come to know and love her and identify with her in a manner that is not tied to the urgency of need.

It is not quite right to call this mode of primary love "sublimated" as if it were a direct transformation or a "taming" of the peremptory drive. This nonperemptory mode of coming to know the object is there from the start and, as model, provides the major pathway from narcissistic to object love. It no doubt also provides the model for sublimation rather than repression, where peremptory drives confront a categorical "no." [10]

Freud conceptualized nonperemptory primary love as identification with the father of personal prehistory. This is primary and direct love and identification, mediated first by the mother, to be sure, and then by the father. It is not the product of loss, conflict, or peremptory need. It occurs before delineation of self and other in the mind of the infant but is, nevertheless, a loving identification with an other. One comes to awareness of self and other with a love of the other always already there.

Why does the name of the father take precedence in nonperemptory primary love when only the mother could be the first object of such love? This question can be taken as text for further adjusting criticism of Freud for underweighting preoedipal engagement and overweighting oedipal issues in attempting to account for a person's ethical stance. If moving beyond the narcissistic symbiotic enclosure with the mother is the major initial developmental task, the nonperemptory mode of loving is already a step in that direction. One loves her not only because she meets one's needs but also on the basis of attributes not necessarily related to the immediacy of one's needs.

This mode of love paves the way for similarly loving the father as the first significant other of the mother/infant unit, and it is the love of the father that ultimately secures one's release from Eden. Furthermore, the events of personal prehistory with the mother, while fundamentally shaping the child's basic balance of trust/distrust or innocence/guilt, only come to light at the point of language. At that point there is a replaying of early steps in differentiation at the level of experiencing the paternal function as prohibitor of symbiosis and, subsequently, of oedipal yearning.

Speech signifies that separateness from the mother has been accomplished through the prior and mute crisis of infancy. That separation is then replayed at the triadic level. The drama of the "prehistorical" mother-child separation is remourned in the oedipal renunciation of peremptory love. In addition, the nature and degree of the separateness achieved at age one—the time of language acquisition—no doubt shapes the way in which the oedipal crisis is traversed. It probably significantly influences, for instance, whether a dominantly positive or a dominantly negative oedipal complex ensues.

As Freud acknowledges in a footnote (*S. E.* 19:31), the identification with the father of personal prehistory *has* to refer to and be based on the nonperemptory love of and direct, immediate, nonconflictual identification with *both* parents. The mother, though, before being constituted as other, is the initial object of both peremptory and nonperemptory demand and desire. It is she who is the primordial no-sayer, including the implicit no-saying of her concrete, physical, "unassimilable" thingliness (Freud, *S. E.* 1:331, 366). It is also she who is the initial object of love, including the nonperemptory love that provided at least a nonconflictual dimension to the process of the child's departure from symbiosis. It is her interest in the child's future as a separate being in his or her own right that, with the advent of language, motivates her to mediate the place of the Other, the place of the no-sayer, and the lawgiver to the father. The father, as the first significant other of the symbiotic unit and therefore representative of the world the child is entering, then becomes the object of the child's nonperemptory love and identification.[11]

By the time the early frustrations and satisfactions with the mother have been traversed; by the time the bad and good mother has become one, separate, other; by the time of language; the father has been installed not only as the ultimate no-sayer but also as the ultimate object of love in the world apart from the mother, which the child is entering. The mother in the place of the Other, the mother as both no-sayer and object of love and identification, is largely covered over in the preverbal and prehistoric past and in the dimension of unconsciousness related to that era. The capacity to make and have a history arrives with language, separateness, temporality, and worldhood. In that world, the father appears as the no-sayer to the prior symbiosis and also the no-sayer to mounting oedipal desire—the dominant no-sayer to oedipal yearnings in both the boy and the girl. At that point, the crucial primal, direct, immediate, nonconflictual love and identification of personal prehistory become the already established love and identification with the father. It is he who demands the most crucial renunciations, and these are accomplished not only out of fear but also out of love.

Freud saw both story lines, the one a fear of retribution and the other an aspect of nonperemptory, freely given love, as pertinent to the development of the capacity to care for others. Of the two, the raw fear of retribution is considerably the less reliable and, by itself, could not sustain an ethical stance. Since Freud took religion to be primarily motivated by a fear of retribution that went hand in hand with infantile, peremptory needs for love, care, and protection, it followed that he saw religion not only as an unreliable basis for ethics but also as a generally pacifying and therefore inhibiting factor in the development of the individual and the race. For Freud it was fear and needy love that motivated religion, with little allowance for the role of nonperemptory, freely given love. Belief in God was at best a sign of inadequate depersonification of the superego and the ego ideal and at worst but a projection of the primitive, narcissistically grandiose ideal ego.

Religion and Developmental History

My argument is this: if Freud's account of early development is as universally valid as I believe it to be, it is unlikely that the universal presence of religion stands as the analogue of only pathological deviation from that development. If Freud had been less closed to religion he would, I believe, have learned from it some things that could have rendered his account of development even more valid, more intricate, and more complete. There would no doubt be general agreement that Winnicott's response to cultural phenomena resulted in such an improved psychoanalytic understanding of development.[12]

The father, the other, out there in the world the child is entering, represents the world, the future, and, in some measure, is figured as the representative of a symbolic father who presides over the world and the future. The nonperemptory primary love and identification that, more reliably than fear, allow the child to accept and internalize the paternal injunctions are not without their own developmental history. It is not just that frustration and fear are mitigated by this love and primary identification; frustration and fear are further mitigated and love, identification, and individuation enhanced when, beyond each crisis of renunciation and mourning, the child comes to know that the renunciation demanded was in the child's own interest and arose from the father's love. In a functional family, the dominant determinants of the father's no-saying to the son's symbiotic or oedipal desires are obviously not the motive of last resort—the "you can't have her, she's mine" of the father of Freud's primal horde.

Of course, at the point of each paternal injunction, the actual father is also hated. But the crux of the matter is not just the balance of love and hate shaped by the prior history of maternal care. It is, in addition, the fact that each renunciation is also a step in acknowledging lack and achieving separateness and thus a more owned and object-related love and hate.

Rizzuto (1979), Meissner (1984), Vergote (1969), and Vergote and Tamayo (1981) have shown that where religion is a part of the child's life, advancing maturity in the child's relationship with God runs parallel with these steps in individuating from parents and family. If there is such a thing as a mature religious experience, the history of its development would be delineated in such studies. Similarly, it would not be unreasonable to expect that the changes that occur in religious belief and practice during psychoanalysis might be those that occur in the ordinary, relatively nondefensive maturation process of believing souls. The God worshiped by mature men and women is a God who is loved and feared but not hated; presumably, this has some parallel in the fact that achieved separateness from good-enough parents also gets essentially beyond hatred of them. One could maintain that mature belief in God, rather than being an indicator of failed individuation, is dependent upon individuation achieved.

Perhaps it is only after individuation has been reaccomplished in adolescence and young adulthood that one is able to grapple, as a separate being, with the questions of birth, the primal scene, loss, guilt, castration, death, sex, nakedness, parents, and siblings that were also the content of primal fantasies and the subject matter of primitive symbolization. However, because of achieved separateness, the awesomeness of those questions and their adult analogues (which would include the question of offspring, future generations, and one's accountability to the human order) is exponentially increased. The reemergence of such questions can be heeded or unheeded. The religious person often feels addressed by them in such fashion that the father of personal prehistory comes to be experienced as the initial mediator of a Father of the World and primitive trust the precursor of adult faith.

The possibility of such mature faith allows us to ask if Lacan, Lacan the nonbeliever, was merely "fond," as Richardson in this volume mentions, "of using religious allusions and metaphors." Though that is what his overt intellectual flamboyance would suggest, one could wonder whether his insisting on terms from virtually the literal language of Judeo-Christianity, like "the Other" and "the name of the father," represented his own either conscious or unconscious insight that literal believers might be participants in a wisdom of the ages more attuned to the actualities of movement from birth and symbiosis to adult belonging and death than modern, outside observers could suspect.

Conclusion

On the assumption that either religious faith or religious nonfaith could be nondefensive, psychoanalysis, in the absence of evidence of defensiveness, should not, with Kristeva, presume that a successful analysis will have traversed the renunciation of faith. As mentioned above, Ricoeur's point is that the renunciation of idols and of defensive attachment to parents and their surrogates that a successful analysis achieves leads to a twofold possibility, that of faith and that of nonfaith. In the face of those possible moves, psychoanalysis ought to be silent.

To defend psychoanalysis is to defend the limitations proper to psychoanalysis. One of these is that in its clinical application there is no ultimate, positive definition of health. The psychoanalyst follows the patient in seeking to clarify suffering directly complained of or attested by symptoms, inhibitions, and defenses. Symptoms and inhibitions *are* defenses. The aim of treatment is a relative absence of defense.

Defense attests to suffering, but not all suffering is defensive. Relative absence of defense describes trust. But trust is not only the product of defense dispelled; it is also the presupposition of the work required for mourning and the ongoing task of sorting the suffering that is subject to alleviation and the suffering that is not. Mature trust, mature faith, whether specifically religious or not, allows for this sorting and for the endurance of inevitable suffering. That is half of the story, the half with which stoics like Freud and most of the rest of us feel at home. The other half we are told of, that faith also provides access to dimensions of love, joy, and peace that surpass understanding, remains, for most of us, most of the time, more problematic.

Notes

1. Here is Geertz's gloss on the Santayana text:

The religious perspective differs from the common-sensical in that . . . it moves beyond the realities of everyday life to wider ones which correct and complete them, and its defining concern is not action upon those wider realities but acceptance of them, faith in them. It differs from the scientific perspective in that it questions the realities of everyday life not out of an institutionalized skepticism which dissolves the world's givenness into a swirl of probabilistic hypotheses, but in terms of what it takes to be wider, nonhypothetical truths. Rather than detachment, its watchword is commitment; rather than analysis, encounter. And it differs from art in that instead of effecting a disengagement from the whole question of factuality, deliberately manufacturing an air of semblance and illusion, it deepens the concern with fact and seeks to create an aura of utter actuality. It is this sense of the "really real" upon which the religious perspective rests and which the symbolic activities of religion as a cultural system are devoted to producing, intensifying, and, so far as possible, rendering inviolable by the discordant revelations of secular experience. It is . . . the imbuing of a certain specific complex of symbols—of the metaphysic they formulate and the style of life they recommend—with a persuasive authority which, from an analytic point of view, is the essence of religious action. [1973, 112]

2. *About Chinese Women* (1977); *Desire in Language: A Semiotic Approach to Literature and Art* (1980); *Powers of Horror: An Essay on Abjection* (1982); *Revolution In Poetic Language* (1984); *The Kristeva Reader* (1986), and *Tales of Love* (1987a). For her intellectual background and a bibliography through 1985, see the introduction to *The Kristeva Reader.* In my judgment *Tales of Love* is the most accessible and clinically pertinent introduction to her work. For further commentary see my "Evening the Score," *Modern Language Notes,* and my review of *In the Beginning Was Love, Journal of the American Psychoanalytic Association,* both forthcoming.

3. This is Richardson's explication herein of Lacan's "there is no Other of

the Other": "To 'live out the consequences of this recognition' is to deny the possibility of God as Other than the Other. Nor can He be identified with the Other as Father, or Law or Name-of-the-Father, for the Other is no more than the laws of language functioning in their cultural-historical embodiment. Nor can He reside there as some center or foundation of meaning, for there is no center, and if meaning implies unity, there is no meaning either." In his article in this volume he also writes, "If God is to be encountered in the Lacanian paradigm, it is not in terms of the symbolic order. . . . His thought, however, permits us to ask whether the God whom Claudel worships is not to be found in the Real, the dimension of ineffable, unimaginable mystery." Richardson thus converts Lacan's declarative statement, "*The gods belong to the field of the real*" (1978, 45) to a question worthy of thought.

4. The identification, according to Freud, "takes place earlier than any object-cathexis" (*S. E.* 19:31). See Kristeva on "An 'Immediate' and Objectless Identification" (1987a, 26). I think identification with the father of personal prehistory must be taken as referring essentially to the basic orientation or foothold in the world achieved during the symbiotic stage, which culminates in the unity established in the still preverbal, preconscious organization of Freud's narcissistic stage or Lacan's mirror stage. It is an organization that likely derives from nonperemptory experience in which, beyond the urgency of pressing need, the infant's beginning self and world can be imagistically and affectively opened up and explored (Smith 1976b). It is at such moments and by reason of such organization that the infant can notice and identify with aspects of the mother other than those tied only to her being the object of peremptory need. This would include noticing and identifying with her way of being in the world beyond that of only the mother-infant unit.

5. Nondefensive identification is accomplished by mourning. André Green wrote, "Identification as relating to mourning of the primordial object . . . is the same process which grounds desire in desire of the Other, since mourning places itself as intermediary in the relationship of subject to Other and in the relationship of subject to object" (1983, 184).

6. I have not been able to document this statement. It could be seen as inconsistent with the difficult negotiations with the church in his final days for the sanctioned burial that he almost missed (see accounts of his death in Mason 1981, 147–50, and Besterman 1969, 27). However, it would be consistent with positions he held that necessitated those negotiations.

7. Freud wrote, "If the application of the psycho-analytic method makes it possible to find a new argument against the truths of religion, *tant pis* for religion" (*S. E.* 21:37). Well, if it turns out that a well-developed religion has endured in every advanced culture more out of nondefensive and mature understanding of self and world, then *tant pis* for Freud.

8. His clarification of the defensive uses of religion is why at least some religious persons (for instance, Will Herberg) will always read Freud and, in spite of his bias against religion, find his work more pertinent to religious struggle and celebration than Jung and many others "sympathetic" to religion.

The more compelling reason is, of course, that if one faces being killed it is preferable that it be at the hands of one who declares himself an enemy rather than one who avows friendliness (Herberg, personal communication).

9. Freud did not stress the self-punishing motives of religious experience as did Nietzsche. Unlike Nietzsche, he was overtly not so much angry or scornful of religion as he was astonished and embarrassed that his fellow beings could be involved in the false consolation of something "so patently infantile" (*S. E.* 21:74).

10. Similarly, the capacity to behold an erstwhile object of danger at a nonperemptory moment is no doubt the major pathway toward being able to anticipate and evaluate a potential danger so that it can be avoided or renounced by an act of judgment rather than by blind flight or fight. More generally, the nonperemptory is the moment wherein the primary functions of ego can appear and *be* autonomous, rather than be imperatively pressed into the service of the drives or defense.

11. For a philosopher's similar account of the transition "from the mother-child relation to the triangle father-mother-child," see Ver Eecke (1984, 78–84).

12. Paul Pruyser (1983) has detailed the pertinence of Winnicott's thinking to religious experience.

References

Besterman, Theodore. *Voltaire.* New York: Harcourt, Brace & World, 1969.

Freud, Sigmund. *The Standard Edition of the Complete Psychological Works of Sigmund Freud.* Edited and translated by James Strachey. 24 vols. London: Hogarth Press, 1953–74.

"Project for A Scientific Psychology" (1950 [1895]), vol. 1.

Psycho-Analytic Notes on an Autobiographical Account of a Case of Paranoia (1911), vol. 12.

Totem and Taboo (1913), vol. 13.

"The Unconscious" (1915), vol. 14.

The Ego and the Id (1923), vol. 19.

The Future of an Illusion (1927), vol. 21.

Civilization and Its Discontents (1930), vol. 21.

New Introductory Lectures on Psycho-Analysis (1933), vol. 22.

Gay, Peter. *An Infidel Jew.* New Haven: Yale University Press, 1987.

Geertz, Clifford. *The Interpretation of Cultures.* New York: Basic Books, 1973.

Green, André. "The Logic of Lacan's *objet (a)* and Freudian Theory: Convergences and Questions." In *Interpreting Lacan,* edited by Joseph H. Smith and William Kerrigan. *Psychiatry and the Humanities,* vol. 6. New Haven: Yale University Press, 1983.

Hartmann, Heinz. "Notes on the Reality Principle." In *Essays on Ego Psychology.* London: Hogarth Press, 1964.

Heidegger, Martin. *Being and Time.* Translated by John Macquarrie and Edward Robinson. New York: Harper and Row, 1962.

Kierkegaard, Soren. *For Self-Examination and Judge for Yourself.* Translated by Walter Lowrie. Princeton: Princeton University Press, 1944.

Kristeva, Julia. *About Chinese Women.* New York: Urizen Books, 1977. (In paperback by Marion Books, distributed by Macmillan, 1986.)

————. *Desire in Language: A Semiotic Approach to Literature and Art.* Edited by Leon Roudiez. Translated by Thomas Gore, Alice Jardine, and Leon S. Roudiez. New York: Columbia University Press, 1980.

————. *Powers of Horror: An Essay on Abjection.* Translated by Leon S. Roudiez. New York: Columbia University Press, 1982.

————. "Within the Microcosm of 'The Talking Cure.'" In *Interpreting Lacan,* edited by Joseph Smith and William Kerrigan. Psychiatry and the Humanities, vol. 6. New Haven: Yale University Press, 1983.

————. *Revolution in Poetic Language.* Translated by Margaret Walker with an introduction by Leon S. Roudiez. New York: Columbia University Press, 1984.

————. *The Kristeva Reader.* Edited by Toril Moi. New York: Columbia University Press, 1986.

————. *Tales of Love.* Translated by Leon S. Roudiez. New York: Columbia University Press, 1987a.

————. *In the Beginning Was Love: Psychoanalysis and Faith.* Translated by Arthur Goldhammer with an introduction by Otto F. Kernberg. New York: Columbia University Press, 1987b.

Lacan, Jacques. *Ecrits.* Translated by Alan Sheridan. New York: W. W. Norton, 1977.

————. *The Four Fundamental Concepts of Psycho-Analysis.* Edited by Jacques-Alain Miller. Translated by Alan Sheridan. New York: W. W. Norton, 1978.

————. *Feminine Sexuality.* Edited by Juliet Mitchell and Jacqueline Rose. Translated by Jacqueline Rose. New York: W. W. Norton, 1982.

LaCapra, Dominick. "History and Psychoanalysis." *Critical Inquiry* 13 (1987): 222–51.

Mason, Haydn. *Voltaire.* Baltimore: Johns Hopkins University Press, 1981.

Meissner, William. *Psychoanalysis and Religion Experience.* New Haven: Yale University Press, 1984.

Piaget, Jean. "The Affective Unconscious and the Cognitive Unconscious." *Journal of the American Psychoanalytic Association* 21 (1973): 249–61.

Pruyser, Paul. *The Play of the Imagination: Toward a Psychoanalysis of Culture.* New York: International Universities Press, 1983.

Ricoeur, Paul. *The Symbolism of Evil.* Boston: Beacon Press, 1969.

————. *Freud and Philosophy: An Essay on Interpretation.* Translated by Denis Savage. New Haven: Yale University Press, 1970.

Rizzuto, Ana-Maria. *The Birth of the Living God.* Chicago: University of Chicago Press, 1979.

Smith, Joseph H. Review of *Semiotic Approaches to Psychotherapy*, by Eugen Bär, and *Language and Interpretation in Psychoanalysis*, by Marshall Edelson. *Psychiatry* 39 (1976a): 404–9.

———. "Language and the Genealogy of the Absent Object." In *Psychiatry and the Humanities*, edited by Joseph H. Smith. Psychiatry and the Humanities, vol. 1. New Haven: Yale University Press, 1976b.

———. "Introduction." In *Psychoanalysis and Language*, edited by Joseph H. Smith. Psychiatry and the Humanities, vol. 3. New Haven: Yale University Press, 1978.

———. "Rite, Ritual, and Defense." *Psychiatry* 46 (1983): 16–30.

———. "Primitive Guilt." In *Pragmatism's Freud: The Moral Disposition of Psychoanalysis*, edited by Joseph H. Smith and William Kerrigan. Psychiatry and the Humanities, vol. 9. Baltimore: Johns Hopkins University Press, 1986.

———. "Evening the Score." *Modern Language Notes*, in press.

———. Review: *In the Beginning Was Love: Psychoanalysis and Faith*, by Julia Kristeva. Translated by Arthur Goldhammer with an introduction by Otto F. Kernberg. New York: Columbia University Press, 1987. *Journal of the American Psychoanalytic Association*, in press.

Tillich, Paul. *Systematic Theology*. Chicago: University of Chicago Press, 1967.

Ver Eecke, Wilfried. *Saying "No"*. Pittsburgh: Duquesne University Press, 1984.

Vergote, Antoine. *The Religious Man*. Translated by Sister Marie-Bernard Said. Dayton: Pflaum Press, 1969.

———. "From Freud's 'Other Scene' to Lacan's 'Other.'" In *Interpreting Lacan*, edited by Joseph H. Smith and William Kerrigan. Psychiatry and the Humanities, vol. 6. New Haven: Yale University Press, 1983.

Vergote, Antoine, and Tamayo, Alvaro. *The Parental Figures and the Representation of God: A Psychological and Cross-Cultural Study*. The Hague: Mouton, 1981.

Vitz, Paul. *Sigmund Freud's Christian Unconscious*. New York: Guilford Press, 1988.

Westphal, Merold. *God, Guilt, and Death*. Bloomington: Indiana University Press, 1987.

3   Reality in Religion and Psychoanalysis

Stanley A. Leavy

I t may appear paradoxical, or at least willful, to begin an essay on reality by illustrative reference to a drama. What could be less of the order of reality than a play? What takes place on the stage, or even more so on the page, is a deliberate illusion. We mistake theater for reality only if we are as childish as that peasant Goethe wrote about who got up in his box at the performance of *Julius Caesar* at the point where the conspirators were about to kill Caesar and cried out "Stop!" But drama has roots in reality, too. The writer, the producer, the director, the stage manager and stagehands, and the actors all make their living in the drama, and the problems of producing and performing are themselves real enough. The story, or action, is fictitious; the actors do not "mean" what they say. Yet a play is no good if it does not speak to the minds of the audience, whether as an exposure to a real-enough even if unfamiliar world—like, say, Arthur Miller's *View from the Bridge,* or even a prolonged fantasy like Maurice Maeterlinck's libretto for *Pelléas and Mélisande.* Accordingly, I shall try to allude to the question of reality in religion and psychoanalysis by first summarizing a famous play.

In Pedro Calderón's drama of 1635, *Life Is a Dream (La Vida Es Sueño),* the hero, Segismundo, has been imprisoned by his father, King Basilio, since infancy and brought up in ignorance of his royal state, to prevent the fulfillment of a prediction made before his birth that he would grow up to destroy his father and the kingdom. His father later repents of this unjust measure and commands that his son, now a young man, be put into a profound sleep, from which he will awake in all of the luxury and power due him by birth and, indeed, as king in his

43

father's stead. His erstwhile keeper will declare to him that his memory of his earlier life is a dream. This belated remedy includes a built-in solution for the difficulties that might arise if the son turns out to be in actuality the monster he was allegedly destined to be: he can be drugged again and returned to prison, and the recent elevation to royalty declared a dream. For Basilio these manipulations are justified, since he believes that "in this world, all who live are dreaming." When the transformation takes place Segismundo is at first convinced that the preceding years as he recalls them have been only a dream, and he assumes his prerogatives.

When his former jailer at length reveals to him that his previous state was not a dream, the newly awakened man rapidly begins to fulfill the baleful prediction; he is enraged and drives Basilio away. Then he turns on a servant who has crossed his will and thrusts him over a balcony. His rage against his father's earlier treatment of him results in wild fury and the threat of revenge: his father has denied him not only love but also his rights as a man. In response to his wrathful behavior, Segismundo is accordingly returned to sleep and to prison. On awakening, once more he is confronted with uncertainty about whether he is dreaming now or was before. It has been less problematic for his father, for whom life itself is a dream, but Segismundo, too, in the most famous lines of the play, concludes that "all of life is a dream, and even dreams are dreams."

It is not necessary to dwell further on the complexities of this remarkable play. They turn not merely on the confusion between dream and waking in the lives of father and son but also on many other disguises and mistaken identities, in which at times no one can be quite sure who is who. In summarizing Calderón's play, I may have given rise to hopes or fears that I will subject it to a psychoanalytic study. It has so plainly an oedipal theme that it fairly cries out for such treatment: a more devoted ego psychologist than I would surely have to ponder on the function of the oppressive father in distorting the son's sense of reality. But I have no such intention and shall limit myself to using the play as background music, so to speak, for an inquiry into psychoanalytic concepts of reality and their implications for religion.

Dreams, Stories, and Reality

Psychoanalysts know that a comparable interplay between dream and waking, fantasy and reality, truth and fiction, constitutes the fabric of the psychoanalytic process in its classical presentation. In a sense, the psychoanalytic process adds to the confusion between dreaming

and waking. The meaning of a dream is revealed through an interpretive method that exposes in the day's residues perceptions formed
during waking, of persons and objects in the concrete environment.
The real world, the objective world that exists whether the dreamer
has perceived it or not, provides the substance of the visual and other
sensory enactments in the dream. Even the most realistic of dreams,
seemingly drawn from concrete experience without modification, on
examination turns out to be the result of quite selectively chosen perceptions, so that we have to assume in the dreamwork a principle of
selection that was not itself part of the external reality. Of yet greater
gravity, the analysis of all dreams also reveals that there are more
distant principles (distant, that is, from common-sense notice) that
govern their formation. All the perceptions, memories, intentions, desires that have gone into the substance of the recalled dream have
yielded to the dreamwork, which condenses, displaces, distorts, and
re-presents them in images often quite distinct from any in the conscious waking life of the dreamer.

Interpretation of the dream may point to perceptions of the real
world of which the dreamer has hitherto remained unaware; they
range from commonplace data, things seen and not taken note of, to
scenes witnessed in early life and seemingly maintained in an affectless
limbo, subject now to revival under the affective influences of current
life, maybe experiences of transference. In these cases, the dream has
restored to waking life repressed perceptions of the objective world.

But the analysis of dreams is only part of the psychoanalytic process. It may be a very small part in individual instances. What is far
more important is the fact that in psychoanalyzing we treat *all* the
messages, stories, memories of the patient as if they, too, were dreams.
That is, we simultaneously attend to spoken statements as factual observations, as valid as any other statements can be, and also examine
them through the refracting medium of our own preconscious
thoughts as screens for fantasy. This is in itself one of the oldest and
still one of the most important of all psychoanalytic findings: that all
statements are at least potentially the bearers of hidden messages, as
we learned in the first instance from dreams. In short, Calderón's un-
happy hero had a point when he said that "even dreams are dreams."

That is, however, not the whole story. Even if we were in the position of Segismundo and could not be sure which state we were in at
any time, we should be able and even required to distinguish between
two states. If we desperately dismissed both as forms of dreaming,
nevertheless thresholds would appear between them, implying differentiation. If we were only dreaming all the time, we would not know

anything about dreams. Although we may from time to time be aware during dreaming that we are dreaming, only a change in state permits the idea: "I was dreaming then." On the other hand, the unconscious process continues during sleeping and waking, transforming the data of perception into forms structured according to the properties of our previous experience and our inborn dispositions, within the horizons of our symbolic world—that is, our inner world of images and meanings, public and private in origin. These transformations are the basis of the unconscious fantasies that are as effective in waking life as in dreaming, at times to the extent of governing our thoughts and our actions.

What is at stake here is the concept of reality—of that which exists in itself and is not just part of private experience. Despite the psychoanalytic reading of the unconscious, dreamlike aspect of experience, we also insist on being able to distinguish that aspect from reality. However distorted the fantasy, it has grown from perceptions, most of them shared by others, or at least capable of being shared, and perceptions must have referents not present in the beholder alone. Of every life it can be said with total conviction: "Something really happened." Events occurring in the life of the individual have values, to be sure, that depend not only on their own nature but also on the state of psychic preparation; but events *do* occur, and there is an external world that exists in its own right.

In ordinary psychoanalytic work, as in ordinary life, we employ a common-sense empirical notion of reality that serves us well enough. It is based on self-existent events and on facts that can be seen, or measured, or photographically recorded, and so forth. If my patient tells me he has been working at the computer all day, I may allow for exaggeration if necessary, but I do not doubt the reality of the computer or the work. If another patient informs me that my office is cold, or unswept, or too small, I may or may not agree with her criticisms, but I do not doubt that she thinks so with some reason. In both cases nothing is to prevent me from reading further into the statements implicit elements of fantasy, but the objective reality in the first instance and the subjective in the second have a being of their own. The concept of "reality testing" rests on the conviction that there is a reality with which the fantasy, the dream, the association can be compared.

This standard of factuality underlies psychoanalyzing like a baseline from which deviations become observable. We psychoanalysts are not to be dissuaded from it by reminders that sometimes the most ordinary events and facts are recognized differently by different observers and that we do not have to follow Dickens's Mr. Gradgrind in his dull and rigid establishment of what "facts" are, because we know, if only subliminally, that every fact we can state, every object we can name, bears a freight of association. Despite such reminders, we accept that what we are told has a foundation in being that excludes its nonbeing. To that extent we distinguish between dreaming and waking, fantasy and reality, fact and fiction, and we provide categories in psychopathology for those who resist the distinction. Those of us who have been primarily concerned with the linguistic and dialogical aspects of psychoanalysis may in our enthusiasm do insufficient justice to the underlying reality, but it nonetheless exists even though it is variously understood.

Transcendent Reality

It is here that the approach to religion needs to begin. Religion differs from other fields of interest to psychoanalysis with respect to its central reality, God. I define religion as the recognition by a community of a real being or of beings transcending sense experience, with whom the members of the community exist in a mutual relationship. Although one hears of "private" or "personal" religion, I do not believe that it can be found entirely separated from a community, past or present. Personal religious commitment finds a symbolic language as it has originated in and been transmitted by a community. On the other hand, religion by my definition is to be distinguished from other group loyalties. They may seem to overlap with religions because they also have common loyalties (to the American flag and constitution, the Freudian tradition, natural science), but they lack the religious essential of relationship with a transcendent being, although from time to time the distinction may be blurred when, for example, a national leader or a social cause is to all intents and purposes worshiped. Further, I cannot identify as religion devotion to an abstract ideal without a historical foundation, nor, on similar grounds, to a pure eclecticism that purports to be a kind of amalgam of the "best" in other religions, nor to an ethical derivative of them. Religion is also not a vague emotion of "religiosity." This is not to deny the value any of these excluded entities may have. If the words "God" and "the gods" are understood as rather general summary tokens for all the various beings considered to be both transcendent *and* related to human beings, it is they that are central to what I mean by religion. They are its primary reality.[1]

On the other hand, psychoanalysts encounter religion in themselves or their patients, or out there in the world, in concrete symbolic forms. Now, it is in the nature of things that symbolic forms within a cultural system influence one another, so that meanings shift slightly or greatly as one moves among religious systems, although the words may be the same. What is more, individuals appropriate religious (or other) symbols in accordance with the lives they have led, and it is in fact here that psychoanalytic effort is exerted: we analysts try to make new sense of the symbols we hear, and especially the *unconscious* sense. In doing so we pay close attention to the historical background of the symbol in the individual life, as well as to the company it has kept or keeps in different epochs of life, and its synchronic transference relations in the present discourse of the analysis as well.

Analysis of the symbolic content of the discourse—taking the word "symbolic" in its larger sense, not in its specifically psychoanalytic use—constitutes most of our work, regardless of the particular school to which we adhere, and regardless of details of technique. Religion is concerned with the transcendent, or divine, as its object, as the central focus of its discourse, whether spoken or unspoken. This is the heart of the matter. It has been a traditional cliché of psychoanalysis that this focus is illusory; that is, it has been held that the idea "God," being unsupported by reality as understood by scientific method and based on the projections of wishes alone, is therefore doomed to vanish when the fantasies underlying it have been analyzed. Here religion is given a different treatment from other symbolic systems, such as art, or politics, or history, in all of which analysts admit the existence of realities to which the systems refer. How is one to understand this difference? What is there about the religious apprehension of reality that has led to this diagnosis (for that is what it is) of illusion or delusion? Is it possible to formulate a concept of reality that need not reduce religious experience to something other than what it claims to be? These are some of the questions I intend to explore here.

On the Conviction of the Nonexistence of God

When I told a too-clever young man that the title of my book on religion and psychoanalysis was to be *In the Image of God,* he wittily asked me: "But how can there be an image of what doesn't exist?" I cannot claim that his foreclosure of the reality of God was the product of his psychoanalytic instruction, which was slight. Rather, it was the normative conviction of his whole intellectual world, in which belief is suspect or ridiculous, or both. Unfortunately, from my contrary point of view, that conviction also predominates in the documents of psychoanalysis. It is not merely that God "is not necessary to our hypotheses," a contention with which no analyst ought quarrel. God is not to be referred to as a reality, much less as *the* ultimate reality that he is for all religions that include a God. That is, while no analyst would infer from the fantasies of a patient about Antarctica that there is no such continent because neither the patient nor the analyst had ever been there, the nonexistence of God may be built into the analyst's deepest convictions. In such a situation the assertion of a patient that God had somehow been present to him could not be faced as more than the account of an illusion, if not a delusion.

Just why psychoanalysis has been tied to atheism, with its corollary that God as transcendent being is illusory, is itself a very interesting historical matter with which I shall not be concerned much here. It has been studied with respect to Freud's unbelief from two points of view in recent times, by the historian Peter Gay in a work in sympathy with Freud's atheism (1987), and by William Meissner, a Jesuit priest who is also a psychoanalyst (1984). The continuing authority of Freud supported the presumption of atheism for several generations of psychoanalysts, although other influences have also prevailed in most instances: in particular, the denial of reality to religious propositions in most Western intellectual and academic circles, as I have suggested earlier. Too many psychoanalytic writers to be enumerated here make their points on matters of religion as if the nonexistence or at least the irrelevance of God, and the illusory nature of belief, had been sufficiently demonstrated to them and their readers and required no further argument.

What I am concerned about, then, is the question of the reality of the object of religion, and what difference that makes to both the practice of psychoanalysis and the psychoanalytic study of religion. My readers may be relieved to know that despite my evident preferences I do not have the ambition of proving to them the existence of God. What I would like to undermine in at least a small way is the usually unspoken conviction that belief in the existence of God is trivial, esoteric, irrelevant to the business of analysis, or intrinsically pathological.

That God exists is the heart of religious belief of any sort we are likely to encounter in psychoanalytic work. But what are we as analysts to do with that belief? The predominant psychoanalytic approach toward belief as it appears in the clinical setting has placed it in the realm of dream and not of waking reality. It is so easy and natural to take that position once we are satisfied with the conviction that reality is limited to that which may be known through sense perception and is open to scientific investigation. To accept that limitation would require the believer to enact miracles in evidence of his or her belief, so that the skepticism of the analyst would have no choice but to yield.

The believer is powerless to give the kind of miraculous evidence that would be required for the scientific definition of the real. If the analyst is unwilling to accept the experience of faith as an index of reality, even if only in a tentative way and for the purpose of advancing the analysis, this sector of the patient's life will be excluded from the analytic process. When the analyst analyzes religious beliefs as illusions, the process is to that extent external to the patient, however satisfying it may be to the analyst.

A first reflection might persuade us that the appeal to sensory evidence is out of place anyhow. We never ask our patients for evidences of reality of that kind, and most of us look on even documentary data as irrelevant to the analysis: a carefully preserved letter to the patient from an angry parent, written many years ago, has nothing to offer beyond what the memory of the letter can provide. Descriptions of the beauty of a lover require no photographs to be convincing. And with respect to all the vicissitudes of relationships, it is the verbal report that counts—including, to be sure, its nuances and its inherent strength or inconsistency. Why do we demand more, or something else, when the relationship with God is in the psychoanalytic focus?

The answer is obvious enough: parents and lovers and all the others with whom people exist in relationship are external "objects," whose reality is open to consensual validation. God is not such an object; God is the reality, according to believers, who transcends external objectivity. God is a class of one. It is there that the skeptical psychoanalyst, like other skeptics, is likely to hold that the patient talking about God is in a dreamworld, from which a successful analysis will awaken him or her. So Otto Fenichel, with monumental confidence, assured us that as his patients progressed in their analysis they became gradually liberated from their religion (1941, 89). And Helene Deutsch had to conclude regretfully that the Catholic teacher she had treated so effectively for her obsessional neurosis was unable to accomplish a real cure since she remained within her religious order as a nun (1951, 189). It is one of the mysteries of the allegiance of groups that no one within the company of psychoanalysts seems to have remarked at the time that a prejudice might have been at work in these convictions.[2]

Psychic Reality, Actuality, the Transitional Object, and Faith

To represent one of the classical psychoanalytic approaches to the theme I am developing, I suggest Ferenczi's "Stages in the Development of the Sense of Reality" (1950, 225–26). There he tried to show on the basis of psychoanalytic theory the passage of the "sense" of reality, meaning its subjective grasp, from the infantile omnipotence to the adult acknowledgment of the external objective world, with the gradual relinquishment of infantile illusions and their expression in, for example, "cursing, blessing, praying." The measure of development is readily available, for "the sense of reality attains its zenith in science." Surely Ferenczi found this sequence because it was assumed in his own mind a priori as the criterion of achieved development. Even if the experience of spiritual reality was foreign to him, which I doubt, he might have considered that erotic reality or aesthetic reality can be as convincing as scientific reality.

Contemporary analysts, not all of them professed believers in any religion, have tried to understand religious phenomena in other terms than these. The concept of "psychic reality" has been pressed into service here: it is scientific in that it is comparable to other judgments of mental operations, and it is metaphysically neutral. "Psychic reality" need not stand on the basis of objective reality open to scientific, rational inspection, nor do its users necessarily posit the atheist position as the norm. That which is real to the individual has a validity of its own. The trouble with it from my point of view is, first, that it says nothing special about belief that is not equally applicable to all other experience; there is nothing in the discourse of the patient that has not emerged from psychic reality. Further, when examined more closely it leaves belief, as a form of experience that cannot be consensually validated, on the same footing as delusion. Let us see, however, a few of the ways in which this attribution of psychic reality has been made.

Heinz Hartmann introduced a pertinent variation in the concept of psychic reality in his "Notes on the Reality Principle" (1956, 44 ff.). He distinguished objective reality from what he called "conventional reality" or "socialized knowledge." The latter is constituted by traditional or institutionalized convictions, such as the religious beliefs of a community. While the work of analysis takes place at the scientific level, according to Hartmann, the conventional reality of the patient is acknowledged. He gives an amusing example: we accept the patient's belief that the prophet Elijah ascended into heaven, but if he contends that his next-door neighbor did the same, we declare him to be psychotic. That unfortunately does not help us with the mental status of Elijah's neighbors, so to speak: what about what they might have said that they had seen? Do we conclude that "conventional reality" originates in private delusion?

William Meissner, who has made the most comprehensive study of modern psychoanalytic attitudes toward religion, has like others before him been influenced by ego psychology. As elsewhere in psychoanalysis, by turning the spotlight from the fascinations of infantile fantasy to the psychic organization within which the fantasies are bound, ego psychology has disposed the analyst to deal with religious ideas less reductively. The image of the avenging father latent in the idea of God ought not to exhaust the meaning of God in our consciousness any longer. Nor is the vision of endless bliss in Heaven reducible without remainder to the memory of maternal care. So far so good, surely.

A further amplification of the meaning of religious belief is rooted in Erik Erikson's concept of "basic trust" as an essential component of early ego formation (see, e.g., 1968, 82). Belief in God is usually accompanied (although not always, and frequently under strictly limiting conditions) by a sense of trust in an ultimate security that cannot be explained as an illusion. But Erikson also made a distinction between "reality" and "actuality" that is applicable here. "Reality" may be limited to the external world, knowable by scientific method, but "actuality" is "the world verified only by the ego's immersion in action." Here Erikson (doubtless influenced by phenomenological philosophy) had in mind the German word for reality, *Wirklichkeit,* from the verb *wirken,* meaning "act," or as its English cognate tells us, "work" (1962, 452–53). If, indeed, we need to confine the word "reality" to the objectively verifiable world (with the "res extensa" of Descartes as its standard), this is a useful distinction, for religious actuality is inseparable from human involvement.

Perhaps the strongest influence on current psychoanalytic reevaluations of religion has come from Donald Winnicott's concept of the transitional object (see, e.g., 1965, 184). Meissner himself has been (1984, and chapter in this volume) much impressed by the concept's usefulness, and so has Ana-Maria Rizzuto (1979). As is well known, Winnicott was the first to show how the toy animal or blanket or other object so precious to the young child that he or she can only traumatically be separated from it is a material symbol, or an affectively toned material metaphor, one might say, for the mother's body. It is effective, therefore, as a step away from the physical presence of the mother that is also a step toward the world of other satisfying objects.

The concept is itself so attractive in its subtlety and its simplicity that it is no wonder it has been seized upon for what is meant to be explanation of artistic and religious experience, among many other things. It facilitates a comprehensible progression from early infantile to adult experience, sacrificing neither the temporal and environmental source nor the possibilities inherent in symbolic development. There must be a universal kind of introspection that reveals in the perception and appreciation of some external objects the kind of preciousness that we can only dimly recall from our childhood but readily see in young children. A shape, a color, a contrast, a touch, a tune—any of them may produce a literally ek-static sense that seems to carry us out of present reality into some genuine, but unactualizable past.

There is a hitch in any argument that attempts to do more in accounting for religious experience by invoking the transitional object than to relate it to other aspects of childhood and adult life. We are given a symbolic continuity by it, but we are not left open to the transcendent. It affords us no access to the possibility of awareness of or contact with an existence *not* given in the symbolic series mother-blanket-aesthetic or religious object. We can include religious objects in the series (e.g., icon, scroll, mezzuzah, crucifix) without hesitation, but we cannot include the faith that animates religious objects both affectively and cognitively. Or, more properly, we can include that faith only if we drop the distinction between religious and other cultural objects, which in my opinion leads to the old reductionism with a new face. It explains the category of the transcendent by eliminating it. Once again we—doctor and patient—have no need for God in our hypotheses.

Psychoanalysis and Religion in the Thought of Hans Loewald

Still another contemporary psychoanalyst, Hans Loewald, has taken up the problem of religion—usually indirectly, while in pursuit of other goals and also remaining well within a naturalistic frame of reference. The difference between Loewald's ideas and those I have already cited seems to me to be that his are genuinely agnostic: they do not claim to account fully for religious experience within the naturalistic framework, thereby precluding the transcendent possibility, nor do they smuggle into the argument theological convictions disguised as clinical observations. The reason for his exceptional freedom from a *parti pris* rests on Loewald's critical philosophical position with regard to reality, and it is there that an exposition of his views must begin.

Hans Loewald wrote in his studies "Ego and Reality" and "The Problem of Defense and the Neurotic Interpretation of Reality" (1980) that we must discriminate between the reality derived from the oedipal (and castration) complex phases of life and that derived from the pre-oedipal phase. In the oedipal experience, reality is that which is opposed to the ego, confronting the ego as something that is to be mastered or submitted to. Most learning has as its intention the rational grasp of an external world that even when it is not construed as lifeless is intrinsically inimical to the desires of the individual. The opposition of the real world has to be overcome in the interests of the developing person, whether by aggressive control or intelligent and rational circumvention, or it must be yielded to. If a God is conceived of at all within such a grasp of reality, he is modeled on the idea of an essentially hostile father, to be propitiated in religion.

In contrast, the earliest grasp of reality is that of the preoedipal child, living within the "mother-child unit." Here there is no opposition of reality to the developing ego; rather, the inner and outer reality correspond, and their gradual differentiation comes to be through the mutual reflection of the two beings. Reality is not something that stands in opposition to the self but is experienced as including the self and being included by it.

I have necessarily only abstracted the careful and comprehensive argument in which Loewald has stated his thesis. The point I wish to make here in adapting it to my purposes is that the kind of discussion that limits reality to the scientifically graspable external or internal world (a comprehension that is by definition carried on in the secondary process) places the object of religious experience outside the realm of reality. By it the believer is a dreamer, for whom belief will vanish when he wakes.

Loewald criticizes this view of the world very specifically. Referring to "the view that culture and reality as a whole is basically inimical to the individual," he goes on to the following:

> The estrangement of man from his culture (from moral and religious norms that nevertheless continue to determine his conduct and thus are experienced as hostile impositions) and the fear and suppression of controlled but nondefensive regression is the emotional and intellectual climate in which Freud conceived his ideas of the psychological structure of the individual and the individual's relation to reality. [1980b, 29]

Psychoanalysis, on the other hand, seeks "to rediscover and reactivate the submerged communication channels leading from the origins of our lives to the solidified, alienated structure of behavior," although its theory "has taken for granted the neurotically distorted experience of reality" (29–30).

At the heart of Loewald's revision of psychoanalytic theory and of the idea of reality that it maintains is his conception of the process of internalization. This is the deepest of developmental processes, and it has its origins in the "global" nature of the mother-child unit. The world within the developing person is the result of interactions in the unit, the "matrix," as Loewald aptly designates it. This is not a defensive process, and the reality that it envisages is a global one that encompasses both the individual and the world around him or her. It is easy to infer from this the sense of relatedness to the universe that animates the religious life, especially in its personal, mystical aspects, and to understand better how the obsessional, technologically absorbed modern spirit has rejected it.

Advances in psychoanalytic theory such as these have facilitated our understanding of religion within the bounds of our science. There are no insuperable contradictions among the new schemata available for this understanding. Erikson's "basic trust" has a theoretical affinity with Loewald's "matrix," and we can conceive of the "transitional object" as a symbolic presence for which both of the others prepare. Perhaps the overall affinity among these concepts lies in their readiness to look on preoedipal positions as lifelong potentialities for the enrichment of experience rather than as evidences of immaturity or disorder. In Loewald's thesis there is a further advantage. He has come from the side of phenomenological philosophy, to look critically at the usually unexamined positivism underlying traditional psychoanalytic concepts of reality. Instead of an "objective," unresponsive, or merely reactive externality that must be confronted, manipulated, and somehow overcome, Loewald proposes a reality in which both the individual subject and the surrounding world, personal and nonpersonal, interact.

As far as the psychoanalytic understanding of religion goes, especially as it appears in clinical work, this is all very good. It may in fact be as far as one has any right to ask the psychoanalyst to go. We analysts are able to situate the subjective experiences that fall within the compass of religion without reducing them to something else, although as I have said, we still must hold them in a kind of ready analogy with other, less controversial achievements of the mind.

However, it is insufficient to leave the matter there, as if there were no more to the question of religion, either clinically or as it is seen by any religious community. For all the increased generosity and vision in the later views, they do not succeed, cannot succeed, in representing religion as it appears to believers. The *anthropological* grasp that these authors present is no small thing itself, but it is one that holds at a distance the idea of the transcendent reality, God. I call it "anthropological" because it can include the idea of God only as a man-made symbol. Contrariwise, at the heart of religion is the conviction that the symbol is not totally man-made, not a golden calf, not just the product of the yearning of the soul, but is a point in which the encounter with a self-revealing transcendent Other is made concrete. Even setting aside the naïve attitude that the religious revelation is unalterably tied to the changeless symbol, we are still left with the religious claim that while man may variously discover God and variously identify him, he does not invent God. What psychoanalytic view have we with respect to *this* reality?

Transcendent Reality as Psychologically Unfathomable

To illustrate and I hope illuminate the problem of reality as it comes up in analyzing religious subjects (both persons and concepts), I choose to begin with further psychoanalytic observations of Hans Loewald on the basis of Christian belief: the death of Jesus as God Incarnate. As on other occasions when Loewald speaks to us about religion, here too he introduces it in a more general setting, as a lateral reference in a very well-known study of internalization:

> It seems significant that with the advent of Christianity, initiating the greatest intensification of internalization in Western civilization, the death of God as incarnated in Christ moves into the center of religious experience. Christ is not only the ultimate love object, which the believer loses as an external object and regains by identification with Him as ego ideal. He is, in his passion and sacrificial death, the exemplification of complete internalization and sublimation of all earthly relationships and needs. [1980c, 260]

The statement poses a psychological question that is itself impossible to answer with certainty: in whom did this internalization take place? In "Western civilization"? To be sure, but do we have even an inkling of how a civilization—meaning a very large number of people in a very large community of only slightly related nations, and over a long period of time—internalized Christ? Or in the "believer"? How does the believer identify with Christ as lost love object? Nontheological answers might be possible for both questions, if only by analogy with identifications and internalizations of mundane origin about which we can be more confident. For example, it might be maintained that the liturgy of the church successfully dramatizes the passion, death, and resurrection of Jesus, and it is through participation in the drama that the believer internalizes the life he has there encountered. To which it might be added, with rather less confidence, that the communication of this process by repeated identifications with the identifiers brought about the inner transformation of whole peoples. In neither of these replies can we have the sense of conviction that we are entitled to have when we use the psychoanalytic method with patients. But we rest on the assurance that internalizations of this kind do take place, and that there is no reason to assume that religious development would be an exception in this respect.

The sticking point lies elsewhere. We want to see more clearly what it was that underwent internalization, and that is tantamount to asking the second question: what is the reality, the objectively definable experience, to which the internalization refers? Here all Christian believers within a very wide mainstream agree. They assent to the tradition that Christ was seen alive, listened to and spoken to, as well as physically touched, after his death and burial. Indeed, in a quite literal sense any Christian community is merely a continuation of the first body of believers who claimed to have seen the resurrected Jesus. The personnel changes, and the doctrines taught vary widely, but the internalized memory does not; the tradition is the vehicle for the internalization, since quite plainly the initial witnesses could not pass on anything else in evidence of their belief, and subsequent firsthand observers, of whom the apostle Paul claimed to be one, have been few.[3]

I selected my example of what is meant by "reality" in religious belief because it is a very obvious one and the most familiar to me. But one need not be a Christian believer to hold to quite comparable convictions. Judaism holds to the tradition that God manifested himself to his people in certain concrete historical acts, including the gift of the Torah through Moses; the Torah itself relates many narratives of events selected because of their implications of miracle, divine interventions later discussed at length by the Rabbis of normative Judaism. In both Judaism and Christianity—and no less in the third biblical religion, Islam—immense accretions of legend, folklore, borrowings from one another and from other religions, and superstitions and magical practices overlie or may even be vehicles of fundamental beliefs, and in popular religion the essentials are often quite subordinate to the legendary. I hope that the point will not be missed, however, that religious belief rests on the psychologically unfathomable—which might be a definition for the "reality," or for the waking state, as it is conceived by the believer, and as it must be respected by anyone who desires to understand the believer's mind. Where we *have* the psychological explanation, the reality has been reduced to a form of dreaming. This is a fully legitimate task of the analytic process itself, to get at an understanding within the analytic situation of the meanings implicit in religious statements of all kinds, including beliefs. But it tells nothing about the reality on which the religion stands.

What limits would this position put to the psychoanalytic study of religion, in the individual or in the body of believers? Just what is "unfathomable" in the content of belief? Clearly, not the manifest content of any religious statement, which like any other communication can be analyzed: it can be compared with other statements with which it has metaphoric and other relations, and it can be set in a historical series with overlapping elements. By such and similar operations unconscious meaning can be derived, which is as valid as that derived from any other kind of statement. Likewise, in the manner by which analysis proceeds, origins can be inferred, and personal historical causality established, at least in a tentative way. What cannot be bypassed, without dismissing the reality of the belief, is the claim that it has a yet more pressing origin in a divine source.

Need the analyst be a believer in order to grant due respect to his patient's grasp of transcendent reality? No analyst could believe in all such manifestations; need he believe in any? To think so would be to make psychoanalysis a branch of theology—a very eclectic theology, perhaps, but a theology nevertheless, and hardly preferable to the dogmatic antitheology of our day, or, to put it more hopefully, of yesterday. Of course the answer is no. Just as it is obligatory for the analyst who is a believer in a religion to be open to the reality maintained by other kinds of believers, and nonbelievers, and always to be able to distinguish what I have called the waking reality of belief from the dream world, so the agnostic analyst needs to do the same in his or her own way, leaving open the possibility that the transcendent otherness that religious persons claim to approach is as real as they claim it to be, as real as chairs and tables and families, as well as sciences and arts. Which comes down to recognizing once again that there are more things in heaven and earth than are dreamt of in our philosophy.

Notes

This essay, in somewhat different form, was read before the Toronto and Western New England Psychoanalytic Societies.

1. Buddhism is a religion that claims not to be a theism. Yet it postulates a fundamental spiritual reality as clearly as any theism does and should be open to the same criticisms with respect to the object of its beliefs.

2. I have called attention elsewhere (Leavy 1982) to Karl Menninger's remark in his 1958 book *Theory of Psychoanalytic Technique* that Fenichel's liberated patients might have been influenced by their analyst's views.

3. I would not want to suggest that this belief has never been contested within the Christian church, as of course it has always been denied or ignored

outside. See as a recent example of what might be called Roman Catholic non-conformity on this question, *The First Coming,* by Thomas Sheehan (1986).

References

Calderón de la Barca, Pedro. *La Vida Es Sueño.* Edited by R. Gaston. Zaragoza: Ebro, 1978.

———. *Life Is a Dream.* Translated by William Colford. Woodbury, N.Y.: Barron, 1958.

Deutsch, Helene. *Psychoanalysis of the Neuroses.* Translated by W. D. Robson-Scott. London: Hogarth Press, 1951.

Erikson, Erik H. "Reality and Actuality." *Journal of the American Psychoanalytic Association* 10 (1962): 451–74.

———. *Identity, Youth and Crisis.* New York: W. W. Norton, 1968.

Fenichel, Otto. *Problems of Psychoanalytic Technique.* New York: Psychoanalytic Quarterly, 1941.

Ferenczi, Sandor. "Stages in the Development of the Sense of Reality." In *Sex in Psychoanalysis.* New York: Basic Books, 1950.

Gay, Peter. *An Infidel Jew.* New Haven: Yale University Press, 1987.

Hartmann, Heinz. "Notes on the Reality Principle." *Psychoanalytic Study of the Child* 11 (1956): 31–53.

Leavy, Stanley. "Questioning Authority." *Cross Currents* 32 (1982): no. 2.

Loewald, Hans W. *Papers on Psychoanalysis.* New Haven: Yale University Press, 1980.

"Ego and Reality" (a).

"The Problem of Defense and the Neurotic Interpretation of Reality" (b).

"Internalization, Separation, Mourning, and the Superego" (c).

Meissner, William W. *Psychoanalysis and Religious Experience.* New Haven: Yale University Press, 1984.

Menninger, Karl. *Theory of Psychoanalytic Technique.* New York: Harper & Row, 1958.

Rizzuto, Ana-Maria. *The Birth of the Living God.* Chicago: University of Chicago Press, 1979.

Sheehan, Thomas. *The First Coming.* New York: Random House, 1986.

Winnicott, Donald W. *The Maturational Process and the Facilitating Environment.* New York: International Universities Press, 1965.

4   "Coufontaine, *adsum*!"
Lacan and Theological Discourse

William J. Richardson

Having been asked to address the theme of "Lacan and Theological Discourse," let me begin in good Lacanian fashion by saying that I have not the slightest intention of addressing that issue and intend instead to discuss the theater of Paul Claudel. Does that surprise you? frustrate, irritate you? Well, that's the way it is!

This sort of thing, I say, is "good Lacanian fashion," for it suggests all at once something about his purpose, his method, and his style. For his purpose, had he received a similar invitation, would almost certainly not have been to write about theological discourse. His concern uniformly was to interrogate the nature of the unconscious as Freud discovered it and to teach others to do the same—nothing else. This was pursued according to one fundamental thesis—namely, that the unconscious is structured like a language, and his celebrated "return to Freud" was a dogged attempt to reread Freud in these terms.

As for his method, he chose, especially in public discourse, to dramatize the unconscious for his listeners as much as to theorize about it, and as Freud shows us in the *Psychopathology of Everyday Life* (a text especially dear to Lacan), nothing dramatizes the unconscious better than the experience of capriciousness, disorientation, and surprise. This accounts for certain characteristics of Lacan's style: its playful, Peck's-bad-boy contrariness, for example, and the maddening, self-conscious obscurity that wants to leave us "no other way out than the way in, which I prefer to be difficult" (1977, 146). If I address your irritation by saying "that's the way it is," the "It" here is the "It" of the famous phrase of the later Freud: *Wo es war soll Ich werden*— not "Where id was, there let ego be," but "Where It was there I must

60

come to be," that is, the It is the unconscious itself, the *Ça (Ça parle, Ça pense—c'est Ça!)*. Were Lacan here, then, I feel sure he would utterly disregard the chosen theme for this volume and simply do his own enigmatic thing, leaving all of us to make of it what we would— or could. *C'est Ça!*

But it would also be characteristic of Lacan to divert us with a disquisition on the Catholic writer Paul Claudel. Let that say that his culture was kaleidoscopic, and he fashioned his discourse out of elements drawn from everywhere: from science, mathematics, art—but especially from philosophy (Parmenides to Heidegger) and literature (Sophocles to James Joyce). Paul Claudel was one of his authors of preference, and Claudel by any standard was one of the most selfconsciously religious of writers (I am told that the well-known satirical journal *Le Canard Enchaîné* once ran an editorial that carried the title "I believe in Paul Claudel" and was signed "God"). I thought, then, it might help us reflect on Lacan's possible relevance to theological discourse (his own intentions notwithstanding) if we considered his reading of one work in particular of Claudel's: *L'otage (The Hostage)*. I shall move back and forth between these two authors as best suits my purpose but will begin with the focus on Claudel, then shift to a focus on Lacan, and conclude by attempting to suggest where the whole business leaves us.

Lacan offered his analysis of Claudel in three lectures during the month of May 1961, as part of the year-long seminar that bore the general title: *Transference* (1960–61). It is worth knowing that in the previous year (1959–60) he had given his celebrated seminar on *The Ethics of Psychoanalysis*. There he had argued that psychoanalysis proceeds according to what he called the "tragic view of life":

> [By that I mean] that negation [which is] identical with the entrance of the subject as such into the [system] of the signifier. . . .
>
> It is because we know better than our predecessors how to recognize the nature of desire at the heart of this experience that . . . an ethical judgment [becomes] possible. It echoes the value of that ultimate judgment: have you acted in conformity with the desire that dwells in you? [1959–60, 362] I suggest that the only thing of which one can be guilty, at least in the perspective of analysis, is to have compromised (*cédé sur*) one's desire. [368]

To dramatize this thesis he concluded that seminar with an analysis of Sophocles' *Antigone*. The "unwritten law" that justified Antigone's defiance of Creon, as Lacan saw it, was not at all what the tradition came to call the "Law of Nature," but simply the law of desire of the

Other in her that she adamantly refused to compromise. That needs clarification, of course, and I shall return to it in a moment, but let it serve as background for Lacan's thesis that Claudel offers us to return to the tragic view of life of the Greeks, in which his heroine, Sygne de Coufontaine, after 1900 years of Christianity, fares poorly in comparison with Antigone.

Let us turn, then, to Claudel and Sygne de Coufontaine. She is the *grande dame* of the Coufontaine family, whose saga is told in Claudel's well-known trilogy: *L'otage (The Hostage)* (1911); *Le Pain dur (Stale Bread)* (1913–14); *Le Père humilié (The Humiliated Father)* (1915–16). Claudel was already forty years old, and the famous conversion of Christmas Day, 1886, from a life of dissolute faithlessness to one of vibrant Christianity was well behind him when in 1908 he wrote to a friend from his diplomatic post in China: "I'm tired of fragmentary works, and I'd like to lock myself up for several years in something of whole cloth. Since I can't write an epic poem, I'd like to compose a cycle of dramas not producing just people, but the *ensemble* of strange, multiple and convergent means whereby these very people are produced for ends foreseen by God."[1] That ensemble became the saga of the Coufontaine family, whose history Claudel begins to follow at the end of the Napoleonic era (1812–14) with the tale of Sygne's tragic choice, which constitutes the story line of *The Hostage.* The sequel, *Le Pain dur,* deals with the story of her son in the 1840s. The third member of the trilogy (*Le Père humilié*) picks up the story of her blind but beautiful granddaughter caught in the political and papal maelstrom of the year 1870 in Rome. I will here consider only the first of these.

It would be a mistake to expect too much from the story line of *The Hostage.* Even Claudel admitted that it was a little absurd. I think of it rather as grand opera, a play of ideas whose beauty comes from the music of its language. Reduced to the barest of bones, the scenario is as follows: It is 1812. Sygne, a woman in her thirties, and her cousin George, ten years her senior, are both descendants of the aristocratic Coufontaine family, whose sympathies remain with the monarchy despite the successes of Napoleon. After the bloodbath of the Reign of Terror, when the parents of both were slain before their eyes, George emigrated to England, but Sygne remained on the estate in order to salvage what she could of its former glory.

As the play opens, George has returned, bringing with him a mysterious old man who happens to be a priest. In a long dialogue, George recounts how he has lost everything in England (his wife had betrayed him, two daughters had died). Together they reflect on the fact that of the whole distinguished family they alone remain, and Sygne, with a smile, whispers: "Coufontaine, *adsum*" ("Coufontaine, here I am")— the ancient family motto inscribed on its coat of arms. Gradually George and Sygne discover the spark of an old love, and before the scene is over, they pledge themselves to each other in deathless fealty:

> *George:* Would you consent to wed me, cousin? . . . [45]

> *Sygne:* Let me take an oath like a new knight! O my lord! My elder brother! Let me swear to you like a nun who takes her vow. . . .
> Our souls weld without alloy the one into the other.
> *George:* Sygne, you whom I found the last of all, do not deceive me. . . . [48]

> *George:* O woman, the last of my race, pledge yourself as you desire to do, and receive from your lord the pledge according to the ancient form.
> [*Sygne*] Coufontaine, receive my glove! (He gives glove)
> *Sygne:* I accept it, George, and you shall never take it back from me. [51]

And so they pledge their love. As the scene ends, George tells Sygne that the old priest he has brought is none other than the Pope himself, "God's representative on earth," whom George has kidnapped from government forces at Fontainebleau. Here he had been held prisoner under Napoleon's orders. George's intention was to use the Pope as a hostage to serve the royalist cause.

Act 2. Enter the villain, Toussaint Turelure, who is repulsive in every way. Son of a sorcerer-father and a domestic servant who had served the Coufontaine family when Sygne was a child, he was the ex-monk who emptied the monastery located on the estate and presided at the butchery of her family in 1793. Now he professes his love for Sygne and proposes marriage, adding that if she refuses he will destroy her cousin George and return the Pope to his enemies, for he is aware that both are in her household. At first Sygne is horrified. In the following scene she tells her confessor, Father Badilon:

> *Sygne:* Since my birth I have lived face to face with this man, ever watching him and protecting myself from him, and making him submit and serve me against his will!
> And constantly through fear and detestation of him there has sprung up a new strength in my breast!
> And now I must call him my husband, this beast! must accept him and offer him my cheek!
> But that I refuse! I say no! even if God incarnate should exact it of me! [104]

But as act 2 progresses, the confessor convinces her that it is her obligation in Christian charity to renounce her pledge to George freely in order that by marrying Turelure she may save the Pope, God's vicar on earth. This she eventually does with great repugnance.

Act 3 picks up the story two years later, on the day when her first-born child is being baptized. Napoleon is on his way into exile, and Turelure, now the civil and military authority in charge of the region of the Seine, has the power to surrender Paris to the royalist forces returning the king to power, in order to save bloodshed. There are two conditions: (1) that the king consent to be a constitutional monarch (hence submit to Turelure's political control); (2) that George de Coufontaine cede all rights to his property, including the right to use his name, to Turelure's firstborn son, who is being baptized on that very day. Turelure designates Sygne to serve as his deputy with full powers to deal with the plenipotentiary of the king. Who is the king's plenipotentiary? None other than her forsaken lover, George.

After a poignant exchange, George becomes enraged; he agrees to the deal but swears to kill Turelure. He leaves; Turelure enters and orders the surrender of Paris. George returns with a gun, there is an exchange of shots, George is killed, but Sygne steps in front of the bullet aimed at Turelure and is mortally wounded in his stead.

The final scene has two versions: according to the first, Badilon ministers to the dying Sygne and tries to evoke an act of charity on her part that would forgive Turelure. At first she refuses but then reneges. According to the second version, which Claudel wrote for the acted presentation, Turelure tries to get her to forgive him in the act of charity that is the price of her salvation, but she refuses and with this intransigent "no" she dies.

The scene proceeds as follows:

> *Turelure:* I am alive thanks to you, dear Sygne. [163] . . . What gratitude I owe you.
> You saved my life at the price of your own.
> O mystery of conjugal love. [164]
> [Sygne responds in obstinate negative silence. Does she want to see their child? No? Does she want to see the priest? No!]
> *Turelure:* You are unwilling to forgive me. You are unwilling that the priest should compel you to forgive.
> You were willing to give me your life. . . .
> But not to forgive me. And yet it is the necessary condition of your salvation. . . . [165]
>
> Let me implore you in the name of your eternal salvation. . . .
> So great is the hate you bear me.

Then what was our marriage? . . .
Sygne, what ought I to think of the "yes" you gave me? . . . [166]

You have been unable to complete your sacrifice. . . .
Damnation, Sygne, eternal separation [awaits you] from the God Who
made you. . . . From the God who summons you to this supreme mo-
ment, and Who calls upon you, the last of your race!
Coufontaine! Coufontaine! do you hear me?
What! You refuse! you betray [your name]!
Rise, . . . it is your Sovereign who calls! What, are you a deserter?
Rise, Sygne! Rise soldier of God! and give Him your glove,
Like Roland on the field of battle when he restored his glove to the
archangel Michael.
Rise and cry: *Adsum,* Sygne! Sygne!
[He appears enormous and mocking as he stands over her.]
Coufontaine, *adsum!* Coufontaine, *adsum!* [167]
[She makes a violent effort, as if to rise, lifts her hand toward heaven and
falls back again. He takes the torch and passes the light before her eyes,
which remain motionless and fixed.]

For Lacan, the whole issue here turns on the meaning of that "no."
To be sure, there are other readings of the play. Some give it a largely
political meaning, a conflict between *ancien régime* and new order in
which Claudel is suspected of being antirepublican. He himself had
some qualms about publishing it, lest it jeopardize his diplomatic career. But for Lacan, the only issue is Sygne's choice. In his view, this
constitutes a return to the tragic sense of the Greeks (1966, 789) in
what amounts to a "Christianity of despair" (1966, 826–27).

To understand what he means by that, we have to backtrack a little
and try to get an overview of what his entire enterprise is about. To do
that we have to have some appreciation for the three categories that
are fundamental to his thought. He calls them: the Symbolic, the Imaginary, and the Real. Perhaps we can do that quickly by reading Claudel's
description of the opening scene:

The Cistercian abbey of Coufontaine, owned by Sygne. The library on
the first floor: a large, lofty room, lighted by four undraped windows
with small greenish panes. At the back between two high doors, on the
whitewashed wall, a large wooden cross with a rude, bronze *Christus,*
which shows signs of mutilation. At the other end, above Sygne's head,
on the remnant of . . . silk tapestry is woven the Coufontaine coat of
arms [bearing the] battle cry and motto: Coufontaine, *adsum.* . . . Sygne
is sitting in a corner at a charming little cabinet completely covered
with account books and neatly arranged bundles of papers. . . . Storm
outside . . . The whistling of the wind is heard. [23–24]

Obviously we all "imagine" this scene as we hear the description as a kind of fantasy, but when Lacan speaks of the Imaginary, he means more than that—he means the entire world of sensible images (primarily, though not exclusively, visual) marked by a bipolar, one-to-one relationship between perceiver and perceived as would be the case if we actually saw what is described (windows, walls, cross, etc.) on stage. The paradigm case for the experience of the Imaginary for Lacan occurs when the infant, born prematurely as a disorganized bundle of impulses, first experiences itself as a unity when it perceives itself as if reflected in an other, a mirror, let us say, or as if in a mirror in the mothering one as a model of unity. Such is the dimension of the Imaginary.

The Symbolic is essentially the order of language. There is no need to resume in detail here: how Lacan took the term from Lévi-Strauss to designate what is specifically human about human culture, precisely language; how he followed Lévi-Strauss to the source of the contemporary science of language, the linguistics of Saussure in order to understand the laws of language; how Jakobson helped him to understand the central role that metonymy (e.g., "the Cistercian abbey of Coufontaine") and metaphor ("the whistling of the wind") play in the functioning of signifiers; and how, finally, he was able to see how Freud's laws for the functioning of the unconscious in dreams (displacement and condensation) are the same structures of metonymy and metaphor that Jakobson discerned. Let it suffice to say that the Symbolic is the ordering of all these laws of language, and when Lacan says that the unconscious is structured like a language, he means that it follows such laws.

But the symbolic order for Lacan is more than just these laws taken in the abstract. They are inscribed in the entire history of the race, coming to us through our phylogenetic past, our racial, national, political, religious, familial, parental, personal past—all suggested here by the wooden cross with its battered Christ on the one hand and the Coufontaine coat of arms with its "Coufontaine, *adsum*" motto on the other.

Lacan refers to the symbolic order differently at different times. Because of its universality and necessity, he speaks of it often as Law, and since the maker of the Law is thought of as Father, the Law becomes the Law of the Father, where Father is the dead Father of Freud's *Totem and Taboo*. Sometimes this becomes the Name-of-the-Father. In another context, the symbolic order becomes the Great Debt, after the manner of Rabelais (1977, 67), which Lacan associates to the Greek notion of Fate (*Até*). Correspondingly, the subject of this debt is a debtor, hence a subject of guilt (June 17, 1961). But most often, the symbolic order is simply referred to as the Other.

What, then, is the Real? It is not "reality," for reality is already structured by the Imaginary and the Symbolic, like the room we are sitting in. The Real is the unstructured, the unimaginable—what simply defies expression of any kind, as a moment of excruciating pain. Think, for example, what must have been the reaction of Sygne aged ten as she actually experienced what she is now able to symbolize:

> Long ago I saw my father and mother, and your father and mother,
>   Coufontaine, stand on the scaffold together,
> Those saintly faces looking down at us, all four bound like victims,
>   our fathers and mothers who were struck down one after another beneath the axe!
> And when it was my mother's turn, the executioner, winding her grey hair around his wrist, dragged her head under the knife.
> We were in the first row and you held my hand, and their blood spurted out over us.
> I saw it all and did not faint, and afterwards we returned home on foot. . . . [33]

The actual lived horror here—unspeakable, unimaginable—is the Real: the unspeakable and unrepresentable. But the Real is also the realm of mystery that science attempts to explore like the outer reaches of the universe.

It is important to note that Symbolic, Imaginary, and Real are never separated; they are bound together in a knot that Lacan calls the Borromean knot: if one link were to be severed, the whole knot would fall apart.

These, then, are Lacan's fundamental categories. How is the subject structured in terms of them? Recall that the infant's first experience of itself is as a mirrorlike reflection and that the initial relation to the mother shares this one-to-one imaginary quality. But when it ceases to be in-fans and begins to speak, there is a rupture of the bipolar relationship with its imaged world. A third dimension is introduced, the order of language, the symbolic order, according to which things may become present in their absence through the power of words.

This rupture is portentous for the infant. There is a negation involved, a negation of the primacy of images in the functioning of its life. Henceforth, all of the child's human relationships will be mediated by the patterns of the symbolic order or, as we saw earlier, "the [system] of the signifier" (which is the same thing). The negation implies a loss of the privileged imaginary bond with the mother, according to which the mother was "all" for the infant. Such a loss is irreparable. It is a cutting off, the severing of a bond—for Lacan, the most elemental form of castration (for both sexes), a wound that is never healed. Indeed, it is a form of death, for it is the first painful experience of that primordial limit of life that Heidegger formulates in terms of "Being-unto-death." "The Law, . . . to be installed as Law," Lacan tells us, "necessitates as antecedent the death of the one who sustains (*supporte*) the Law" (June 10, 1961). At any rate, when Lacan speaks of the "tragic experience of life," it is this "negation," this loss, that is "identical with the entrance of the subject as such into the [system of the signifier]" (1959–60, 362) to which he refers.

At the heart of this experience of negation (in Lacan it is coincident with what Freud calls "primary repression") is the "nature of desire": "It is because we know better than our predecessors how to recognize the nature of desire at the heart of this experience that a revision of ethics is possible. [In fact,] an ethical judgment is possible which echoes the value of the ultimate judgment: have you acted in conformity with the desire that dwells within you?" (1959–60, 362).

Thus, when the bipolar bond with the mother is ruptured, there is a loss for the infant. It suffers a lack of that fullness of union with the mother that had existed on the imaginary level—that is, on the level of images. There is, then, a "lack" or "want" "of being" (*manque à être*) in the infant, and for Lacan it is in precisely this "want-to-be"—this "want-ing"—that the "nature of desire" consists. Henceforth, what the subject desires is to restore the shattered unity, to find again that lost object which is the imaginary fullness that is gone now, gone forever. But the quest must be filtered through the constrictions imposed by the laws of the symbolic order, discernible in the laws of language. Desire, too, then, carries the scar of castration and is signed with the seal of death. At any rate, as desire, it will follow the rhythms of a "dialectic of desire" as this was first elaborated by Hegel.

Accordingly, Lacan insists that the "desire of man is desire of the Other" (1977, 264): in the first place, this means that the subject desires to be the desired of the Other (at first, the mother). The subject wants to be the object of the Other's desire, and, to the extent that the phallus is taken to be the privileged signifier of desire, to be the phallus for the mother as Other. In the second place, desire of the Other means that the desire of the subject is the desire of the Other insofar as the Other is subject of the unconscious. In any case, it is desire in this double sense of desire of the Other that the psychoanalysts of today allegedly understand better than their predecessors.

We must see, now, how all this affects Lacan's interpretation of

Sygne's "no" in such a way that for him it constitutes a return to Greek tragedy. Certainly it will be in sharp contrast to the way Claudel himself understands her behavior. Claudel sees her trial as coherent with his Christian worldview and a confirmation of his own act of faith. For him, the "hostage" of the title is the Pope, "representative of God" on earth, caught between the hostile powers of the State and the claims of ancient privilege in a dying aristocracy. What is important is the Pope's freedom, and this is assured by the "heroic sacrifice" of Sygne. Her sacrifice, he claims, has, after all, its historical precedent (e.g., Clotilde in her marriage to Clovis). Sygne's problem was that her courage failed. He tells us: "The sacrifice she offered was incomplete. She did not pardon [Turelure] in her heart. She did not open herself completely as Christ did to Judas."[2]

Yet this rather detached assessment yields to an understandable ambivalence in Claudel: "What seems to me difficult to justify, what causes me a kind of horror each time that I see the play . . . is the dreadful cruelty of the sacrifice suggested to poor Sygne by her spiritual counselor in complicity with the most secret resources of this proud and ardent heart."[3] Yet the final gesture of the raised hand, prima facie evidence to the contrary, contains for him a sign of hope:

> . . . Faith, the commitment of one's whole person to the sovereign, is in that raising of the right hand. This resumes the entire play and [indeed does so] in a grand surge of confidence, hope and love, which, as we may hope, saves her. I repeat here once more what I said concerning *L'Anonce faite à Marie:* it is not saints that I wanted to present but feeble human creatures grappling with grace.[4]

For Claudel himself, then, Sygne's final gesture, for all its enigmatic ambiguity, is a saving one. Human evidence to the contrary, grace will somehow prevail.

For Lacan, these formulas are meaningless. What he perceives as the final intransigence of Sygne is a return to the Greek experience in a manner far more profound than anything that their concept of *ananké* could account for. Antigone, for example, had the consolation of believing in a god or gods of fate (*Até*), some divine law that sustained her in her trial. For Sygne, however, "it is against her will, against everything that determines it, not just in her life but in her whole being, that [she], by an act of freedom, must go counter to everything that sustains (*tient*) her being down to its most intimate roots" (June 3, 1961). Her suicidal gesture betrays a sense of "absolute dereliction" and "abandonment" by divine power. She has been driven to the "destruction of her being by having been torn from all her attachments of speech and of faith" (June 3, 1961). Here, the issue is not only that she has failed to be true to her desire, but also that this infidelity touches her at the very roots of her subjectivity, in that cleavage by which she is constituted as a subject.

Her attachments derive from her spoken commitment to George. In act 2 she argues with Badilon:

> *Sygne:* This morning we pledged our faith to one another.
> *Badilon:* You are not married.
> *Sygne:* Married! Ah, this is more than any marriage!
>   He gave me his right hand, as liege to vassal,
>   And I took an oath of fealty in my heart.
> *Badilon:* An oath in the night. Promises only, and neither deed nor sacrament.
> *Sygne:* Shall I take back my word?
> *Badilon:* High above the human word is the Word which speaks in Pius. [102]

But that is just the point. For Lacan, the Word that speaks in Pius is no more than the Word of the Other, of the Father, of the Great Debt that imposes guilt without redeeming grace. It is not divine.

When Lacan speaks of the Word, he likes to invoke the tones of St. John's Gospel. For example: "The psychoanalytic experience has rediscovered in man the imperative of the Word as the law that has formed him in its image." This sounds conventional enough, but then he adds: "[The Word] manipulates the poetic function of language to give to [man's] desire its symbolic mediation" (1977, 106). The Word, then, is no more than the symbolic function itself, mediating desire by metonymy. In the lectures of 1961, Lacan tells us: "For us the Word has become incarnate. It has come into the world and contrary to the saying [*parole*] in the Gospel, it is not true that we have not received it. We have recognized it and we are living out the consequences of this recognition" (June 17, 1961). We do recognize: "*Verbum* is language. . . . In the Greek text, *logos* is also language and not speech [*parole*]. After that, God makes use of the word—'let there be light,' He says" (1954–55, 327). I take him to mean that language precedes any use God may make of it and, therefore, is in its own order ultimate. "[This] is what I mean when I say that no metalanguage can be spoken, or, more aphoristically, that there is no Other of the Other" (1977, 311).

To "live out the consequences of this recognition" is to deny the possibility of God as Other than the Other. Nor can He be identified with the Other as Father, or Law or Name-of-the-Father, for the Other is no more than the laws of language functioning in their cultural-historical embodiment. Nor can He reside there as some center or foundation of meaning, for there is no center, and if meaning implies unity, there is no meaning either. You can understand, then, why he says that "the verifiable formula for atheism is not 'God is dead' but rather 'God is unconscious'" (1963–64, 59).

The Word of Pius, then, is no different from the Word of the Other, the Word as Other. And it is the Word of the Other that makes Sygne's situation so desperate. It is from the deep rooting in language constituted by her promise to George that she is forced to uproot herself, and, indeed, by a choice that is supposed to be free. This is the sense of her betrayal, not only of George but of herself as a speaking subject. The result is not simply an experience of "frustration" but rather the full import of Freud's own word *Versagung,* the abandonment of her word, the default of a promise. By reason of our subjection to the Word, it is possible for us to curse (*maudire*) ourselves, "not simply as particular destiny [in terms of an individual] life but as the very way by which the Word engages us, as encounter with truth, as the hour of truth" (June 17, 1961). The result is total alienation.

Who, then, is the hostage that gives the play its title? For Claudel, it is the Pope. But for Lacan, the Pope is a feeble, futile, innocuous figure. The legitimacy that is restored is "only lure, fiction, caricature and in reality prolongation of an order [already] subverted" (June 3, 1961). The true hostage, as he sees it, is Sygne herself, for she is captured by the Word and forced to offer sacrifice to the negation of what she believes in. She is asked to make her own the very injustice that horrifies her. "Man has become hostage of the Word because . . . God is dead" (June 17, 1961). "At this moment there opens up that gaping hole [*béance*] in which nothing else can be articulated than the beginnings of [that phrase of Oedipus at Colonus], *mé phynai*—'Oh, to never have been born'" (June 17, 1961).

For Claudel, then, Sygne's final gesture takes place in an economy of grace that transcends the order of human symbolization or imagining. For Lacan, the betrayal consists precisely in her refusal of the demands of the symbolic order. Is there anything to be said in Lacanian terms about an order of grace? I have tried to suggest elsewhere (1986) that if God is to be encountered in the Lacanian paradigm, it is not in terms of the symbolic order for the reasons given. His thought, however, permits us to ask whether the God whom Claudel worships is not to be found in the Real, the dimension of ineffable, unimaginable mystery.

If I may close with the same flippant insouciance with which I be-

gan, let me conclude by posing some questions that seem to me relevant to theological discourse but that I have no intention of trying to
answer:

1. If God and the economy of grace are to be found not in the Symbolic but only in the Real, how can there be any serious theological
discourse about them at all?

2. How are we to give a theological meaning to human desire in
the light of Lacan's conception of desire as want-to-be yearning only
for a lost object that was never really possessed and certainly can
never be found?

3. How are we to understand an ethics that takes as its ultimate
judgment: "Have you acted in conformity with the desire that dwells
in you?," on the grounds that "the only thing of which one can be
guilty, at least in the perspective of analysis, is to have given up on
[*cédé sur*] one's desire?"

4. If the subject is constituted as subject only by the negation identical with the entrance of the subject as such into the [system] of the
signifier—that is, by the cleavage through which it becomes sub-
missive to the law of the Father and the Other becomes subject of the
unconscious—who is it that says, who is it that *can* say, "*adsum*"
("here *I* am")?

Notes

1. Paul Claudel–Francis Jammes–Gabriel Friseau, *Correspondance 1897–
1938* (Paris: Gallimard, 1952), 130. Cited by Waters (1970), 80.
2. Note in *Le Figaro,* October 29, 1934, cited in *Oeuvres Complètes,* 10
(1956), 313.
3. Ibid.
4. Letter to M. de Pawlowski (1914), cited in Avré (1961), 67.

References

Avré, Barna. *L'otage de Paul Claudel. Essai de psychologie littéraire.* Quebec:
    Le Soleil, 1961.
Claudel, Paul. *Oeuvres complètes.* Vol. 10. Paris: Gallimard, 1956.
———. *The Hostage* (1911). Translated by Pierre Chavannes. New Haven: Yale
    University Press, 1917.
Lacan, Jacques. *Le Séminaire: Livre II (1954–55). Le moi dans la théorie de
    Freud et dans la technique de la psychanalyse.* Edited by Jacques-Alain
    Miller. Paris: Seuil, 1978.

————. *Le Séminaire: Livre VII (1959–60). L'ethique de la psychanalyse.* Edited by Jacques-Alain Miller. Paris: Seuil, 1986.

————. *Le Séminaire: Livre VIII (1960–61). Le Transfert!* Students' notes.

————. *The Four Fundamental Concepts of Psycho-Analysis* (1963–64). Translated by Alan Sheridan. New York: W. W. Norton, 1978.

————. *Ecrits.* Paris: Seuil, 1966.

————. *Ecrits: A Selection.* Translated by Alan Sheridan. New York: Norton, 1977.

Madaule, Jacques. *Le drame de Paul Claudel.* Paris: Desclée de Brouwer, 1947.

Richardson, William J. "Psychoanalysis and the God-question." *Thought* 61 (1986): 68–83.

Waters, Harold A. *Paul Claudel.* New York: Twayne, 1970.

5   Confrontation with Neutrality in Theory and Praxis

Antoine Vergote

Ethics is inherent in being human. There is therefore an ethics of psychoanalysis. The human being is not necessarily religious, even though religion itself maintains that the person finds his or her deepest truth and salvation only in community with the divine; in monotheism: with God. Although religion is not constitutive of the human, as is the case with ethics, according to the religious person it is essential for humanity, and undoubtedly it is also very important in the history of culture; thus the status of religion is for the science of man—of which psychoanalysis is a part—an object of ambivalent interest.

According to the measure in which psychoanalysis reveals something fundamental about the person, one may expect that it can say something meaningful about religion, just as it can with art. And because religion involves the whole person it is, on the other hand, proper to think that psychoanalysis can also learn something from religion, just as it has been informed by popular stories, literary works, and data drawn from cultural anthropology. From the point of view of the religious believer who takes psychoanalysis seriously, there is reasonable hope that it will clarify religious insight and that this clarification will have practical value.

For the practice of the analyst, the correct view of the relation between psychoanalysis and religion is the precondition for understanding and possibly commenting on any religiously affected judgments present in either the believing or doubting (unbelieving) analysand.

This chapter deals first with the relationship of psychoanalytical theory to religion. Then, several examples will indicate how religion can be an important moment in the analytical process.

74

Psychoanalytical Theory

QUESTIONABLE ALOOFNESS

In comparison with other data, religion is seldom mentioned in the scientific publications of psychoanalytical associations. This silence contrasts conspicuously with the interest Freud had in the phenomenon. Indeed, the more Freud's thinking evolved, the more the matter of religion seemed to concern him. In 1927 (*Future of an Illusion*), 1930 (*Civilization and Its Discontents*), and 1939 (*Moses and Monotheism*) he devoted comprehensive arguments to the topic. Several of his students also concerned themselves with psychoanalytical studies of religious phenomena. There are probably several reasons for the aloofness of later analysts. Those who derive all their insights from the one master, Freud, and have little or no religious culture, seem to consider religion as definitively explained by Freud, and thus no longer a topic for scientific discussion. Others hold the thesis that in practice psychoanalysis is neutral with respect to religion, and they choose not to endanger this neutrality through a theoretical confrontation. Unpleasant memories of Jung's psychic-religious mysticism may have added to the fear that any accommodation between religion and psychoanalysis is doomed.

Nevertheless, many of the insights of psychoanalysis touch upon fundamental dimensions of religion. Freud saw this, but he thought that religious representations were only the expression of an obscured psychological truth. In reaction to Freud, Jung wanted, theoretically and practically, to restore the religious ground to psychological data. But his theory, that true psychology is religion, lets both domains so run together that, in my opinion, they lose their unique identity. Thus it is not easy to avoid these two opposing positions, which merge religion and psychology but from opposite directions.

Although this is not the place to treat Jung's views, I would like to express my own conviction clearly. Jung integrated religious representations in the psyche so completely, as an inborn constitutive element thereof, that the relation with a divine reality is actually folded back in psychic inwardness. The religious person is interested only in his or her own inner world. I therefore consider Jung's positive position concerning religion to be atheism obscured by mythic-psychological terms. One may apply to Jung that which Lacan confirmed in connection with his own religious interpretation: radical atheism is the recognition that God belongs to the unconscious. Leaving the discussion of Lacan's psychological interpretation to one side, I want however to note that the same danger is inherent in psychoanalysis as is

present in Jung's psychology. A psychoanalytical theory that interpretively absorbs religion into an explicit atheism risks becoming an
inverted counterpart of Jung and likewise risks falling into a mysticism
of a new army of salvation. A psychoanalysis that considers God an
outdated idol and wishes to take the place of religion is likely to
present itself as an idol. Psychoanalysis retains its identity only when it
makes no claims to a doctrine of salvation, or to human self-develop-
ment, or to happiness, and when it does not have the philosophical
pretension to declare life to be impossible nonsense.

A PSYCHOANALYTICAL EXPLANATION OF RELIGION?

Freud rightly opposed the modern blurring and diluting of the concept religion: the "whitewashed" rational reference to an anonymous
divine principle. He was also correct in refusing to see the deepest
source of religion in a cosmic-mystical feeling of oneness and in refusing to interpret this sort of mysticism as the highest form of religion: a
religion purified of all human motivations and representations. When
one considers religion as an objective cultural phenomenon, as Freud
did, then indeed the above conceptions seem to be only shadows of an
extinct religion or perhaps vague impulses toward it. Each person is
free to make his or her own philosophical reinterpretation of that
which presents itself in the history of culture as religion. If psychoanalysis is to concern itself with religion it must begin by identifying
religion on the basis of what is made known in the history of religion.
Neither the Jewish nor the Christian religion—nor the many others—
allows itself to dissolve into a vague speculative deism or into the sensation of merging with the cosmic whole. A religion is a network of
pronouncements about a supernatural and/or divine being(s), about
ethics, about prayers, and about symbolic signs and actions through
which the person comes into living community with the divine. Similarly, Freud emphasized that the divine being is a father figure. Religion
is the most complex cultural phenomenon, according to Freud, and
the explanation thereof cannot be reduced to one factor (*S.E.* 13:100).

But does psychoanalysis entirely explain religion? Freud was convinced that he had given an adequate explanation and thus had justified
his rejection of religion. In discussing his forceful attempt some critical
observations need immediate attention. If, as Freud says, psychoanalysis is not a complete anthropology (*S.E.* 14:50), to say nothing of a
Weltanschauung (*S.E.* 22:158), then a priori its ability to explain religion without remainder is disputable. Freud seems more consistent
with the limits which he himself placed on psychoanalytic expertise
when he writes that psychoanalysis is neutral with respect to religion

(Freud and Pfister 1963, February 9, 1909). One may not even restore religion to a *Weltanschauung,* he also writes (*S. E.* 22:161–62), because it is not clear how it could in this capacity unify its three functions: its doctrine, which answers questions concerning the origin and the ultimate meaning of existence, its response to human desires ("consolation"), and its ethical prescriptions. Those who know something of religious literature are also offended by the description that Freud gives of religious desires in *The Future of an Illusion* (1927). And those who know something of cultural anthropology and of biblical science cannot take seriously, in spite of their esteem for Freud's genius, his interpretations of myth, totemism, rites, the history of religion, the Bible, and Christology.[1] Epigones who simply parrot Freud in these areas make a fool of psychoanalysis in the eyes of the scientific world. The impression cannot be denied that Freud approached religion with a prejudice that contrasts with his readiness to listen to his patients and to revise his positions continually.

Two basic motives are behind Freud's project of a psychoanalytic explanation of religion. As a convinced disciple of Enlightenment rationalism he saw religion in the first place as an archaic phase of cultural infancy. He thought this emancipatory interpretation could be legitimated by an "applied psychoanalysis," which itself could explain the origin of culture, ethics, and religion. Such use of psychoanalysis in the service of personal convictions held a special advantage for the psychoanalytic theorist. If it could be demonstrated that in religion there is the manifestation of the archaic in the human person, then there would seem to be a clear proof for what the theorist wants to show in clinical studies: the abiding activity in the human being of unconscious representations, especially that of the Oedipus complex.

As is well known, Freud introduces in *Totem and Taboo* a genetic-psychological theory concerning the transition of nature to culture and the existence of religion. In brief, it comes down to this: the sons of the Ur-father murdered him in order to capture the wives that he had reserved for himself. Tormented by feelings of guilt, the sons later idealized the father. They recognized his law, and they made peace among themselves for pragmatic reasons. The posthumously idealized Ur-father was then gradually divinized. Archaic religious illusions thus seem to be a remainder of the primordial beginning (the *arche*). One might ask oneself in amazement how consciousness of guilt, and thus ethical law, could come into being from the murder of a lawless father in a lawless "horde." Are we not caught in a vicious circle, noted by Freud himself in his citation of a folk tale (*S. E.* 18:89): Christopher carries the child Jesus; the child Jesus carries the world; what supports the feet of Christopher? Freud's imaginary interpretations of cultural anthropological and biblical data are clearly in the service of the psychological purpose in which many human scientists in his time were trapped.

Lacan brought a fundamental correction to psychoanalytical theory through the introduction of the related ideas on the symbolic, the symbolic order, and the realm of the signifiers. By these he means that the human subject involves himself or herself in a whole of mutually differentiated meaning-founding signs (signifiers)—namely, language or the system of signs analogous to language. They are presupposed and, far from being susceptible to psychological clarification, they dominate psychological development. Even unconscious representations are, according to Lacan, "structured like a language." Through this theory Lacan has brought psychoanalysis in line with the turn taken by the human sciences, which across the board have broken with the mythical view of earlier psychology that had considered itself the basis of all human sciences. The Freudian explanation of religion by a psychogenetic theory of its origin can only be seen as a grand error. We need not treat here the demand for a more adequate theory.

THE PSYCHOANALYTICAL VIEWPOINT

The problem concerning the insight psychoanalysis can bring to religion has thus become clearer. First, psychoanalysis may not speak about the truth claims that religion makes, at least not immediately. Its limited expertise does not allow that. Freud, moreover, recognizes this in his critical work *The Future of an Illusion,* where he concludes with the affirmation that religion, seen as a product of desire, might be true, although he considers this to be highly unlikely. Religious claims upon ultimate truths can neither be proved nor refuted, notes Freud, because they do not belong to the order of scientific rationality. Of course, some more proximal issues pertaining to religion can be shown to have neurotic components. But Freud did not on the whole engage such issues. He tended to interpret religion globally and simply to set the whole of theological thought aside as irrelevant. It was for him only a speculative superstructure that obscured the true kernel. An eloquent example of the a priori way in which he treated the world of religious meaning occurs in his interpretation of Sophocles' Oedipus drama. He unabashedly dismissed the oracle, which gives the drama its real mythical-religious meaning, as the hypocritical cunning of the poet (*S. E.* 16:368).[2] His commentary also tied itself in knots in the attempt to force upon Oedipus a guilt consciousness; he replaced the *terror* in the face of divine fate with moral *horror.* In order that psychoanalytical theory might share in the truth and wisdom that are granted to a classic master work, Freud wanted to see in the drama the visible display of the oedipal drive-wishes that were later understood as repressed.

Freud's overhasty reduction of specifically religious rationality to a hidden psychic underground is a typical expression of his psychologism. Lacan turns the relation around. Consistent with his recognition of meaning-founding signifiers, and of their psychological impact, he emphasizes the remarkable logic of theology, and he affirms the importance thereof for the psychoanalytical understanding of the person. But, extending his position, he believes he finds the rationality of theology in the structure of the unconscious. This is all very vague and therefore food for esoteric speculations! "God is unconscious" (Lacan 1978, 59; 1972, 73, 65). Such a statement reminds one of Jung's questionable psychology of the inborn archetypes. More consistent than Jung, Lacan really holds that this position definitively justifies atheism. I cannot discuss here this foggy atheistic theology. However, I would like to point out that in any such discussion, one would have to begin with a serious analysis of the surrealistic ambiguity contained in the thesis "the unconscious is structured like a language" (Vergote 1983a).

Despite the heterogeneity between religious pronouncements and psychoanalytical theory, there is a common ground where they touch each other. It could not be otherwise because both have the intention of saying something essential about the person. That is why Freud and Lacan give so much attention to religion. Fundamental themes and typical forms of relations indeed characterize religion and psychoanalysis: desire, the meaning of the father figure, law, and guilt. In line with Freud's depth psychology, we may hold as guiding principle the idea that a psychic depth dimension is the ground where psychoanalysis and religion meet each other. We may say that psychoanalysis refers important themes, which also come up in religion, back to the primordial experience of the person, whereas religion lifts them up to a relation with God, which is conditioned but not determined by the psychic depth dimension. This schema can be compared with psychoanalysis of a psychopathology. Psychoanalysis goes to work analytically. It goes from the present back to the psychic causes that lie in the past. From these causes, however, the present cannot be theoretically constructed.[3] Psychic causes only conditionally determine. They must be distinguished by the expression: conditional determinism. Freud's reductionist psychoanalysis of religion has therefore been heuristically fruitful. It handed down principles applicable to a dynamic psychology of religion and to religious themes manifested in psychopathology.

This thesis will be illustrated by a short discussion of the most prominent themes common to religion and psychoanalysis. In order not to fall into coarse simplifications I will limit myself to the Christian religion.

DESIRE

In religion the person is involved with his or her desires that reach beyond the range of scientific reason. That is the principal thesis of the work to which Freud gave the eloquent title *The Future of an Illusion.* In fact, he treats here only the different desires and anxieties of the distressed person, and not the desire that is the dynamic power in the religious philosophy of Plato, in the Pauline desire for God, or in Christian mysticism. It is true that religious desire proper seems to originate and to receive its first form in the drive-wishes of the child, who is born helpless and who turns to the caring affection of a father and mother for satisfaction of its needs. But does not psychoanalysis also point out that in this situation a relation is founded that transforms neediness into a blossoming love and recognition? And what is more, that the remembrance of need satisfaction becomes an experience of pleasure that brings into existence in the psyche the erotic capacity? This mutation—through which the person is lifted out of the vital cycle of neediness and satisfaction without, however, neutralizing these states—brings about an active openness that breaks through the reality toward which scientific reason is directed. Furthermore, the entrance into language, with its possibility of negating limitation to the here and now and with its never-completed description of reality, gives an unending dynamism to desire. Religious language then grafts new meaning terms to this endless desire, which further opens the desire by directing it precisely toward that which religion presents as more real than the reality grasped by scientific reason. Psychoanalysis, which with Freud holds that the capacity for love is a characteristic of psychic health, can hardly investigate whether religious desire-love indeed gives evidence of this capacity. Psychoanalytic theory makes it possible to shed light upon the link between erotic and religious desire. At the same time it also provides working concepts that enable one to distinguish between sublimated desire-love and the hidden, displaced eroticism of religious hysteria or erotomania.[4] Here the analyst needs to listen carefully to the documented witnesses of religious love and desire and take into consideration the religious frame of reference. When the analyst fails to appreciate the desire-founding and transforming power of religious signifiers, he or she is only doing wild psychoanalysis.

In *The Future of an Illusion* an analysis of actual religious desire and love is completely absent, even from the description of the impulse thereto in human love. Freud analyzed only a religious conviction primarily motivated by desires that lie so close to immediate human needs and anxieties that one indeed immediately thinks of their illusory character. Why illusory? First, because they are contradicted by reality. These believers themselves experience the reality that God does not intervene in earthly affairs in order to meet their drive-wishes. Second, this sort of belief in God is also an illusion from the perspective of the Christian representation of God. The disillusionment that is brought about by experience of reality can then make a person susceptible to the deeper meaning of the religious message. The clarification that psychoanalysis brings to these forms of religion is thus limited to making understandable the influence that neediness can continually exercise on desires. This explanation, however, does not fully explore the idea of God. When one reflects upon the complex phenomenon that a religion always is, one must recognize the wide gulf between need motivations and the idea of God as it takes its meaning in the whole of the religious network.[5]

THE UR-SCENE AND ORIGINAL GUILT

Every religion contains statements about the origin of the world, life, and human persons, from a more or less divine Ur-beginning. This fundamental characteristic of religion is so interwoven with the linguistic nature and the time consciousness of the human being that at first glance it seems to fall outside the reach of psychoanalytical interpretation. Yet the idea of beginning resembles one of the main fantasms known to psychoanalysis: that of the Ur-scene. It is called a fantasm because it is a representative image which appears only at the edges of consciousness and is usually so repressed that only in analysis is it spoken about. The content is that one imagines oneself in some way to have been a witness to the parental sexual act of which one is the fruit. In this fantasm the awakened curiosity concerning the intimacy between parents and the infantile interpretations thereof play a role. The kernel however lies deeper: it is the impossible attempt to place oneself at a moment in time before one existed in order to be present at one's own beginning. This fantasm receives its full meaning in the context of narcissism. Narcissism always produces resistance to the idea that one is not necessary, that one's existence is received and not somehow a product of one's own doing. Clinical experience reveals that the schizophrenic, who is still trapped in such original narcissism, cannot reconcile himself to the actual contingency. Freud rightly interprets this condition when he says that the schizophrenic wants to be his own father.[6] The contingency of existence and consciousness of being in debt to another for existence are damaging to narcissism.

It is in this context that the name "father" has its most basic meaning. Certainly, the mother is also the origin. But the close vital and affective link between mother and child calls forth more the natural continuity as it exists in life-giving nature. In many cultures and in their religious symbols the mother and the earth represent each other, while that which is fecundating and which falls from above symbolizes the father. As origin, he is, more clearly than the mother, the other. Perceived as other by the child, the father specifically signifies the contingency of the origin, an origin that is a real beginning and no longer a manifestation of the continuity of life. It must also be remembered that the dynamic of the Oedipus complex is defined by the appearance of the father as third; he makes structuring triangulation possible, and this for both sexes. Because the father is the other, because he is the detached beginning that signifies the break in the natural unity of life, it is important for the child to experience that he or she is recognized through the initiative and interested association of the father; we may say: through the establishment of a link of love whereby he fully adopts the child. What psychoanalysis has to say concerning the meaning of the father is also confirmed by many cultural-anthropological studies.

The whole of Freud's psychoanalysis of religion is an attempt to clarify the idea of God as an imaginary enlargement of the father figure. But in the two directions he pursues, the true meaning of the father is completely missing. *The Future of an Illusion* recognizes in the father only the imagined omnipotent and benevolent person who accommodates the helplessness of the child. And in *Totem and Taboo* the Urfather is the brute male animal without any fatherlike disposition to recognize the "sons" and without a desire for their salvation. Talk of a murder of the "father" is then only a strange misconception. It is a myth recounted in a scientific setting, and one feels obliged to interpret it psychoanalytically. Does there not lie at the base of this fantasmagorical psychogenetic theory of culture a narcissistic fantasm articulated by Freud himself? Namely, wanting to be one's own father, instead of being willing to recognize the father as prior? Freud looks at the father only from the standpoint of the rivalry of the sons, not from the standpoint of the father himself. Moreover, his problem was: there is no room for two.[7]

The psychoanalytic interpretation of the name of the father points to the place to which the divine name of the father is anchored;[8] such interpretation, however, has not been worked out by psychoanalysis to the point that the latter is recognized. There is a striking agreement between the name of the father as it functions in the family structure and the same concept as it structures the religious relation, most obviously in the Christian faith. On the one hand the affirmation of God implies the radical recognition of the contingency of human existence, through the belief that one's origin lies in the free personal will of the creator. On the other hand, the belief in a God who calls into existence, who reveals himself, who recognizes humanity, and who makes a covenant with them also accommodates the desire to have a personal origin, to be affirmed and to be loved. The conflicts traversed by and frequently resolved by religious belief often are the same conflicts that characterize the relation with the father. For example, in religious belief—as in family relations—there is the tension between (1) the knowledge of being established in a lineage that yields trust and certainty and (2) the resistance to the narcissistic wound brought about by the pronouncement that one has no power over one's existence, neither for its coming into being nor for its completion.

Because psychoanalytic theory cannot infer the idea of God as father from the name of the father, the relationship between the human and divine name of the father poses a theoretical problem. In the absence of strict reasoning it is possible to cover this up with the stopgap term "projection." Many theorists, however, see the name of the father as a cultural reality, a signifier that is not explained by psychoanalysis but functions only as a signifier in psychoanalysis. As cultural reality it gives form to the archaic depth dimension of the psychism. What is peculiar to religion, then, is that it explains the name of the father through the affirmation that it has its origin in the not-to-be-explained divine name of the father. Psychoanalysis as such can only remain silent in the face of this claim of faith.

LAW AND GUILT

Psychoanalytic theory and religion also demonstrate striking similarity in the connection they make between the father figure, the law, and desire. This similarity intrigued Freud, and, in addition to his intention to explain religion, it is the problem that he wanted to solve in *Totem and Taboo.* The problem of human guilt made him think that from the beginning something is fractured in the person. He concluded that work with the affirmation that the Christian doctrine of original sin is, in religiously disguised form, the recognition of a historical reality that he sought to reconstruct as the original "murder of the father." In this initial break he believed he had found the deepest ground of the human disposition toward neurosis.

A study on ethics and psychoanalysis would give ample witness that drive-wishes only develop into meaningful human desires if they allow themselves to be regulated by ethical law. The Oedipus complex is the structuring core of this. An explanation can be offered of why the father figure is par excellence the representative and giver of the law. In the name of Yahweh, Moses proclaimed God's personal choice of the Jewish people; in this way God realized fatherhood over his people and established a link of lineage. Then Moses proclaimed the law on the basis of the fatherlike authority of Yahweh. The law is the condition for divine lineage. The negative formulations of the commandments express powerfully that the law must realize a transformation of human drive-wishes. The negativity must have the same result that the first commandment, positively formulated, clearly expresses as Yahweh's religious desire: for people to love God with all their human possibilities.

All religions contain an ethical law, all consequently awaken consciousness of guilt, and all have rites of confessing guilt. In a religion that establishes a personal relation with God, the consciousness of guilt is more clearly a personal guilt with respect to God. Because such a religion does not remain intertwined in the earthly community but offers transcendence through the proclamation of God's love and the demand for love of God, liberation from guilt is also an essential element of it.

Psychoanalysis cannot deduce religious guilt from the general human consciousness of guilt because the religious guilt itself is aroused from the unique proclamation of the religion. Psychoanalysis can, however, assist the understanding that this proclamation has power over the person because it is grafted on experiences that express an aspect of the core of the person's being: the link between law, the father, and desire. This psychic substructure of religion also makes possible the manifestation of a guilt neurosis in religious experience.

Religion in Analytic Therapy

Two practical consequences follow from the above. The nearness and distance between psychoanalytical theory of the person and religion imply that in treatment of the religious analysand, religious fear-laden and wish-laden representations will often be intertwined with the neurotic, while in treatment of the religiously indifferent analysand they will seldom come up. The previous discussion likewise touches upon principles that provide guidance for the analyst's possible interventions. Despite the analyst's own views on religion, psychoanalytic ethics require him or her to maintain neutrality in the face of the convictions of the analysand, to listen just as attentively to religious statements as to others, and to help the analysand to work through religious conflicts when these indeed are a part of psychic conflicts. This can be a delicate task because the analyst must be able to allow the analysand to take the lead or take final responsibility for making the sometimes subtle distinction between what objectively belongs to religion and what is a neurotic appropriation thereof. This does not mean that the analyst should refrain from questioning or interpreting what he or she believes to be clearly neurotic. However, the analyst's interventions should be unbiased—not based on a conviction that all religious belief and practice are inherently neurotic. If one is not capable of such lack of bias, because of ignorance or personal uneasiness with religion, then one should maintain silence rather than violate the ethics of psychoanalysis or inhibit, through misunderstanding, the progress of the analysis.

Analysis of religious ideas that are implicated in neurosis usually leads to doubts in the area of faith. In an analysis no domain of life can remain withdrawn from the conflict in a no-man's-land. Whether the analysand keeps and refines his or her belief or renounces it depends upon a combination of several factors: upbringing, the gravity of the neurotic elements, one's personal ethics, and sometimes also the analyst. Stubbornly held and repeatedly discussed doubts can be a trap for the analyst. They are attached to underlying psychic conflicts, but like all theoretical ruminations, they form a defense mechanism against drive-wishes that one unconsciously wants neither to accept nor to renounce. The shifting of examination of psychic conflicts to the area of theoretical reflection upon conflicts is a compulsive neurotic symptom to which the neurotic at times can attach himself, even if he does not suffer from the typical obsessional neurosis. When the analyst intervenes in the presence of religious representations that are involved in the neurosis, the analysand often reacts with extended discussions about belief and disbelief. In his potential interventions the analyst must be careful not to be seduced into the conflict to which he is challenged. In the following example, especially, there is provocation related to such unconscious strategic reflections.

MEGALOMANIA IN RELIGIOUS CONFLICTS

In the analysand's stubborn repetition of reasons not to believe in God, frequently a certain conviction is expressed concerning a representation of God as a fantastic monster, which calls to mind the greedy Ur-father of *Totem and Taboo.* If God exists, it is continually repeated, then he can only be the jealous enemy of humanity. He condemns all human pleasure as an insult inflicted upon himself; all human self-affirmation falls short of the glorification that he demands for himself alone; he considers all science as a violation of his exclusive omniscience. The person who believes in him, it is argued, can only resign himself to helplessness, submissiveness, ignorance, and the renouncing of pleasure.

Analysands who do so argue know at some level that that of which they speak is only a sham of the God of the Christian religion in which they were brought up. They know it indirectly but also do not want to know it. If this were not so, then they would indifferently turn away, without delay, from religion, or they would investigate the matter further. Yet they do neither one nor the other; instead, in the analysis they continue to quarrel inwardly with their monster-God. This representation of God thus has a function in their psychic economy. Others maintain that a God who is indifferent with respect to suffering is but a narcissistic, self-sufficient God; however, the analysands of whom I am speaking here do not go deeper into the faith question posed by suffering but remain indecisive.

In the presence of such absurd representations of God it is clear that one cannot speak of religious belief. Yet the analysand remains libidinally attached to this representation and cannot let go. The analyst might think that the analysand's fear of what he sees as a revengeful God is so oppressive that he is unable to find the strength to free himself from his delusion. Moreover, the analysand is able to articulate the fear and is able to recognize its absurdity. But the fear chiefly serves to give dramatic intensity to his rebelliousness. Even if the fear decreases, the rebelliousness remains simmering on a back burner. As is eventually shown in analysis, the representation of God to which such an analysand refers is necessary for him as the great antipode against which to measure himself in imagination and heart. The reference to God supports the narcissistic fantasm of divine greatness. In the patient's imagination he wants the power, the omniscience, the creative genius, and the glorification that religion grants to God. The dilemma is that whether God does not exist or does exist, one cannot take his place. In the quarrel that is manifested as religious doubt, the analysand goes back and forth between the kind of inner contradictions that always characterize desire-fantasies. But contradiction as such is not expressed. Consciousness is limited to the religious claim of belief in God and to the accusation of the absurdity of such belief. It is up to the analyst, at the appropriate time, to articulate the underlying fantasm and the imagined contradiction.

Here God is undeniably the term that gives content and intensity to the megalomania that Jones correctly interprets as the "God complex,"[9] which according to him lives hidden in narcissism that is largely repressed. In the conscious, quarreling game with this complex, made possible by the religious referent, the analysand comes close to religious delirium. However, the reference to a religion outside himself, which is nevertheless denied, probably at the same time protects him from a real psychotic delusion.

As one might suppose, in this type of analysis many delusions of greatness are articulated that are not immediately concerned with the rivalry with God: dreams of worldly fame, of effortless brilliant creativity, of power and esteem through riches, and so forth. The oldest and most effective, and also the most tormenting, wish representations are those of a unique phallic power and pleasure. These also imply the strongest challenge to "God."

It is not the so-called religious doubts that induce such an analysand to undergo analysis but the tormenting doubts concerning sexual performance, job performance, and love relations. Here the "God complex" forms the background. However, when religious reflections receive clear expression, then the analyst cannot, in my opinion, remain silent and move on, as if they were only a superstructure of a sexual or other problem. If the analyst remains silent about the neurotic core of the "religious" dilemma, then the unconscious source of the problem remains unanalyzed.

It is not religion but religious enmity that is in this case neurotic. Deep envy, as analyzed by Melanie Klein, also works itself out in this kind of relation to God. Here the envy receives its sharpest expression, because here it shows its fullest meaning. The analysand hates the idea of religious belief because that is the deepest wound to his narcissism. It is difficult to imagine such an analysis succeeding without the working through of the fantasm-filled religious enmity. To be liberating, analysis is not called upon, of course, to convert the religious enmity into religious belief. Such conversion can only occur when religion itself offers other possibilities to the analysand.

GUILT NEUROSIS

Religious guilt neurosis is a complex form of obsessional neurosis. I will limit myself here to a few indications that illustrate the above principles.[10]

It is often thought that the obsessional neurotic suffers from feelings of guilt. Nothing is less true. The tormenting obsessive thoughts and actions indeed go back to what can be metaphorically called an unconscious feeling of guilt. This expression is of course inadequate, for by their very nature feelings are consciously perceived. The analysis manifests that obsessional neurosis is an unconscious strategy for warding off guilt feelings by apparently insignificant rituals, displaced verifications, obsequious behavior, and masked pleasure-seeking through the symptoms themselves. However, in religious guilt neurosis the patient really suffers from a consuming and unconquerable feeling of guilt with respect to God. Here, too, the patient knows indirectly, without being able to accept it, that the God of his religion is not the cruel judge who prosecutes him. The patient genuinely maintains a belief in God, but "something" prohibits belief in God's inclination toward forgiveness. The patient entrusts his or her sins to this inclination toward forgiveness without actually finding inner peace in the experience of reconciliation. The big difference with the instance of religious conflicts in megalomania is that in religious obsessional neurosis there is genuine belief in God, although it is warped by neurosis. In the prior example there was no belief in God because the reference to the God of religion was only or primarily a function of a contested but desperately maintained megalomania.

Analysis, then, does not consist in a theological clarification of the representation of God. Such clarification, moreover, often has already happened, without much benefit. Unconscious drive-wishes and frightening imaginings are the distant sources of the neurotic representation of God as well as of the conscious guilt anxiety. Yet the neurotic element in religious belief is here more than an epiphenomenon. Because it is anchored in the unconscious, belief in its turn gives its own content and power to the unconscious representations. In all suffering there is always an enjoyable attachment to the delusion of complete guiltlessness with respect to God and with respect to one's own conscience. To experience oneself as powerless in this respect is a great setback for narcissism. The person pushes the religious laws and the obedience to the extreme, in order to assure God's good will for him (legalism). In this the person also strenuously tries to achieve the narcissistic image of his (or her) perfection, in correspondence with the harsh superego transferred unto God. But because of the constant revolt of the instinctual desires he experiences, he cannot reach the ideal perfection he imagines God requires. The difficult acceptance of this setback for his narcissism, without cynically folding back up into oneself because of the narcissistic setback, is an important moment in the therapeutic work. The interpreting interventions of the analyst can be effective only with respect to the intertwining of the unreal ideal of the ego, the corresponding representation of God, and the resulting guilt anxiety. The interventions thus necessarily concern religion as the analysand experiences it, precisely in the aspects that give expression to and support the delusive ideal. The analyst will not be in a position to make these interventions if—like Freud—he or she cannot differentiate between guilt neurosis and religious guilt confession. In *Civilization and Its Discontents* Freud described the religious confession of sin as self-accusation. This predominates in religious obsession. In guilt neurosis, indeed, the person indefinitely repeats the self-accusation, without reaching peace of mind, for he remains enclosed in an exacerbated narcissism and imprisoned in an unconsciously motivated representation of a fierce divine judge. Rather than self-accusation, religious confession is primarily an avowal made to a God who gives the person the right to enjoyment, accepts his weaknesses, and invites him to call him "Father" with confidence.

When the analysand arrives at the edge of the dark forest full of demons in which the guilt anxiety has trapped him, he indeed sees the liberating light, but usually he also experiences the ground sinking beneath him. He no longer knows who he is and feels empty because he no longer has a predictable image of himself onto which he can hold. Earlier, his constant anxiety had caused suffering, but at least it also had left no room for the frightening feeling of inner emptiness. The paradoxical experience of liberation and emptiness reflects the truth of Freud's statement, which annoyed many: however much the patient desires liberation, he is as attached to his sickness as he is to himself. The religious obsessional neurotic loses something of himself when he escapes from guilt anxiety. He goes through a moment of depression. The anxiety of guilt is not one of the underlying causes of depression, as is too often claimed. On the contrary, depression here is due to the specific feeling of emptiness that results from the dismantling of the impossible ego-ideal and from the demolition of the dramatically guilt-ridden but intensely lived relationship with God.

That depressive moment agrees with a phase of the "desert experience," which mystical seekers of God describe: the phase where they realize their impotence to experience the love of God as they desire and as is demanded of them by their faith. There is, of course, a difference between the two instances. With the mystic the experience of emptiness is defined by a consciousness of the distance between him and his God; for the religious obsessional neurotic, the emptiness is in response to the loss of an unconscious pathological ego-ideal. The obsessional neurotic was not in the ascending movement of the mystical way, and now, freed from his guilt anxieties, he is still not proceeding along this way. But if the analysand remains a believer, he will experience something of the mystic purification, which consists in a finding in oneself a decentralized fulfillment of the God-directed relation. It is not the task of the analyst to point the patient toward this solution of the depressive moment. The believing analyst can only trust that the still-believing analysand will find this possibility in himself and in the nonneurotic dynamic of his belief. The unbelieving analyst should at least be aware of the discontinuities and mutations in the religious life itself so that he can listen to the patient with understanding.

PSYCHOLOGICAL PROCESS OR DIVINE HAPPENING?

In the analysis of believers, religious experiences can be recalled that—through the unveiling of the divine secret—can give life a new direction. Trusted religious words, previously lifeless, unexpectedly become redeeming words that disclose what the analysand sees as true reality and give a divine luster to pale existence. This is spontaneously experienced as the unexpected appearance of God in one's own life as a special personal revelation; the analysand realizes that though he was not seeking it and possibly even excluded the possibility and its benefit, he had been silently expecting it. These insight-yielding experiences are sometimes so intensely realistic that God is experienced as present concretely, here and now, although the analysand cannot speak of a perception, as is the case in visions.

The reading of religious texts can reinforce the intensity of the belief in the truth of such an experience and can guarantee its reality character. Does not the prophet Jeremiah say that God personally called him while he walked in the field behind the plow? And did God not make it clear that Jeremiah was predestined for his religious vocation while in his mother's womb? Mystics honored by the tradition also give witness to the wonder-filled experiences by which God had favored them. They are undoubtedly on guard to examine whether their experiences and visions are not a bewitching of the senses or seductive diabolical parodies. When their experiences withstand the critical test of orthodoxy and when they appear beneficial to religious progress, mystics interpret them as brought about by God.

Analysis happens through free association in speaking with the analyst, who listens as the expert in matters of hidden psychic representations and desires. Religious experiences are not easily shared, less easily even than awful sexual memories and experiences that one does not wish to be heard in an astonished or judging manner. One tends to want to keep the religious experiences outside the analysis, as a personal secret that is not of psychological interest. Once trust is genuinely established, they are brought into the discussion. The attention-directedness proper to discourse in analysis then unavoidably brings with it critical questioning of the religious experiences. Free association leads to the recalling of the context and the forgotten prehistory: old religious memories that had been forgotten, a secret desire that one had not discerned, words to which one had apparently paid no attention but which have continued to have influence—a whole network of unsuspected factors seem then to be related to the religious experience. Is the sudden breakthrough of all this so unexpected that this religious experience is perceived not as a product of underground psychic powers but as a manifestation of the special working of the Other? The patient will at first unavoidably tend to distrust these religious experiences as a quasi-hallucinatory happening.

If that had not already happened, then analysis strips such religious experiences of their preternatural character. This can be an alarming and humiliating insight. The patient feels somewhat cheated by himself and by God. Most patients, however, eventually realize that in these experiences they felt spoken to in the deepest and best parts of themselves. They are often able to deal with the wound to self love. The outcome depends upon the manner in which the experience is actively taken up in the analysand's life, and in part upon the understanding that the analyst has for the happening. Prejudice can hinder the process. This is not to say that the analysand must be persuaded that the discovery of religious truth took place in the experience, for he obviously cannot deny its quasi-hallucinatory nature. But this is not to declare, as Freud did, that the experience was simply "nothing more than" a hallucination (*S. E.* 21:67–72).

Religion affirms God's activity in the person. Psychoanalysis does not have the scientific competence to speak against such religious convictions. It does throw light upon psychic reality within religious phenomena. The religious temperament does not pay spontaneous attention to psychic reality because it directs the believer's attention toward divine activity; thus, it is inclined to see such activity as visible and perceivable even in exceptional phenomena. One who recognizes psychic reality or who experiences it in analysis demystifies the preternaturally divine ground of such exceptional phenomena. As a believer he or she must conclude that God is active in and through human, psychic factors. The miraculous is then disenchanted. Theology can then consider belief as purified of its attachment to affectively beneficial but nevertheless shadowy signs and experiences.

Psychoanalysis as science observes only psychic reality—neither the presence nor the absence of God. In this psychic reality it also recognizes the operable references to a divine reality. Concerning that reality it can only maintain silence, in its theory as well as in its practice.

In religion and in psychoanalysis it has been a misunderstanding to see either psychoanalysis or religion as having the only claim to the same cultural heritage.

Notes

Translated by Daniel J. Frett.

This essay also appears in Dutch in *Psychoanalyse. De mens en zijn lotgevallen.* Edited by A. Vergote and P. Moyaert et al. Kapellen: DNB/Uitgeverij Pelckmans, 1988.

1. I have treated this in my "Religion after the Critique of Psychoanalysis" (1980).

2. For a critical study of Freud's interpretation of Sophocles, see Bollak (1986).

3. In spite of his deterministic philosophical view, Freud repeatedly uses the term "neurosis choice." Although this expression does not indicate a free choice, it does point out that disposition, contingent experiences, and associated reactions and interpretations work together and receive their pathological meaning by a sort of subjective act.

4. I have treated this in detail in *Guilt and Desire* (1988, 121–67).

5. For the development of this see my *Religion, foi, incroyance: Etude psychologique* (1983b, 35–109).

6. In his discussion of the narcissistic illusion of greatness, which he calls "Der Gottmens-Komplex" (the complex of the human being God; my translation), Ernest Jones likewise comments: "In der Regel sind sie natürlich Atheisten, da sie die Existenz eines anderen Gottes nicht dulden können" (Generally, they are of course atheists, for they cannot bear the existence of another God) (1928, 28–29).

7. In *Moses and Monotheism,* too, Freud continually returns to the theme of "taking the place of the other." Freud's idea that the "great man" "must kill the father" is likewise well known.

8. The expression "the name of the father" has been introduced into psychoanalytic literature by Lacan. The reference to the Christian prayer expression ("In the name of the Father. . .") is obvious and might be misleading. In the Christian image, which takes over the Hebraic biblical term, "name"

stands for the person himself. The Christian prayer therefore means that the believer unites himself ("in . . .") with the God Father he identifies and confesses as such. Lacan's expression stresses that the word "father" is a signifier that identifies the paternal function within the symbolic order of the family structure and consequently has a psychologically structuring effect. Personally, I would insist on the meaning of the father-mother polarity for the child and the adult and for the representation of God. In this respect I may refer to empirical researches done with a semantic scale: Antoine Vergote and Alvara Tamayo, *The Parental Figures and the Representation of God: A Psychological and Cross-Cultural Study* (1980).

9. See note 6.

10. For an exhaustive study see Vergote (1988, 43–97).

References

Bollak, Jean. "Le fils de l'homme. Le mythe freudien d'Oedipe." *L'ecrit du temps* 12 (1986): 3–26.

Freud, Sigmund. *The Standard Edition of the Complete Psychological Works of Sigmund Freud.* Edited and translated by James Strachey. 24 vols. London: Hogarth Press, 1953–74.

Totem and Taboo (1914), vol. 13.

On the History of the Psycho-Analytic Movement (1914), vol. 14.

Introductory Lectures on Psycho-Analysis (1916–17), vol. 16.

Group Psychology and the Analysis of the Ego (1921), vol. 18.

The Future of an Illusion (1927), vol. 21.

"A Religious Experience" (1928), vol. 21.

Civilization and Its Discontents (1930), vol. 21.

New Introductory Lectures on Psycho-Analysis (1933), vol. 22.

Moses and Monotheism (1939), vol. 23.

Freud, Sigmund, and Pfister, Oskar. *Psycho-Analysis and Faith: The Letters of Sigmund Freud and Oskar Pfister.* Edited by Heinrich Meng and Ernest L. Freud. Translated by Eric Mosbacher. London: Hogarth Press, 1963.

Jones, Ernest. *Zur Psychoanalyse der christlichen Religion.* Leipzig: Internationaler Psychoanalytischer Verlag, 1928.

Lacan, Jacques. *Le Séminaire: Livre XI. Les quatre concepts fondamentaux de la psychanalyse* (1964). Paris: Seuil, 1973.

———. *Le Séminaire: Livre XX. Encore* (1972–73). Paris: Seuil, 1975.

———. *The Four Fundamental Concepts of Psycho-Analysis* (1963–64). Edited by Jacques-Alain Miller. Translated by Alan Sheridan. New York: W. W. Norton, 1978.

Vergote, Antoine. "Religion after the Critique of Psychoanalysis." *Annual Review of the Social Science of Religion* 4 (1980): 1–29.

———. "From Freud's 'Other Scene' to Lacan's 'Other.'" In *Interpreting Lacan,* edited by Joseph H. Smith and William Kerrigan. *Psychiatry and the Humanities,* vol. 6. New Haven: Yale University Press, 1983a.

―――. *Religion, foi, incroyance: Etude psychologique.* Liège: Mardaga, 1983b.

―――. *Guilt and Desire: Religious Attitudes and Their Pathological Derivatives.* New Haven: Yale University Press, 1988.

Vergote, Antoine, and Tamayo, Alvara. *The Parental Figures and the Representation of God: A Psychological and Cross-Cultural Study.* The Hague: Mouton, 1980 (also Louvain: University Press).

6   The Role of Transitional Conceptualization in Religious Thought

William W. Meissner

T he problem I would like to address in this essay arises within the context of the interface between psychoanalytic and religious thinking. Each of these areas represents separate disciplines and ranges of discourse, each with its separate reference points, modes of conceptualization, and symbolic connotation. Speaking within the context of an accepted belief system and the record of revelation, religious thought addresses itself to a realm of conceptualization that it takes as having existential validity and substantial truth value. The belief system and the theological reflection on it assert unequivocally that there is a God, within the Judeo-Christian tradition that there is a personal God, that he is active and interactive in the contexts of created and human activity (e.g., through the media of creation, divine providence, and grace), and that the ultimate reference for these symbolic terms must be some form of existential reality. The given frame of reference for such conceptualization is the objective, existing, and real world of human experience.

On the opposite side of the conceptual chasm, psychoanalysis stakes its claim to an inner world of man's psychic experience that expresses itself in wishes and fantasies and is more or less rooted in the subjective polarity of man's experience. In addressing human religious experience and conceptualization, psychoanalysis makes no commitments to a framework of existence or objective realities but confines its focus and the implication of its arguments to the intrapsychic realm. It asserts no more than the subjective and the intrapsychic and at least prescinds from the objective or extrapsychic implications of its formulations. If psychoanalysis speaks of God, it addresses itself to no more than a God-representation with all of the dynamic, wishful, and fantasied concomitants of that central psychic representation. The question of any relation, connection, or implication between the representational God in psychic reality and an existing living God in the realms of external reality is simply unaddressed.

I should note that this way of stating the problem puts a benign face on matters. In its more extreme forms, the psychoanalytic perspective has led many analysts to go beyond this purview and to assert on the basis of psychoanalytic arguments that the existence of a God and, indeed, with him all the panoply of religious processes, entities, and realities must be cast into doubt, or at least left in the realm of agnostic obscurity. In this perspective, then, the entire spectrum of religiously endorsed and theologically elaborated conceptualizations is put under attack. Little wonder, then, that theologians or religious thinkers of any persuasion should approach psychoanalysis with suspicion and wariness. The conflict and tension between these respective perspectives is cast in terms of the dichotomies of the intrapsychic versus the extrapsychic, of psychic reality versus external reality, and of subjectivity versus objectivity.

In an effort to construct a conceptual bridge over this chasm between religious and psychoanalytic thinking, I have tried to extend Winnicott's genial formulations regarding transitional phenomena as pointing toward a useful and potential conceptual space that provided a medium for a dialectical resolution of these tensions between the subjective and the objective (Meissner 1978b, 1984). In the present essay, I would like to extend that analysis and at the same time clarify and respond to some objections raised against my approach.

Freud's Answer

Freud clearly set his face against illusion of all kinds and cast himself more or less self-consciously in the role of the destroyer of illusions. In his letter to Romain Rolland in 1923 he wrote, "A great part of my life's work (I am ten years older than you) has been spent 'trying to' destroy illusions of my own and those of mankind" (Freud 1960, 341). Rolland had his own illusions, particularly about religion, which Freud felt compelled to attack (Freud 1930, 1936). If Rolland was a creator of illusions, particularly religious and mystical illusions, Freud would be their destroyer. Even a belief in the goodness of human nature was too much of an illusion for Freud to stomach (1933). Popular causes did not fare well. He regarded Herzl, the father of Zionism, as one of a dangerous breed of men "who have turned dreams into reality" (Falk 1978).¹ As for the Marxist vision of a classless society, Freud lost little time in declaring it idealistic and an illusion—another variant on the religious theme (1933).

Freud had only one exception to his disparagement of illusion: artistic creations, in Freud's view, were forms of illusion that were not based in reality but nonetheless had a valuable role to play in view of their connection with fantasy (Freud 1930). The artist can find satisfaction in creating and expressing fantasies through special capacity for sublimation. But these satisfactions are limited to a select few and at best provide no protection against the slings and arrows of outrageous fortune. Artistic creativity and appreciation are based on internal psychical processes. Of the life of fantasy, Freud says:

> The connection with reality is still further loosened; satisfaction is obtained from illusions, which are recognized as such without the discrepancy between them and the reality being allowed to interfere with enjoyment. The region from which these illusions arise is the life of the imagination; at the time when the development of the sense of reality took place, this region was expressly exempted from the demands of reality-testing and was set apart for the purpose of fulfilling wishes which were difficult to carry out. At the head of these satisfactions through phantasy stands the enjoyment of works of art—an enjoyment which, by the agency of the artist, is made accessible even to those who are not themselves creative. People who are receptive to the influence of art cannot set too high a value on it as a source of pleasure and consolation in life. [*S.E.* 21:80–81]

Freud seems to be saying that the illusion of art, however feeble and transient, is nonetheless valuable because it allows men to step aside from the pressures of reality and to gain satisfaction from it. Was he suggesting that illusion was not in principle to be disparaged and discounted because it conflicted with reality (after all, art and reality in this sense are opposed), but rather that it is to be decried and destroyed only where it interferes with the human capacity to deal with the struggles of life? In another place, Freud even comments: "To tolerate life remains, after all, the first duty of all living beings. Illusion becomes valueless if it makes this harder for us" (*S.E.* 14:299). For Freud to make this exception is curious, since the claim that Winnicott and religious believers make is that this is one of the positive contributions of religious belief to the human condition.

The strongest, and therefore the worst, illusions of all were those of religion. Religious illusions were a dragon to be slain with the hard steel of the sword of science. In his views religious beliefs were opposed to reality and provided one form of withdrawal from painful reality. His attack on religion was uncompromising. He wrote:

> It regards reality as the sole enemy and as the source of all suffering, with which it is impossible to live, so that one must break off all relations with it if one is to be in any way happy. The hermit turns his back on the world and will have no truck with it. But one can do more than that; one can try to re-create the world, to build up in its stead another world in which its most unbearable features are eliminated and replaced by others that are in conformity with one's wishes. But whoever, in desperate defiance, sets out upon this path to happiness will as a rule attain nothing. Reality is too strong for him. He becomes a madman, who for the most part finds no one to help him in carrying through his delusion. It is asserted, however, that each one of us behaves in some respect like a paranoic, corrects some aspect of the world which is unbearable to him by the construction of a wish and introduces this delusion into reality. A special importance attaches to the case in which this attempt to procure a certainty of happiness and a protection against suffering through a delusional remoulding of reality is made by a considerable number of people in common. The religions of mankind must be classed among the mass-delusions of this kind. No one, needless to say who shares a delusion ever recognizes it as such. [Freud, *S.E.* 21:81]

Freud here moves beyond the language of illusion to say that religious belief is in fact a delusion. As far as Freud was concerned, religious illusions carried over into the territory of psychosis. Freud was actually cognizant of a distinction between the terms "illusion" and "delusion." An illusion is not simply an error, even though it may be a false belief. The basic defining characteristic of illusions is that they derive from wishes. As such, illusions are neither necessarily false nor in contradiction to reality, but when they do contradict reality they become delusions. Freud wrote: "We call a belief an illusion when a wish-fulfillment is a prominent factor in its motivation, and in doing so we disregard its relations to reality, just as the illusion itself sets no store by verification" (*S.E.* 21:31). But it is also clear that Freud regarded religious beliefs as standing in contradiction to reality at a number of points, and to that extent they were for him unequivocally delusions.

Thus Freud weighs in heavily on the side of those who would tip the problematic of transitional conceptualization heavily in the direction of the subjective or intrapsychic pole and correspondingly minimize the objective or extrapsychic dimension. At this pole of the dialectic, religious ideas and beliefs have no external validity, no objective reality, no degree of verifiable truth, but they are instead pure products of the inner world and particularly of the dynamics of wish fulfillment. They are, therefore, unequivocally delusions.

Delusion versus Illusion

The question of the distinction between delusion and illusion has been carried further by Grünbaum (1987). He argues that if we were to grant Freud the premises of his argument, it would probably follow that theistic beliefs were delusions rather than simply illusions. Further, the psychogenetic, epistemological, and semantic aspects of Freud's concept of delusion allow such beliefs to be either idiosyncratic or socially shared. Insofar as Freud considers religion to be an infantilizing mass-delusion, it would be the prime example of the latter variety.

But Grünbaum takes issue with Freud's concept of a mass-delusion, pointing out that it is not at all congruent with the notion of delusion found in the standard psychiatric sources. In a standard psychiatric dictionary (Hinsie and Campbell 1970), the notion of delusion is linked with that of hallucination in the sense that there is no demonstrable fact corresponding to the content of the belief, just as a hallucination is a sense perception without a corresponding external stimulus. Delusion is thus defined as "a belief engendered without appropriate external stimulation and maintained by one in spite of what to normal beings constitutes incontrovertible and 'plain-as-day' proof or evidence to the contrary." Thus far, no conflict with Freud, but then, "Further, the belief held is not one which is ordinarily accepted by other members of the patient's culture or subculture (i.e., it is not a commonly believed superstition)." Moreover, a later edition of the same dictionary regards a false belief as delusional only if it is idiosyncratically maintained and consequently makes social consensus a deciding factor. Grünbaum quotes the dictionary definition as follows:

> Delusion—a false belief that is firmly maintained even though it is contradicted by social reality. While it is true that some superstitions and religious beliefs are held despite the lack of confirmatory evidence, such culturally engendered concepts are not considered delusions. What is characteristic of the delusion is that it is *not* shared by others; rather it is an idiosyncratic and individual misconception or misinterpretation. Further, it is a thinking disorder of enough import to interfere with the subject's functioning, since in the area of his delusion he no longer shares a consensually validated reality with other people. [Campbell 1981; quoted in Grünbaum 1987, 174]

The disparity in points of view and understanding of the nature of delusion seems evident, and Grünbaum raises some critical questions. Can we say that no matter how primitive, superstitious, irrational, or unrealistic a belief may be, as long as it is culturally shared, we would not call it delusional? How do we go about establishing that an idea is part of a social reality; do we count noses? Do we need to have a majority of noses in order to regard a belief as socially accepted? What do we regard as social reality in pluralistic societies like the United States, where there are such radically divergent and incompatible belief systems held by various groups—secular humanists, the moral majority, evangelicals, various religious groupings, abortionists, right-to-life groups, and on and on? Grünbaum further objects that limiting the concept of delusion to idiosyncratic thinking disorders that are socially maladaptive within a culture is dangerously close to the view of some Soviet psychiatrists that sees political dissent as a form of psychiatric disorder, and also makes no allowance for highly maladaptive and pathological shared beliefs of certain groups, such as the Temple of God cult that extinguished itself so gruesomely at Jonestown, or the Islamic fundamentalists who are currently engaging in seemingly fanatical, self-destructive religious wars. When the Ayatollah Khomeini declared President Carter to be Satan, he was undoubtedly declaring a culturally shared perception and belief. In dictionary terms this belief would not be regarded as delusional, whereas in Freud's terms it would represent a mass-delusion, presumably along paranoid lines.

In terms of the previous discussion, the divergence in the understanding of the notion of delusion seems to split along lines of the dichotomy between subjective and objective polarities. Freud's criteria of delusion are essentially subjective, that is, they are basically wish fulfillments that do not correspond to reality. The psychiatric view places the emphasis on objective criteria more directly—that is, that the criteria of delusional belief rest on the extent to which it corresponds with validating external evidence or is congruent with a shared social or cultural reality. I would argue that there may be a third alternative, which encompasses both of these sets of criteria. If we were able to situate ourselves in the position of an ideally objective and culturally independent observer and thus pass judgment on particular beliefs or belief systems, we would certainly take the wishful or fantasy-derived dimension of a given belief into consideration in making our evaluation, and regard such beliefs as delusional in the degree to which they either prescinded from, contradicted, or were impervious or resistant to any qualification by demonstrable objective evidence or realities. There is always question of the consensual validation of extrinsic and objective evidence, but given such an epistemological possibility, it provides one basis for the determination of delusional beliefs.

But from that ideal vantage point we would also be in a position to make some evaluation of the cultural and social contexts within which a belief system functions. For example, regardless of the intensity and conviction of the participants, an impartial outside observer can readily assess as beyond the pale of rational, reasonable, nonpathological thought processes the internecine slaughter and paranoidlike, prejudicial attitudes between Irish Catholics and their Protestant brethren, or the hate-filled, fanatical, blindly destructive rage of Moslem fundamentalists and their Jewish antagonists. The very intensity of the fanatical emotions that accompany the convictions of such protagonists also speaks to us of their pathological import. In some degree, our assessment would take into consideration the psychological needs, emotionally disturbed states of rage and fear, as contributing influences that shape the relevant belief systems in a delusional form. Thus the criteria of such judgment may be more complex and problematic than those implied in either Freud's assessment or the usual psychiatric assessment. It may not be entirely adequate to settle for more or less polarized criteria—they may not satisfy our assessment of living human situations in which beliefs, values, attitudes, and commitments on a grand scale play such a vital and determinative role. I would submit that the criteria we seek, therefore, are neither exclusively subjective nor objective, which is to say that they may be both inclusively subjective and objective.

Winnicott's View

Winnicott approached the question of the understanding of illusion through his analysis of transitional objects as a childhood developmental phenomenon (Winnicott 1953). Winnicott's contributions have spawned a considerable literature on the vicissitudes of the infant's use of transitional objects and the development of transitional phenomena (Grolnick and Barkin 1978; Hong 1978). Various authors have discussed various forms of transitional objects and stages of the evolution of transitional phenomena in the infant's experience. Tolpin (1971) advanced the psychoanalytic understanding of the use of transitional objects a step further by viewing the transitional-object stage as a vehicle for the development of the infant's capacity for self-soothing and anxiety-regulating. In her view, the transitional object is gradually internalized in minute stages and thus contributes to the establishment of intrapsychic self-soothing structure. She describes a similar function and process of internalization for the development of anxiety-regulating capacities and structures. Hong has extended this analysis to the positing of stages of transitional development as they emerge sequentially in the first two years of life.

My interest here is in the contribution of the understanding of transitional phenomena to the area of illusion. Winnicott argues that illusion is an important aspect of the human capacity to involve oneself in the world of experience, a capacity that expresses itself in the creative shaping of a humanly meaningful environment and in facilitating in psychic terms the interlocking processes of accommodation and assimilation. In his analysis of the developmental contexts of transitional-object experience, Winnicott argues that in the optimal configuration of interaction between mother and child the "good-enough mother" is sufficiently attuned to the infant's needs so that she is available at a point at which the need demands satisfaction. The conjunction of the infant's need and response by the real object—mother—creates a situation of illusion in the child in which, from the point of view of his experience, he has created the need-satisfying object. Thus, as Winnicott observes, to the eyes of the external observer the response comes from the outside, but not from the point of view of the baby. But at the same time it does not come exclusively from within, that is, it is not a hallucination.

This area of the infant's experience is simultaneously subjective and objective. Winnicott thus stakes out an important dimension of human experience, over and above involvement in interpersonal relationships and the inner realm of intrapsychic experience and functioning. He articulates an intermediate area that he designates as "experiencing," which lies at the intersection of psychic and external reality. He writes, "It is an area that is not challenged, because no claim is made on its behalf except that it shall exist as a resting-place for the individual engaged in the perpetual human task of keeping inner and outer reality separate yet interrelated" (1971, 2).

In Winnicott's view, the claims of illusion and of this intermediate realm of experiencing reach far beyond the developmental context. He comments:

> It is usual to refer to "reality-testing," and to make a clear distinction between apperception and perception. I am staking a claim for an intermediate state between a baby's inability and his growing ability to recognize and accept reality. I am therefore studying the substance of *illusion*, that which is allowed to the infant, and which in adult life is

inherent in art and religion, and yet becomes the hallmark of madness when an adult puts too powerful a claim on the credulity of others, forcing them to acknowledge a sharing of illusion that is not their own. We can share a respect for *illusory experience,* and if we wish we may collect together and form a group on the basis of the similarity of our illusory experiences. This is a natural root of grouping among human beings. [1971, 3]

In the developmental context, the child's illusion of magical omnipotence and control over the transitional object must gradually give way to increasing degrees of disillusionment and of gradual modification by degrees of optimal frustration, leading gradually toward accommodation to reality. This dialectic and tension between illusion and disillusionment continues to be elaborated throughout the whole of human experience and life. The project of gaining knowledge and acceptance of reality is never fully completed. Every human being, each in his own way, is caught up in the tension and struggle of relating inner to outer reality. The relief and resolution of this interminable tension can be gained only within the intermediate area of illusory experience, which for the most part even in the life of the adult remains unchallenged, particularly as it finds expression in the arts and religion. Winnicott comments:

> Should an adult make claims on us for our acceptance of the objectivity of his subjective phenomena we discern or diagnose madness. If, however, the adult can manage to enjoy the personal intermediate area without making claims, then we can acknowledge our own corresponding intermediate areas, and are pleased to find a degree of overlapping, that is to say common experience between members of a group in art or religion or philosophy. [1971, 14]

Winnicott emphasizes the role of the capacity for illusory experience as it develops and evolves in the play of the child and then in the creative and cultural experience of the adult. Winnicott (1971) himself emphasizes certain aspects of the playing experience that underscore its illusory character. The area of playful illusion does not belong to the child's psychic reality, nor is it part of the external world. In it the child gathers objects (toys) that he invests with meanings and feelings derived from his subjective world. Play has an inherent excitement that derives not from instinctual arousal but from the precarious interplay between the child's subjectivity and what is objectively perceived and received. Winnicott notes a direct development from the appearance of transitional phenomena to the capacity for play, from isolated play to shared playing, and from shared playing to the capacity for cultural experience. The child who plays well demonstrates a capacity for blending illusion and reality that comes from an earlier level of his development and reflects a relatively smooth integration of both libidinal and aggressive impulses. The capacity to utilize both libidinal and aggressive energy harmoniously is essential not only in the play of children but also in the more adult forms of creative activity.

Transitional Phenomena

I would like to expand the implications of transitional phenomena to embrace more mature and adult forms of creative and cultural expression. Art in all its forms and religion are primary areas where such activities find a place. The notion of transitional phenomena in this sense incorporates areas of human understanding in which the symbolic function plays a role. Symbols play a vital role not only in cultural phenomena but also in important areas of human social commitment and affiliation. Politics and religion are prime examples of where symbols play a central role.

The question I am posing has to do with the extent to which Winnicott's understanding of transitional phenomena can serve as a meaningful model for the analysis of religious experience and ideation. The analysis of culture he provides stands in stark opposition to Freud's. For Freud, the purpose and value of culture were instinctual restraint and channeling, a matter of intrapsychic conflict; for Winnicott, the cultural dynamisms originate in the mother-child dyad and continually evolve in other interpersonal and social contexts as a matter of establishing and maintaining a sense of self. For Freud, civilization and culture are necessary evils that result in neurotic adjustments; for Winnicott, they are indispensable sources of human psychic development and selfhood that keep the personality from slipping into schizoid isolation and despair (Gay 1983).

The infantile vicissitudes of transitional phenomena lay the basis for the child's emerging capacity for symbolism. In a sense, the piece of blanket symbolizes the mother's breast, but, as Winnicott suggests, its actual transitional function is as important as its symbolic value. He observes, "Its not being the breast (or the mother), although real, is as important as the fact that it stands for the breast (or mother)" (1971, 6). The use of transitional objects, then, is more a step toward the symbolic function than itself a form of symbolism. When symbolism is achieved, the infant has already gained the capacity to distinguish between fantasy and fact, between internal and external objects, between primary creativity and perception, between illusion and reality. For purposes of the present discussion, I would argue that the use of symbols takes place within the intermediate area of experience that Winnicott designated as illusion.

By the same token, real external objects and experiences can become vehicles for the expression of similar subjective intentions and significances and can thereby take on an added, symbolic dimension. The symbolic quality of such experiences and objects participates in the intermediate realm of illusion, which is compounded from elements of external reality intermingled with subjective attributions that express the human capacity to create meaning. The exercise of the symbolic function takes place at at least two levels, the conscious and the unconscious (Godin 1955). Consciously, we can express meanings by actions (gestures, behaviors) or by attributing meaning to external objects. Unconsciously, the meaning of the action or attribution is not immediately evident and can only be ascertained by interpretation within a broader social or historical context. An animal phobia expresses a fear, but the object of the fear is masked. As Godin remarks:

> These two levels of symbolic expression are closely linked and complementary to one another. The symbolic function is always exercised by an encounter between an interior urge, which results from the whole organization of a personality, and its actualization in exterior expressions of which most (but not all) are modelled by the surrounding culture, traditions and social conventions. The symbolic act, therefore, unites, not only several degrees of reality (matter and spirit), but several levels of human reality (conscious and unconscious, individual and social). [279]

This capacity for symbolic experience makes culture possible since it provides the matrix within which the cultural experience takes place. That experience is not merely subjective (as derivative of and determined by intrapsychic dynamics only), nor is it exclusively objective (as a reflection of extrinsic and objectively determined qualities of the object); it is compounded of objective qualities, as of a painting or statue or piece of music, and the subjective experience that the individual psyche brings to it. I will suggest that the same compounding of subjective and objective is characteristic of religious experience, in the first instance, and religious understanding (theology), in the second.

Human psychological development can be envisioned as a lifelong "transitional process" involving a dynamic interchange between the self as an open system and the external world (Rose 1978). This suggests a dynamic equilibrium between a more or less fluid self and external reality, not simply limited to the transitional-object phenomena of childhood but continuing on into adult life. The process of everyday adaptation requires an element of creative originality and imagination as part of a continuing transitional interplay between self and reality. Consequently, adaptation is itself a creative process, rather than merely utilizing creative resources. Each human being selects, abstracts, and creates an idiosyncratic and unique *Umwelt* through which he integrates his sense of reality. This exchange between the inner and outer worlds takes place in unique and important ways in the realm of cultural, and specifically religious, experience.

It is not difficult to see the impact of Winnicott's notions of the transitional object and the transitional phenomenon as they extend into the realm of cultural experience. It is also important to recognize the extent to which Winnicott's approach differs from Freud's view of illusion. Freud's emphasis on the distortion or contradiction of reality in the service of wish fulfillment is basic to his view of illusion. But what Freud sees as distortion and contradiction of reality, Winnicott sees as part of man's creative experience. What Freud sees as wish fulfillment in accordance with the pleasure principle and in resistance to the reality principle, Winnicott views as an inherent aspect of human creativity.

In Winnicott's view, then, illusion plays a role in the developmental transition to reality: without the capacity to utilize transitional objects and to generate transitional forms of experience, the child's efforts to gain a foothold in reality will inevitably be frustrated. Thus illusion is not an obstruction to experiencing reality but a means of gaining access to it. In the same sense, the symbolic dimension of human understanding represents an attempt to see beyond the immediate, the material, the merely sensual or perceptual, to a level of deeper meaning and human, if not spiritual, significance.

Religious Experience as Transitional

All religions make use of religious symbols—the crucifix, the Torah, the bread and wine, the menorah, the star of David, and so on. Such objects become the vehicles for the expression of meanings and values that transcend their physical characteristics. This symbolic dimension, however, is not a product of the objects themselves; it can come about only by some attribution to them by the believer. Consequently, the objects as religious symbols are neither exclusively perceived in real and objective terms nor simply produced by subjective creation.

Rather, they evolve from the amalgamation of what is real, material, and objective as it is experienced, penetrated, and creatively reshaped by the patterns of meaning attributed to the object by the believer.

Consequently, the object has its symbolic function only for the believer and his belief system. We are once again in the transitional space in which the transitional experience is played out in the context of religious illusion. Such symbols, even in their most primitive and material sense, serve the articulation and maintenance of belief that are important for the human experience of believing. Human beings are, by and large, incapable of maintaining a commitment to something as abstract as a religious belief system without some means of real—sensory, visual, or auditory—concretization. The individual Catholic's belief in the real presence of Christ in the Eucharist could hardly be maintained, or at least could be maintained only with extreme difficulty, if participation in the Eucharistic liturgy were not surrounded with a panoply of concrete symbolic expressions of what is basically a highly theological and suprasensory understanding. Communion itself, the act of consuming the sacred host, is a form of concrete symbolic action.

As is the case with other forms of traditional experience, this process can be misdirected into infantile or pathological channels. Greenacre (1969, 1970) has provided a workable model of the relationship between the transitional object and the development of a fetish. A word of caution may be useful at this point regarding the use and implication of terms. Just as the realm of transitional experience and conceptualization is not synonymous with the transitional object, so the application of terms pertaining to the transitional realm or to fetishistic distortions is not synonymous with the infantile or pathological experience of either. The terms are used analogously to suggest modes of thinking that are in some respects similar but in other respects different. There is no sense in which God can be regarded as a transitional object, but the mode of conceptualization by which we think of God may involve transitional components. If we speak of a fetishistic dimension in thinking about religious objects, this does not imply that the phenomenon is a piece of fetishistic pathology.

I would contend that just as the transitional object of the child can degenerate into a fetish, transitional religious experience can be distorted into less authentic, relatively fetishistic directions that tend to contaminate and distort the more profoundly meaningful aspects of the religious experience. Greenacre (1969, 1970) describes the similarities and differences between these modes of relating, one relatively adaptive and serving the developmental process, the other pathological and serving neurotic and perverse needs. The fetish evolves as a necessary prop to the individual's capacity to function as an adult, particularly with regard to sexual involvement and expression. She describes the fetish "as a patch for a flaw in the genital area of the body image" (1969, 334). Both the transitional object and the fetish contribute to the maintenance of illusion, and both involve a degree of symbolic magic. The magic of the transitional object serves developmental needs and is gradually eliminated as those needs are diminished and otherwise fulfilled. The fetish involves a more complicated and need-driven magic, which does not easily abate. Greenacre emphasizes the gradations between them: "They are phenomena at two ends of a spectrum of predisposing and variously combining conditions, between which there is a series of gradations of intermediate forms with different qualities and intensities" (1970, 341). Greenacre only hints at the application of these ideas to our subject, when she mentions "the role of the transitional object in relation to illusion, symbolism, and to creativity in general. It is also important in the development of religious feeling and, with the fetish, plays a part in religious practices" (342).

The model, derived from areas of development and psychopathology, can find analogous application to the understanding of religious experience. The transitional mode of experiencing and conceptualizing can be distorted by the excessive injection of subjective needs, needs which may be pathologically derived. The needs when pathological are not necessarily synonymous with the needs involved in the pathology of the fetish. They may reflect unresolved dependency needs, passivity, narcissism, conflicts over aggression, guilt, shame, inadequacy, identity conflicts, and so on. The religious object can become the vehicle for projective or transference processes that involve the object in a defensive or need-satisfying system. When such a defensive course is followed, religious objects or practices begin to take on a magical quality that perverts their authentic religious impulse and meaning. Religious objects, prayers, and rites become magical talismans in the service of magical expectations and infantile needs. In this sense religious objects can be reduced to talismans, religious rites can become obsessional rituals, and religious faith can be corrupted into ideology. The more these "fetishistic" or otherwise defensive components pervade the individual believer's beliefs and the belief systems of the religious community, the more they might be presumed to veer toward Freud's vision of religious systems as delusional.

Religious symbolic systems are, at least in the Judeo-Christian tradition, derived from a twofold source that is at once subjective and objective. The subjective dimension comes from the dynamic constituents of human understanding and motivation, while the objective dimension is contributed by a revelation with the presumption of a divine presence and action behind it. Leavy articulates this dimension of religious belief systems as follows:

> Faith is by nature—human nature—presented symbolically, and religions are symbol systems. The believer, knowingly or not, owes his or her religious language to a revelation that is the spring of the tradition, coming from outside the believer's mind. The ultimate references of faiths are not themselves products of regressive fantasies, but symbolic representations of ultimate truths. [1986, 153]

It is within this dimension of religious experience that the psychological and the theological intersect, and it is likewise within this area of conceptualization that I have proposed the transitional form of understanding as providing the basis for bridging concepts that might facilitate a dialogue between the psychoanalytic perspective and the religious perspective (Meissner 1984).

I would like to explore the further ramifications of this form of conceptualization with two central areas of religious thinking: first, the God-representation; second, the understanding of faith itself. I have previously discussed the dynamics of the representation of the image of God and its transitional components (Meissner 1977, 1978b). A more extensive empirical and developmental understanding of the God-representation has been presented in the work of Rizzuto (1979). In these analyses, the God-representation is described as a form of transitional representation that the child, and later the adult, creates in the immediate psychic space of illusory experience. Although it arises within the matrix of human subjectivity, it is not simply hallucinatory. The process by which the image of God is created as a personalized transitional representation continues throughout the life cycle.

This image, which is both created and discovered, shares the transitional space with other cultural representations. Nonetheless, the God-representation has a particular valence insofar as it is uniquely connected to the believer's sense of self and to the sense of meaning and purpose in his existence and ultimate destiny. Further, the vicissitudes of the God-representation reflect ongoing processes of exchange and interchange taking place in relationship to the individual's evolving self-representation. This process is authentically dialectical insofar as the God-representation transcends the limits of the subjective realm and is beyond the limits of magical control. Rizzuto attacks the Freudian argument head-on and states the case for the transitional and illusory quality of the God-representation in the following terms:

> I must disagree. Reality and illusion are not contradictory terms. Psychic reality—whose depths Freud so brilliantly unveiled—cannot occur without that specifically human transitional space for play and illusion. To ask a man to renounce a God he believes in may be as cruel and as meaningless as wrenching a child from his teddy bear so that he can grow up. We know nowadays that teddy bears are not toys for spoiled children but part of the illusory substance of growing up. Each developmental stage has transitional objects appropriate for the age and level of maturity of the individual. After the oedipal resolution God is a potentially suitable object, and if updated during each crisis of development, may remain so through maturity and the rest of life. Asking a mature, functioning individual to renounce his God would be like asking Freud to renounce his own creation, psychoanalysis, and the "illusory" promise of what scientific knowledge can do. This is, in fact, the point. Men cannot be men without illusions. The type of illusion we select—science, religion, or something else—reveals our personal history and the transitional space each of us has created between his objects and himself to find "a resting place" to live in. [209]

This statement needs to be immediately amended by a reassertion that the realm of transitional conceptualization is doubly derived—that is, both objectively and subjectively. The God-representation is not simply the product of creative imagination. The belief system preexists the individual believer and is posed by an extrinsic, culturally determined declaration and imposition that asserts the real existence of the objects of belief. One might conclude that such belief systems cannot be delusional in any individual sense but include the context of belief as part of the subculture of the religious group. It is either not delusional at all, or it is some form of mass delusion—Freud's conclusion. Participation and membership in the community of believers require belief not only in the image of God as a subjectively derived psychic representation but also in the reality and existence of a God who creates and brings all things into being.

In this arena, the degree to which the subjective dimension comes to dominate the conceptualization runs the full gamut—from the belief of the child and the theologically naïve, for whom the God-representation is determined almost exclusively by subjective and psychodynamic derivatives, to the sophisticated conceptualization of the scientific theologian, whose conceptualization of the nature of God is founded predominantly in the data of revelation and is elaborated in a form of scientific theological rationalization. While the theology of Western Christianity takes the existence of God as a datum of revelation, the nature of that understanding and its conceptualization are elusive. The accounts of the nature of the godhead extend from the personal narratives of the Old Testament to the "Ipsum Subsistens Esse" of St. Thomas—pure existential act—or, if you prefer a more contemporary version, Tillich's "ground of being." The elusiveness of the concepts is reflected in the traditional ways of knowing God: the *via affirmationis* by which any perfections found in the created order must also exist in God, the *via negationis* is which any perfections predicated of God cannot exist in him in the same way as they exist in creatures, and finally the *via eminentiae,* which claims that whatever perfections are predicated of God must exist in Him in a transcendental form that supersedes the imperfections and limitations of the created order. These three modalities are assumed to be simultaneously operative in any linguistic usage pertaining to the godhead. How these theological formulations that elaborate and articulate the belief system impinge on and determine the God-representation remains an interesting and difficult question. They constitute some dimension of the objective polarity.

I would stress, however, that in the realm of true belief, neither the subjective nor the objective pole of this experiential continuum is ever altogether eliminated. For the naïve believer, whose God-representation is determined in large measure by the transferential derivatives from parental figures, subjectively determined imaginings about God are articulated within a community of belief in which the existential dimension adheres as an important aspect of the belief system. For the scientific theologian, on the other hand, his theologically elaborated and derived conceptualization of the nature of God is never so completely abstract as to remove himself from the correlated psychic determinants. Within the Judeo-Christian condition, moreover, the theological elaboration points in the direction of and opens itself to a more specifically psychic elaboration, particularly by way of the theological doctrine of the Trinity and the conceptualization of the fatherhood of God. It would seem to me that if the balance and integration between the subjective and objective components of our understanding of the God-representation are kept in mind, the risks that Leavy poses of the reduction of the image of God to a form of magical fetish would be far from what is intended by a transitional conceptualization. Leavy is quite right in opposing the essence of such religious ideas to those of general cultural ideas; but the opposition has more to do with the nature of the entities involved than with the form of the conceptualization. God, after all, is of a different order of existence from the teddy bear in the nursery or the Beethoven quartet. If one insists on the Freudian understanding of "illusion" as deception rather than as creation, as a leaning away from reality rather than toward it, one forces the argument into dichotomous renderings and negates the very suppositions of the notion of transitional phenomena and transitional conceptualization.

The faith experience has a number of attributes that characterize it as a form of transitional experience. The believer does not regard his faith as a matter of wishful hallucination or of purely subjective implications. Rather, his faith speaks to him of the nature of the world in which he lives, of the meaning and purpose of his existence there, and, in most religious traditions, of the relationship of that world and himself to a divine being who creates, loves, guides, and judges. However, faith cannot at the same time demonstrate the independent reality of the spiritual world to which it lays claim. Consequently, as I have emphasized, the experience of faith is not totally subjective or totally objective; rather, it represents a realm in which the subjective and the objective interpenetrate—both the subjective and objective poles of experience contribute to the substance of belief. The question I am addressing here is not that of the truth value of the believer's faith. The point, rather, is that to envision his faith solely in subjective terms, as Freud essentially did, is to do a disservice to the believer and actually to distort the substance of his belief.

Obviously, the vicissitudes of this process are complex and extremely variable. The extent to which individuals accept the belief system of an established religious community varies considerably. Ultimately at issue are the establishment and maintenance of the individual's sense of identity in relation to and in the context of a community that he comes to accept as part of his view of himself, his life, and his world, the reciprocation of which lies in the acceptance of his individuality as part of the community of believers.

The need and capacity to integrate oneself with such a community must be balanced against the need to rebel and to find and express one's individuality. In some basic sense, the individual, personal faith of the believer is always somewhat removed from, and in tension and dialectical interaction with, the belief or dogma of the religious community. At the extremes, one finds expressions of religious rejection, alienation, and rebellion, on the one hand, and complete submission and religious compliance, on the other. Between them lie infinite degrees of variation within which most human beings live out their religious convictions. The faith of any human being, then, is both received from the religious community of his affiliation and created as a matter of internal and subjective expression. In this sense faith can be regarded as taking shape within the realm of illusory experience, and the faith of religious communities as being realized through the sharing of illusory experience within a given group of believers. Within any religious group, such sharing of illusion is a matter of degree that allows for both individual variation and a community of sharing.

But the assertion of faith carries with it a transcendent element, addressing itself to the most developed form of religious experience. The assertion of faith is not merely a reassertion of basic trust; it is, rather, a creative assertion of something beyond trust and far more significant. Its regression is, if anything, recapitulative: it returns to the rudiments of trust in order to go beyond them. Thus faith ultimately renounces the imperfection and finitude of basic trust in order to reach beyond it and thereby recapture it more profoundly. This is the creative moment of faith.

To bring this discussion back to its starting point, I have tried to address the difference between the religious-belief system and the paranoid-delusional system (1978a, 1984). I posed the question in terms of Schreber's delusions:

> How, then, does one draw a line between the theocosmological delusions of Schreber and the belief system of religious men? Schreber's *Memoirs* read in part like an elaborate theological tract. His delusional system is a highly evolved and systematized attempt to organize and understand his experience in terms of a coherent theory. Organized [religious] doctrine represents a similar attempt to interpret human experience and give it meaning in terms of a divinely instituted plan and guidance. Both delusional and [religious] belief systems reach certain untestable conclusions which cannot be contradicted by available evidences. How in fact would one go about disproving Schreber's delusion that he was being transformed into a woman? How would one disprove the Christian assertion of the real presence in the Eucharistic sacrifice? [1978a, 93]

In so stating, I have exposed my breast to the unrelenting thrusts of logical criticism. Grünbaum (1987) argues (as have many through the centuries) that the doctrine of transubstantiation predicates the change of the bread and wine into the literal body and blood of Christ. But this is indeed a hard saying—one that violates perceptual evidence and puts faith to the test. None of the usual properties of flesh and blood are apparent to those receiving the sacrament. The theological argument that distinguishes between substance and accidental properties (the argument is *not* properly part of the doctrine!)—that is, that transubstantiation affects the Aristotelian substance and does not affect the properties—is no more than an immunizing strategy, a kind of face-saving rationalization to preserve the doctrine in the face of a lack of evidence.

This is not the place for a theological debate. But certainly the opinions of religious thinkers cover a broad spectrum regarding the "real presence." It is not at all difficult to get a heated argument going among theologians as to what exactly "real presence" means. Does "flesh and blood" really mean what we ordinarily take it to mean—as, for example, when we go to the butcher shop? Does it imply something spiritual, taking "flesh and blood" to mean the reality of Christ's salvific presence through grace—an expression of his spiritual or divine existence? Does it have a merely symbolic meaning that should not be translated into literal material terms?

How, then, does the Christian belief in the Eucharist differ from the delusions of a Schreber? The question has relevance to our argument, for, if we take the question out of the transitional sphere and address it in the objective realm, Grünbaum's objections and questions have a point. In the objective and extrinsic realm, flesh and blood are flesh and blood—you can feel them, taste them, and so forth. If, on the other hand, the doctrine is to be taken in the purely subjective realm, we may be dealing with something hallucinatory or at least delusional. Only in the transitional realm is it possible to articulate the doctrine in terms of the metaphorical, symbolic, spiritual, and credal sense that it intends. It is only in these terms, I would argue, that any meaningful understanding of the doctrine from a psychoanalytic perspective can be achieved. I can remind the reader at this point that the psychoanalytic perspective is not at all concerned with the truth or falsity of the belief; it is concerned with the understanding of the meaning of the belief in the context of individual psychic reality and in reference to the individual's sense of personal identity, selfhood, and the ultimate meaning, purpose, and belonging of his existence. If beliefs and belief systems facilitate psychic growth and contribute to the maintenance of psychic health and mature responsible living, they are not pathological—any more than the illusory play in the transitional space between mother and child is pathological. Or for that matter, any more than Freud's own cultural creation—psychoanalysis.

Note

1. This is a statement not of Freud's opposition to Zionism but of his reaction to Herzl's visionary rhetoric. Freud would later serve on the board of

trustees at the Hebrew University and would have welcomed the establishment of a Department of Psychoanalysis there (Rosenbaum 1954); he actively supported the founding of the university and was generally supportive (E. Freud 1970).

References

Campbell, Robert J., ed. *Psychiatric Dictionary.* 5th ed. New York: Oxford University Press, 1981.

Falk, Avner. "Freud and Herzl." *Contemporary Psychoanalysis* 14 (1978): 357–87.

Freud, Ernest L., ed. *The Letters of Sigmund Freud and Arnold Zweig.* New York: Harcourt Brace Jovanovich, 1970.

Freud, Sigmund. *The Standard Edition of the Complete Psychological Works of Sigmund Freud.* Edited and translated by James Strachey. 24 vols. London: Hogarth, 1953–74.

"Thoughts for the Times on War and Death" (1915), vol. 14.

The Future of an Illusion (1927), vol. 21.

Civilization and Its Discontents (1930), vol. 21.

New Introductory Lectures on Psycho-Analysis (1933), vol. 22.

"A Disturbance of Memory on the Acropolis" (1936), vol. 22.

———. *The Letters of Sigmund Freud.* Edited by Ernest Freud. New York: McGraw-Hill, 1960.

Gay, Volney P. "Winnicott's Contribution to Religious Studies: The Resurrection of the Cultural Hero." *Journal of the American Academy of Religion* 51 (1983): 371–95.

Godin, Andre. "The Symbolic Function." *Lumen Vitae* 10 (1955): 277–90.

Greenacre, Phyllis. "The Fetish and the Transitional Object" (1969). "The Transitional Object and the Fetish: With Special Reference to the Role of Illusion" (1970). In *Emotional Growth,* vol. 1. New York: International Universities Press, 1971.

Grolnick, Simon A., and Barkin, Leonard, eds. *Between Reality and Fantasy: Transitional Objects and Transitional Phenomena.* New York: Aronson, 1978.

Grünbaum, Adolf. "Psychoanalysis and Theism." *The Monist* 70 (1987): 152–92.

Hinsie, Leland E., and Campbell, Robert J., eds. *Psychiatric Dictionary.* 4th ed. New York: Oxford University Press, 1970.

Hong, K. M. "The Transitional Phenomena: A Theoretical Integration." *Psychoanalytic Study of the Child* 33 (1978): 47–79.

Leavy, Stanley A. "A Paschalian Meditation on Psychoanalysis and Religious Experience." *Cross Currents,* Summer 1986, pp. 147–55.

Meissner, William W. "The Psychology of Religious Experience." *Communio* (1977): 35–59.

———. *The Paranoid Process.* New York: Jason Aronson, 1978a.

————. "Psychoanalytic Aspects of Religious Experience." *Annual of Psychoanalysis* 6 (1978b): 103–41.

————. *Psychoanalysis and Religious Experience.* New Haven: Yale University Press, 1984.

Rizzuto, Ana-Maria. *The Birth of the Living God.* Chicago: University of Chicago Press, 1979.

Rose, Gilbert J. "The Creativity of Everyday Life." In *Between Reality and Fantasy: Transitional Objects and Transitional Phenomena,* edited by Simon A. Grolnick and Leonard Barkin. New York: Jason Aronson, 1978.

Rosenbaum, Milton. "Freud—Eitingon—Magnes Correspondence: Psychoanalysis at the Hebrew University." *Journal of the American Psychoanalytic Association* 2 (1954): 311–17.

Tolpin, Marian. "On the Beginnings of a Cohesive Self." *Psychoanalytic Study of the Child* 26 (1971): 316–52.

Winnicott, Donald W. "Transitional Objects and Transitional Phenomena." *International Journal of Psycho-Analysis* 34 (1953): 89–97.

————. *Playing and Reality.* New York: Basic Books, 1971.

7 Paranoia and Piety: Reflections on the Schreber Case

Merold Westphal

No doubt Freud's most famous nonpatient is the paranoid Dr. Schreber. There are two reasons why the case study Freud wrote in 1911 has a claim on our attention insofar as we are interested in the light psychoanalysis can throw on religion. One is its manifestly religious content. Schreber's paranoid delusions have primarily to do with God, at least in their manifest content. In the second place projection plays a central role in Freud's interpretation, and projection is as important to his account of religion as introjection is to his account of morality (Ricoeur 1970, 233, 236).

To be sure, Ricoeur suggests that in this case "more light is thrown on the function of projection than on its mechanism" (238 n.). But if, as we shall shortly see, the proper task of the psychoanalytic study of religion is to focus precisely on the function religion plays in the lives of individuals and societies, this limitation of the Schreber case will not diminish its value in the present context. It will focus our attention on the way religious ideas can function as a defense against guilt by legitimizing what would otherwise be immoral.

But how do we know what kinds of questions to ask, what avenues of exploration are likely to prove most fruitful? In the first place, we need not restrict ourselves to patently pathological phenomena such as the three Christs of Ypsilanti (Rokeach 1964). Freud's assumption, and the working hypothesis of my essay, is that "even thought-structures so extraordinary as these [paranoid ones] and so remote from our common modes of thinking are nevertheless derived from the most general and comprehensible impulses of the human mind," and that Schreber's case is to be located in "the familiar complexes and motive forces of mental life" (*S.E.* 12:18, 35).

This is in keeping with Freud's general practice. Just as Plato seeks to see the structure of the soul writ large in the structure of society, so Freud hopes to find the workings of the "normal" psyche writ large in the mental processes of neurotic and psychotic patients. The last footnote in the Schreber case refers us to the 1907 essay, "Obsessive Actions and Religious Practices," where Freud first makes this point with explicit reference to religion. There he says that "one might venture to regard obsessional neurosis as a pathological counterpart of the formation of a religion, and to describe that neurosis as an individual religiosity and religion as a universal obsessional neurosis. The most essential similarity would reside in the underlying renunciation of the activation of instincts that are constitutionally present; and the chief difference would lie in the nature of those instincts, which in the neurosis are exclusively sexual in their origin, while in religion they spring from egoistic sources" (*S.E.* 9:126–27; cf. 21:43–44, 115). We are entitled to look in the exotic details of the Schreber case for light on the quotidian piety of ordinary people.

But we are not entitled to look for answers to questions about the truth of religious beliefs. Perhaps the most important step toward a fruitful investigation of the relation of psychoanalysis to religion is the recognition that psychoanalysis is unable to resolve the truth questions posed by religious claims. No one has stated this more eloquently than Paul Ricoeur.

> My working hypothesis . . . is that psychoanalysis is necessarily iconoclastic, regardless of the faith or nonfaith of the psychoanalyst, and that this "destruction" of religion can be the counterpart of a faith purified of all idolatry. Psychoanalysis as such cannot go beyond the necessity of iconoclasm. This necessity is open to the double possibility, that of faith and that of nonfaith, but the decision about these two possibilities does not rest with psychoanalysis. . . . The question remains open for every man whether the destruction of idols is without remainder; this question no longer falls within the competency of psychoanalysis. It has been said that Freud does not speak of God, but of god and the gods of men; what is involved is not the *truth* of the foundation of religious ideas but their *function*. . . . [Ricoeur 230, 235; my italics]

This epistemic limitation of psychoanalytic critique can be seen in the two problems Freud encounters while seeking to overcome it. In the first place, he recognizes that illusions may well be true. Suppose, for example, that theistic belief grows out of our childlike helplessness and expresses a deep longing for a father (*S.E.* 21:18, 24, 33, 72). Because "wish-fulfillment is a prominent factor in its motivation," such belief can be called an illusion (21:31). This naturally arouses our suspicion (26, 34), but illusions "need not necessarily be false—that is to say, unrealizable or in contradiction to reality. For instance, a middle-class girl may have the illusion that a prince will come and marry her. This is possible; and a few such cases have occurred. . . . just as [illusions] cannot be proved, so they cannot be refuted" (31).

Seeking to close the gap between illusions, which might be true, and delusions, which are essentially contrary to reality, Freud invokes the positivism of his day. "But scientific work is the only road which can lead us to a knowledge of reality outside ourselves" (31). The falsehood of religious beliefs depends on their not lending themselves to the verification (falsification, testing) procedures of empirical science. Unlike Constance, God is not on the Bodensee, waiting to be seen (25).

But this move is doubly awkward. On the one hand, there is nothing psychoanalytic about the positivist principle, and the need to invoke it only highlights the inability of psychoanalysis to settle questions of religious truth. (See Lecture XXXV of *New Introductory Lectures on Psycho-Analysis, S.E.* 22.) On the other hand any attempt to state the principle, as Freud has just done, is subject to familiar, but nonetheless embarrassing problems of self-reference. For the positivist principle is not itself testable.

Still, Freud might argue, while the suspicions generated by psychoanalysis may not ultimately settle questions of religious truth, they make a penultimate contribution by flagging certain beliefs as requiring special attention. If psychoanalysis cannot be the jury that decides the issue, it can be the grand jury that assures that the matter will go to trial. Here Freud encounters a second problem. For psychoanalytic suspicion is more evenhanded than he either suspects or would like it to be. If there is in each of us the helpless child who says "that it would be very nice if there were a God who created the world and was a benevolent Providence, and if there were a moral order in the universe and an after-life" (*S.E.* 21:33), is there not in each of us an adolescent who thinks that it would not be very nice at all, that it would be much nicer if there were no one on whom we are dependent and to whom we are responsible? Is it not Freud who teaches us how deeply ambivalent we are toward the father and how the roots of hostility are, if anything, deeper than those of longing? Before a genuinely Freudian grand jury, indictments of suspicion are at least as likely to be issued to the unbelieving as to the believing soul. As Freud never tires of pointing out, psychoanalysis agrees with religion that we are *all* miserable sinners (*S.E.* 9:123; 13:72; 21:111–12, 120). With thinkers like Nietzsche and Sartre, he is one of the great secular theologians of original sin.

The believing soul can easily misinterpret this result. Like the child whose chief consolation in punishment is the awareness that a sibling is also in trouble, the believing soul may take spiteful comfort in the evenhandedness of psychoanalytic suspicion. Or, like the capitalist and the communist in relation to each other, the believing soul may welcome attention to the enemy's faults as a way of distracting attention from his or her own. But the fact remains that psychoanalysis is "iconoclastic"; it gives rise to suspicion about the life of faith. Pointing fingers at others is an act of desperation.

Nor is there genuine comfort to be found in the discovery that the believing soul is off the hook so far as truth is concerned, that psychoanalysis cannot show religious beliefs to be false. For if Ricoeur is right and the psychoanalytic "destruction of idols" is directed not to the *truth* but to the *function* of religious beliefs, neither defense nor solace can be derived from the conviction or even the fact that the beliefs are actually true. In the light of psychoanalytic critique, my beliefs may be true and my faith nevertheless idolatrous. If in ethics it is essential that I do the right thing for the right reason, in religion it is essential that I speak the truth in love (Eph. 4:15), since knowledge without love is nothing (1 Cor. 13:2). The *function* is as important as the *truth,* the *how* as crucial as the *what.*

At just this point the passionate unbeliever and the passionate believer come together in their critique of idols. Kierkegaard helps us to see the significance of switching the question from truth to function. "If one who lives in the midst of Christendom goes up to the house of God, the house of the true God, with the true conception of God in his knowledge, and prays, but prays in a false spirit; and one who lives in an idolatrous community prays with the entire passion of the infinite, although his eyes rest upon the image of an idol: where is there most truth? The one prays in truth to God though he worships an idol; the other prays falsely to the true God, and hence worships in fact an idol" (1941, 179–80).

This oft-quoted vignette is intended to render concrete the distinction between objective and subjective truth.

> *When the question of truth is raised in an objective manner, reflection is directed objectively to the truth, as an object to which the knower is related. Reflection is not focussed upon the relationship, however, but upon the question of whether it is the truth to which the knower is*

related. If only the object to which he is related is the truth, the subject is accounted to be in the truth. When the question of the truth is raised subjectively, reflection is directed subjectively to the nature of the individual's relationship; if only the mode of this relationship is in the truth, the individual is in the truth even if he should happen to be thus related to what is not true. [178; Kierkegaard's italics]

A careful reading of Kierkegaard will indicate that this distinction is meant to deny neither the reality nor the importance of objective truth. Its purpose is rather to deny the sufficiency of objective truth by pointing to the idolatry that can so easily coexist with it. By speaking of the how in terms of subjective *truth,* Kierkegaard suggests that in shifting attention from (objective) truth to function we are not leaving the question of truth behind after all. In addition to the truth of propositions, their correspondence to reality, there is the truth of persons, their correspondence to the content of professed beliefs. If, for example, I profess belief in the God of the Jewish and Christian Bible but pray selfishly, making God and neighbor into means to my ends, I am not in the truth even if my metaphysics should turn out to be objectively impeccable. For the God to whom I pray is an idol, a wish-fulfilling figment of my imagination (since the God of the Bible is not a means to my ends), and my practice and my profession are at odds with each other. How can I be in the truth if I am living a lie?

In spite of his own wishful thinking about helping to decide the question of objective truth, Freud seems to recognize that his contribution lies in the area of subjective truth. In chapter 3 of *The Future of an Illusion* he asks about the value and worth of religious beliefs to believers in a way that points to the work they do, their function in the life-world of faith (*S.E.* 21:15, 20). He immediately proceeds in chapter 4 to place religious ideas in relation to the human needs and motives they serve, linking need to work, motive to function (21–24). He identifies two primary tasks that religious ideas perform, consolation vis-à-vis the overwhelming power of indifferent nature (16) and compensation vis-à-vis the renunciations civilization exacts in the collective struggle with nature (7, 10, 18).

Beyond this general orientation to the function of religious beliefs, he calls special attention to the immoral uses that religion often serves.

It is doubtful whether men were in general happier at a time when religious doctrines held unrestricted sway; more moral they certainly were not. They have always known how to externalize the precepts of religion and thus to nullify their intentions. The priests, whose duty it was

> to ensure obedience to religion, met them half-way in this. God's kindness must lay a restraining hand on His justice. One sinned, and then one made a sacrifice or did penance and then one was free to sin once more. . . . It is no secret that the priests could only keep the masses submissive to religion by making such large concessions as these to the instinctual nature of man. . . . In every age immorality has found no less support in religion than morality has. [37–38]

In this way the god of wish fulfillment is "only seemingly stern" (19).

We can summarize the foregoing as follows: (1) Psychoanalysis is iconoclastic in relation to religion. It generates suspicion about the life of faith. (2) The everyday religion of "normal" people cannot be exempted from this suspicion, for psychoanalysis claims that the pathological phenomena that are its point of departure bring to light processes at work in all of us. (3) Psychoanalytic suspicion leaves the question of religious truth (objectively speaking) unanswered. Its special insights are restricted to the motives that give rise to religion and, correlatively, to the function religion plays in people's lives. (4) Far from giving comfort to the believing soul, this last restriction means that piety can be pernicious even if its beliefs are true. Truth may be an adequate defense in a libel suit; but here it is not.

With these guidelines about the kind of questions it would be most appropriate to ask, we turn to the Schreber case. His first illness, which began in 1884, concerns neither Freud nor us because it ran its short course, Schreber assures us, "'without the occurrence of any incidents bordering upon the sphere of the supernatural'" (*S.E.* 12:12).[1] The second illness, which began in 1893, is where the interest lies. Its first phase was characterized by delusions of persecution. Schreber was the victim of "soul-murder" for the purpose of sexual abuse at the hands of his physician, Dr. Flechsig. Beginning in 1895, however, the delusions of persecution were replaced by delusions of grandeur as Schreber became the wife of God. He was to be changed into a woman so that he could redeem the world by giving rise to a new race. Freud writes, "The position may be formulated by saying that a sexual delusion of persecution was later on converted in the patient's mind into a religious delusion of grandeur" (18).

This summary is doubly misleading. It is already clear that the delusion of grandeur is as sexual as it is religious, for Schreber is to become a woman in order to be impregnated by God. But it is also clear that the earlier delusion of persecution is as religious as it is sexual. For, as Freud himself immediately adds, "The part of persecutor was at first assigned to Professor Flechsig, the physician in whose charge he was; later his place was taken by God Himself" (18). Both stages are at once sexual and religious. The question concerns the relation of the two. Freud's answer comes in three steps.

The medical reports of Dr. Weber, Schreber's subsequent physician at the Sonnenstein Sanitorium, are appended to Schreber's *Memoirs* (267–83, 315–27). As Freud reads them, they suggest "that the motive force of this delusional complex was the patient's ambition to play the part of Redeemer, and that his *emasculation* was only entitled to be regarded as a means for achieving that end" (*S.E.* 12:18). Freud vigorously rejects such a view. While acknowledging that this means-end relationship is how things eventually get expressed, he insists on the primacy of the idea of being transformed into a woman. One piece of evidence is Schreber's account of the time in 1893, shortly before falling ill for a second time and two years before the idea of being the Redeemer by being God's wife had emerged, when the idea occurred to him as he was waking one morning "'that after all it really must be very nice to be a woman submitting to the act of copulation'" (13).

The other evidence relates to the sequence of his delusions. "For we learn that the idea of being transformed into a woman (that is, of being emasculated) was the primary delusion, that he began by regarding that act as constituting a serious injury and persecution, and that it only became related to his playing the part of Redeemer in a secondary way. There can be no doubt, moreover, that originally he believed that the transformation was to be effected for the purpose of sexual abuse and not so as to serve higher designs" (18).

If the presence of homosexual libido is the point of departure for Freud's interpretation (32–33, 45–46), the second step is Schreber's rejection of it. Freud writes, "Before his illness Senatspräsident Schreber had been a man of strict morals: 'Few people,' he declares, and I see no reason to doubt his assertion, 'can have been brought up upon such strict moral principles as I was, and few people, all through their lives, can have exercised (especially in sexual matters) a self-restraint conforming so closely to those principles as I may say of myself that I have done'" (31). Schreber constantly speaks of the moral Order of Things, and it is clear that at least at the outset he finds homosexuality to be contrary to this order. Freud is surely correct when he says that the idea "'that after all it really must be very nice to be a woman submitting to the act of copulation'" is "one which [Schreber] would have rejected with the greatest indignation if he had been fully conscious" (13).[2]

That, of course, is exactly what he does during the persecution stage of his illness (33), which brings us to the third and decisive step in Freud's answer to the question about the relation of sexuality and religion in Schreber's illness. His delusions, including their religious content, are defenses against his homosexual desire. Freud's claim is "that the exciting cause of the illness was the appearance in him of a feminine (that is, a passive homosexual) wish-phantasy, which took as its object the figure of his doctor. An intense resistance to this phantasy arose on the part of Schreber's personality, and the ensuing defensive struggle, which might perhaps just as well have assumed some other shape, took on, for reasons unknown to us, that of a delusion of persecution. The person he longed for now became his persecutor, and the content of his wishful phantasy became the content of his persecution" (47). Freud finds this type of defense typical of paranoia (59–60, 62).

The mechanisms at work here are fairly obvious. The unacceptable homosexual desire is *projected* onto Dr. Flechsig, who now wishes to use Schreber as a woman. This permits both a *denial* of the unwelcome wish-fantasy, and a corresponding and supportive *reversal* of affect. In place of "I love Flechsig" we find "I hate Flechsig (since he is persecuting me)" (63).[3] Schreber is morally innocent in relation to both his homosexual desire and his hatred of Flechsig.

We should not be too quick to assume that the hatred of Flechsig is subsequent to the projection that makes a persecutor of him and not a prior, independent motivation for the projection. Schreber himself tells us that the empirical Dr. Flechsig is not really the target of his hostility (40, including n.3). And Freud not only has no doubt that Flechsig is a surrogate for Schreber's father or brother (47, 50) but also calls attention to the typical oedipal ambivalence this brings with it (28–29, 50–52, 55).

Freud's attempt to explain the mechanism of paranoia by superimposing the pathological triad, fixation, repression, and return of the repressed, upon the developmental triad, autoeroticism, narcissism, and object love, raises more questions than it answers (60–62, 67–69). But if we remember Ricoeur's suggestion that the Schreber case throws more light "on the function of projection than on its mechanism" (Ricoeur 1970, 238 n.), we will not be discouraged. For the function of the delusion of persecution is quite clear. It is a strategy to relieve Schreber of the anxiety he would experience (both as guilt and as fear of punishment)[4] if he had to acknowledge his homosexual desire; and it allows him to retain the fantasy of playing the female role in copulation. He can think incessantly about it without feeling guilty about it. Like parapraxes, dreams, and neurotic symptoms, this paranoid delusion is a compromise (*S.E.* 15:66, 130; 16:301, 359). Schreber must repudiate his fantasy, but in return for this he is able to retain it. And just as his delusion allows him to remain innocently preoccupied with his homosexual fantasy, so it permits him to give innocent but vehement expression to his hatred of his father.

We have already noted that God replaces Flechsig as the primary persecutor, so we will not be surprised to find that much of the verbal abuse with which Schreber replies to the threat of sexual abuse is directed toward God rather than Flechsig (*S.E.* 12:25–27). Although the project of soul-murder and emasculation are contrary to the Order of Things, God has yielded to Flechsig's influence and has become his accomplice or possibly the instigator of the plot (39, 19). In a moment not entirely devoid of (unintended) humor, Freud tells us how easily God becomes the second surrogate for Schreber's father, Daniel Gottlieb Moritz Schreber. After all, the latter "was a *physician*" (Freud's italics) and indeed "a most eminent physician, and one who was no doubt highly respected by his patients." Recalling the euhemerism of the ancients, Freud writes, "Such a father as this was by no means unsuitable for transfiguration into a God in the affectionate [sic] memory of the son" (51–52).

This is the point at which the religious dimension enters the Schreber case, and we must ask about its significance. In one sense it adds nothing to our understanding of the case. Within the framework of the persecutional compromise formation, God plays exactly the same role as Flechsig, and it is not clear that he (Schreber's God is clearly masculine) is better suited to play it. His only possible advantage is that Schreber knows that the threat to him is not an empirical one, and in the case of God there is no need to distinguish between the actual Flechsig and the threatening Flechsig soul.

There is, however, a point of some interest. While Schreber is not terribly clear about the nature of soul-murder, he describes it as taking possession of another's soul and refers to "Goethe's Faust, Lord Byron's Manfred, and Weber's Freischütz." He then adds, "Commonly, however, the main role is supposed to be played by the Devil, who entices a human being into selling his soul to him . . . yet it is difficult to see what the Devil was to do with a soul so caught, if one is not to assume that torturing a soul as an end in itself gave the Devil special pleasure" (Schreber 1955, 55; cf, *S.E.* 12:38). The threatening Flechsig is a demonic character from the outset. Moreover, the God who displaces him is regularly described as the "posterior realms of God" or the "lower God," Ahriman by name (*S.E.* 12:23–24, 44). But Ahriman is the Zoroastrian devil. So it is not surprising that Dr. Weber should describe Schreber, in summarizing his complaints, as "the plaything of devils" (14).

The question this raises in the present context, of course, is not that of metaphysical dualism or the existence of Satan. It is the question of the function of the demonic in the religious life-world. The function that comes to our attention here is the scapegoat function. I do not mean the scapegoat of Leviticus 16, who is punished for the sins of the people, but the scapegoat who unites the following two dictionary definitions: "3a: a person or thing bearing the blame for others . . . b: a person, group, race, or institution against whom is directed the irrational hostility and unrelieved aggression of others" (*Webster's Third New International Dictionary of the English Language Unabridged*).

Nietzsche has taught us to notice the difference between the two kinds of scapegoat. Nobler than the holy God are the Greek gods, "those reflections of noble and autocratic men, in whom *the animal* in man felt deified and did *not* lacerate itself, did *not* rage against itself! For the longest time these Greeks used their gods precisely so as to ward off the 'bad conscience' . . . the very opposite of the use to which Christianity put its God." Joyfully meditating on Zeus's view of humankind as "wretched through folly," Nietzsche shouts at us— "foolishness, *not* sin! do you grasp that?" But even the foolishness must be misfortune, and so the Greeks say, "'He must have been deluded by a god' . . . In this way the gods served in those days to justify man to a certain extent even in his wickedness, they served as the originators of evil—in those days they took upon themselves, not the punishment but, what is *nobler,* the guilt" (*Genealogy of Morals* II, 23; cf. *Ecce Homo,* "Why I Am So Wise," 5, and *Thus Spoke Zarathustra* I, "On the Adder's Bite").

E. R. Dodds gives us a splendid example in "Agamemnon's Apology." Agamemnon does not deny the deed by which Achilles was wronged, only that it was his. "'Not I,' he declared afterwards, 'not I was the cause of this act, but Zeus and my portion and the Erinys who walks in darkness: they it was who in the assembly put wild *ate* in my understanding, on that day when I arbitrarily took Achilles' prize from him. So what could I do? Deity will always have its way'" (Dodds 1971, 3).

It is useful for the sacred to take on this demonic character. For when it does I remain blameless both in the wrong I may do (or wish to do) and in any punishment I may receive. Both the doing and the receiving are reduced to the category of misfortune, and I am immune from moral categories.[5] To the degree that I am able to project my awareness of my own deeds and desires onto a malevolent deity, I carry out a teleological suspension of the ethical that frees me from all moral accountability. I may not live free from pain, but I can live free from guilt and shame.

Suppose I am a TV evangelist who is engaged in sexual misconduct. Given the standards I profess I will feel guilty. This might lead to a change in my ways, but I might try to defend myself with a little help from projection. First I might find my Flechsig, another mortal onto whom I can transfer responsibility. If there should happen to be another TV evangelist whose sexual misconduct I can expose and denounce, I may be able not to notice for a while the behavior of my own that has made me so eager and so happy to discover his sins. But suppose he and his friends return the favor and I am publicly exposed. How can I acknowledge the behavior without accepting either the blame or the discipline that my church imposes on me? Easily. I say the devil made me do it and return to my ministry as quickly as possible.

Here we are in a world noticeably different from Schreber's. We are dealing with actual behavior rather than mere desires. (Freud, of course, finds this difference rather minor so far as guilt is concerned.) More important, we are dealing with perfectly "sane" behavior rather than with anything certifiable. But is not projection the visibly operative defense mechanism in both cases? Do not the two demonologies function in quite the same way? And does the sanity of the latter case keep it from being sick? Whenever the sacred becomes the scapegoat who takes the blame (as distinct from the punishment) for human behavior, the religious becomes the enemy rather than the ally of the ethical.

This brings us back to Freud's earlier observation about the historical frequency with which religion has been partner to immorality. What the Schreber case shows us (so far) is one process by which this can happen. We may or may not agree with the sexual ethics of Schreber and our TV evangelist, which in neither case is idiosyncratic. That is not the point. What is at issue is what they do with their own best moral judgments. In neither case do they bring forth reasons to revise the morality that underlies the guilt they need to fend off. What they rather do is find a way, by their employment of the sacred, to exempt themselves from their own basic moral convictions.

Thus, if religious justification is to be found for state-sponsored terrorism in the war against *secular* modernity or *godless* communism, it will not be because terrorism is found in general to be justified. It will rather be because what counts as terrorism when "they" do it does not count as terrorism when we do it. Of course, "The devil made me do it" is not a very promising strategy in such an instance, though demonizing the enemy as the "great Satan" or the "evil empire" could be quite helpful. Does the second stage of the Schreber case provide any further resources for such a project?

It has already been suggested that while the sacralizing of the scapegoat (replacing Flechsig with God) is of some interest to us it is of little advantage to Schreber (since Flechsig is already a transempirical, demonic figure). But that is true only as long as he remains within the parameters of his persecutional delusion. Freud explicitly rejects the view that the megalomania of the second stage arises to rationalize the persecution of the first, as if the patient were to say, Since God is so terribly preoccupied with me I must be someone terribly important (*S.E.* 12:48–49). The real import of the move from Flechsig to God, as Freud and Schreber both clearly see, is the path it opens to a superior compromise-formation, the delusion of grandeur or the Messiah complex.[6] The replacement of Flechsig by God

> seems at first as though it were a sign of aggravation of the conflict, an intensification of the unbearable persecution, but it soon becomes evident that it was preparing the way for the second change and, with it, the solution of the conflict. It was impossible for Schreber to become reconciled to playing the part of a female wanton towards his doctor; but the task of providing God Himself with the voluptuous sensations that He required called up no such resistance on the part of his ego. Emasculation was now no longer a disgrace; it became "consonant with the Order of Things," it took its place in a great cosmic chain of events, and was instrumental in the re-creation of humanity after its extinction. [48; cf. Schreber's own account, 19–20]

What, then, are the strengths of Schreber's delusion of grandeur as a defense against the anxiety aroused by his homosexual desire toward and hatred of his father? First, his homosexual wish-fantasy becomes morally acceptable and need no longer be repudiated, though the initiative remains with God and not with Schreber himself. Since it is God who requires this teleological suspension of the ethical, Schreber can accept it in good conscience. As Dr. Weber describes it, " 'It is not to be supposed that he *wishes* to be transformed into a woman; it is rather a question of a "must" based upon the Order of Things, which there is no possibility of his evading, much as he would personally prefer to remain in his own honourable and masculine station in life'" (17).

Weber's summary seems a fair one in the light of Schreber's own account of this second stage. "'I shall show later on that emasculation for quite another purpose—a purpose *in consonance with the Order of Things*—is within the bounds of possibility, and, indeed, that it may quite probably afford the solution of the conflict'" (20). "'On the other hand, God demands a *constant state of enjoyment,* such as would be in keeping with the conditions of existence imposed upon souls by the Order of Things; and it is my duty to provide Him with this . . . [Freud's ellipsis] in the shape of the greatest possible generation of spiritual voluptuousness. And if, in this process, a little sensual pleasure falls to my share, I feel justified in accepting it as some slight compensation for the inordinate measure of suffering and privation that has been mine for so many past years'" (34; cf. 20–21). Schreber indeed develops this "slight compensation" into an unconstrained identification of heavenly bliss with voluptuousness so that, in Freud's summary, "the state of heavenly bliss is to be understood as being in its essence an intensified continuation of sensual pleasure upon earth!" (29).

The second strength of the second defense strategy is that bringing his desire "to be a woman submitting to the act of copulation" into consonance with the Order of Things makes possible a reconciliation with God and Father. The homosexual desire remains projected onto God, but since this is now acceptable it ceases to be the basis for war against God. Whereas before he and God exchanged mockery and scorn, now he receives "direct inspiration from God, just as we are taught that the Prophets were" (16; cf. the identifications with Jesus Christ and the Virgin Mary noted above).

Freud calls attention to the link between these two strengths. Prior to the mission as Redeemer, Schreber "had been inclined to sexual asceticism and had been a doubter in regard to God; while after it he was a believer in God and a devotee of voluptuousness" (32). I might add that during the first stage of delusion Schreber was not so much a doubter as an outspoken enemy of God, but the point does not change. As the wife of God he is able for the first time to say yes both to his sexuality and to his father. It is no wonder he speaks of finding "'the solution of the conflict'" (20).

But there is still a third advantage. Freud accepts "the popular distinction between ego-instincts and a sexual instinct" (74); and he calls attention to the way Schreber's "ego found compensation in his megalomania, while his feminine wishful phantasy made its way through and became acceptable" (48). Schreber thinks that "God does not have any regular communication with human souls" and it is "only in exceptional instances that He would enter into relations with particular, highly gifted persons" (22–23). Thus, in Dr. Weber's summary, Schreber finds himself to be " 'the most remarkable human being who has ever lived upon earth'" (17).

In his delusion of becoming the wife of God Schreber wins (1) moral legitimacy for his homosexual desires, (2) freedom to love rather than to hate his father, and (3) world-historical status as a Redeemer of cosmic importance. This solution is clearly superior to the persecutional compromise-formation, so much so that it may seem puzzling to refer to it as a compromise-formation at all. But the element of compromise remains. There is a cost for the benefits just listed. Schreber is not free to act out his sexual desires. The consummation of his marriage to God is postponed to an indefinite future. For the present he is free only to fantasize about it (constantly and innocently). And, since the world in which all these benefits accrue to Schreber is indeed a fantasy world, the second cost is that of losing touch with reality (as socially defined). In the transition from persecution to grandeur, Schreber's defense does not become less delusional. He remains a psychotic personality.

We are inquiring about the function of religion. We are seeking to understand its potential for legitimizing immoral behavior in the world of ordinary people in the light of its capacity for justifying immoral fantasies in the world of psychotics. I believe that the second stage of Schreber's illness is not just a better solution to his personal problem but points as well to a better, more efficient way for "sane" people to justify their immorality religiously. Two of Freud's most basic assumptions, noted at the outset of this essay, invite or even compel us to this transition. One is that the mental operations of neurotic and psychotic people are not so very different from those of "normal" folk. The other is that the group psychology of social phenomena, which we might call socioanalysis, is not so very different from individual psychoanalysis.

Consider the case of holy war. According to Dr. Weber's summary, Schreber came to accept the sufferings of his persecutional stage by coming to view them as "all on behalf of a holy purpose" (13–14), or as it is translated in the *Collected Papers,* a "sacred cause" (Freud 1963, 109). Holy war is a sacred cause not entirely unlike Schreber's. Against the background of demonizing the enemy, it elevates the agent to the role of God's specially chosen instrument, projects onto God the agent's megalomaniacal will to power, and thereby transforms action in accordance with that will to power from immorality into duty, the very upholding of the Order of Things.

There are differences to be sure. (1) In holy war the ego instincts of aggression are dominant, and any sexual gratification (e.g., rape) that may be involved is secondary. (2) The ego instincts involved are collective or tribal rather than individual. (3) The gratification of those instincts takes place in the real world, not just in fantasy. (4) While one may be called upon to suffer on behalf of this sacred cause, it is primarily others who are called upon to do the suffering.

With reference to the last point, John Howard Yoder has remarked, "The real temptation of good people like us is not the crude and the crass and the carnal, as those traits were defined in popular puritanism . . . but that of egocentric altruism; of being oneself the incarnation of a good and righteous cause for which others may rightly be made to suffer" (quoted in Hauerwas 1983, 131).

Thus, from the Crusades to the Holocaust, Jews have been made to suffer for the sake of Christian heroism or Aryan supremacy. Under such slogans as the "white man's burden," "manifest destiny," and the struggle against "atheistic communism," dark-skinned peoples have been subordinated to colonial and neocolonial domination. (In speaking of the wish-fulfilling construction of the Heavenly Father, Freud mentions the claim by "pious America . . . to being 'God's own Country'" [*S.E.* 21:19].) In ironical reversals by which the once persecuted become the persecutors, South African blacks and Palestinians are today made to suffer for the cause of Afrikaner culture and the Jewish state, respectively. Then there are Hiroshima and Nagasaki (not to mention current superpower willingness to sacrifice millions of civilians on the altar of national security) and the many varieties of Islamic Jihad. The list goes on and on.

No wonder Joan Baez sings, "If God is on our side, we'll start the next war." For in each of these cases, many, if not all, of those willing to make others into nothing but means to their own tribal ends have justified their behavior as required by a sacred cause. In fact, they have followed the Schreber recipe to a tee. They have come to see themselves first as threatened by a demonic enemy, and then as the specially chosen vehicles of a divine purpose. The question is why, if Schreber is plainly paranoid, these other cases are not also seen as paradigms of psychosis. The Schreber case challenges us to ask hard questions about phenomena such as these, especially those that are closest to us and make us feel most uncomfortable. For when other beneficiaries of such holy causes assure us that they are not using God as a means to their own ends but are rather instruments chosen by God to carry out divine purposes, we do not take these assurances as self-authenticating. Why should our own assurances be exempted from similar suspicion?

Ricoeur is right. Freudian psychoanalysis is iconoclastic vis-à-vis religion. Its hermeneutics of suspicion shows how easily the gods people serve are their own constructions, carefully designed to exempt the faithful from moral standards that they cannot refute but will not obey. Is this "destruction of idols" without remainder? Is this the whole story about religion, as Freud wanted to believe? I think not, but rather than try to defend my own answer to the question, I want to reflect on how the question should be asked. For if the question is properly asked, it will be clear that more than writing essays is needed to show that there is more to religion than the analogues to psychological pathology recognized by Freud.

Since Schreber's paranoia involves such defense mechanisms as projection, denial, and reversal, it is natural to put the question in terms of the possibility of nondefensive beliefs and practices. But defense mechanisms are not always thought to be pathological, and very early Freud sought to distinguish normal from pathological defenses (Laplanche and Pontalis 1963, 105). Some have suggested, for example, that sublimation is a healthy response to the threat of anxiety (Sappenfeld 1961, 23–24; Boden 1974, 247 n. 7). What is necessary is to identify the pathological element in the mechanisms of defense.

Perhaps it is repression, the key to all the defenses, including sublimation. By keeping certain unwelcome perceptions about myself (ourselves) beneath the level of consciousness, I permit or require myself to live in a world of falsehood and unreality. More specifically, I do not allow myself to see the ways in which I construct (or edit) the sacred so as to make it but a means to my (our) ends, a legitimation of my (our) immorality.[7] If there is to be any religion purified of idols that survives psychoanalytic iconoclasm it will have to be a nondefensive religion in the sense of being free from repression.[8] This does not mean that I will do whatever I please, for repression in the Freudian sense is not to be equated with simple self-restraint. It means that I will be honest about myself and will not hide the shameful aspects of myself from myself in order to allow them to continue in operation. It means I will not negotiate a compromise in which, for a price I am willing to pay, I can purchase exemption from my own best moral insights. Or, if this sounds too triumphalist, it means that my religion will be a force in the service of such honesty, which will no doubt never be total, rather than in the service of defensive dishonesty. It means that my religion, like that of the Hebrew prophets and of Jesus, will be as suspicious of idols as is Freudian psychoanalysis. It is only because his iconoclasm is as uncompromising as Freud's that Kierkegaard is able to point in the direction of such religion with more conceptual integrity than any other modern thinker.

But more than conceptual integrity is required to show that Freud's story, while tragically true, is not the whole story. To show the logical possibility of religion in the service of nonrepressive honesty is a task as easy as it is theoretical. To show the real possibility of such religion (by showing its actuality) is a task as difficult as it is practical.

Notes

1. Whenever Freud quotes from Schreber's *Denkwürdigkeiten eines Nervenkranken,* he includes the Schreber page in his own text. Since the pages of the German text are given in the margin of the English translation, the reader who wishes to see these passages in context or to compare the translation in the *S.E.* with the translation by Macalpine and Hunter can easily do so. I give Freud's quotations of Schreber from the *S.E.*

2. Morton Schatzman has called our attention to more evidence in support of this claim than Freud was aware of (Schatzman 1973, especially chapters 5–6). If Freud, like Schatzman, had studied the "terrifying theories of child-rearing" (Wollheim 1988) of Schreber's father, Daniel Gottlieb Moritz Schreber, he would not so easily have spoken of "the affectionate memory of the son" for his father, nor have suggested that the partial recovery that made possible the son's release from institutional care was due to "the fact that his father-complex was in the main positively toned" (*S.E.* 12:51–52, 78). Of course, the very grim picture of the elder Schreber that emerges from Schatzman's research is not incompatible with a genuine love of the son for his father, as Freud would have known from his own case, or with a tender longing for The Father in a more encompassing, symbolic sense. But Freud could never have left the lines just quoted stand as they are had he been aware of the facts to which Schatzman has called our attention.

Analogous questions about the relation of Schreber to his mother have been raised on the basis of information now available (Allison et al., especially chapter 11 and pp. 232–66). In each case the question raised is the same as the question raised by Masson (1984), whether Freud systematically underestimates the role of an individual patient's specific history.

3. A comprehensive account of Freud's understanding of defense and defense mechanisms is hard to come by. There is not even agreement over what should be included in the list of such mechanisms. Defense is usually said to be directed against internal, instinctual perceptions, but one early account describes symptoms as defenses against both temptation or illicit desire and the

external punishment that it is feared will follow (*S.E.* 9:124). For discussion and sample lists, see Laplanche and Pontalis (1963, 103–11), Sappenfeld (1961, 22–25), and Boden (1974, 244–49). Projection plays the lead role in the present case. It appears in all the lists. Supporting roles are played by reversal and denial, which are sometimes hard to distinguish from each other and from projection. I deny that I love or hate X by projecting the love or hatred onto X and then affirming that X loves or hates me.

4. That guilt and the fear of punishment are to be sharply distinguished, though they are often conjoined, I have argued in *God, Guilt, and Death,* chapter 4. Subjective guilt or moral anxiety is my approval of the other's disapproval of me. In guilt I acknowledge that I deserve to be punished. The diminished feeling of self-worth that this involves can exist even where fear of actual punishment is not present.

5. Kierkegaard helps us understand the advantage of reducing punishment to misfortune. "Punishment is not pain in and for itself; the same pain or suffering can happen to another merely as a vicissitude of life. Punishment is the conception that this particular suffering is punishment. When this conception is taken away, the punishment is really taken away as well" (1970, 52).

6. Though Schreber eventually comes to identify himself with Jesus Christ, it is clear that his divine mission as the wife of God makes him more nearly the Virgin Mary (*S.E.* 12:28, 32, including n. 1).

7. In the case of sublimation I do not allow myself to see the ways in which even my morality serves to gratify my immoral desires, a point on which Nietzsche is perhaps more helpful than Freud.

8. At least free from repression in this sense. Perhaps it is too sweeping to identify repression with pathology. Perhaps, instead, we should say that just as not all defenses are pathological, so the repression involved in them is not necessarily pathological. It all depends on what gets repressed, and why. Since repression does involve self-deception, however, the concept of healthy repression will have to be carefully formulated. In any case, repression that serves to legitimize what we would otherwise take to be immoral can only be healthy if our morality is sick.

References

Allison, David B., de Oliveira, Prado, Roberts, Mark S., and Weiss, Allen S. *Psychosis and Sexual Identity: Toward a Post-Analytic View of the Schreber Case.* Albany: SUNY Press, 1988.

Boden, Margaret A. "Freudian Mechanisms of Defense: A Programming Perspective." In *Freud: A Collection of Critical Essays,* edited by Richard Wollheim. Garden City, N.Y.: Doubleday, 1974.

Dodds, E. R. *The Greeks and the Irrational.* Berkeley: University of California Press, 1971.

Freud, Sigmund. *The Standard Edition of the Complete Psychological Works of Sigmund Freud.* Edited and translated by James Strachey. 24 vols. London: Hogarth, 1953–74.

"Obsessive Actions and Religious Practices" (1907), vol. 9.

"Psycho-Analytic Notes on an Autobiographical Account of a Case of Paranoia" (Dementia Paranoides) (1911), vol. 12.

Totem and Taboo (1913), vol. 13.

Introductory Lectures on Psycho-Analysis (1916–17), vols. 15–16.

The Future of an Illusion (1927), vol. 21.

Civilization and Its Discontents (1930), vol. 21.

New Introductory Lectures on Psycho-Analysis (1933), vol. 22.

————. *Three Case Histories.* Edited and introduced by Philip Rieff. New York: Collier, 1963.

Hauerwas, Stanley. *The Peaceable Kingdom: A Primer in Christian Ethics.* Notre Dame: University of Notre Dame Press, 1983.

Kierkegaard, Soren. *Concluding Unscientific Postscript.* Translated by David F. Swenson and Walter Lowrie. Princeton: Princeton University Press, 1941.

————. *Soren Kierkegaard's Journals and Papers,* vol. 2. Translated by Howard V. and Edna H. Hong. Bloomington: Indiana University Press, 1970.

Laplanche, J., and Pontalis, J.-B. *The Language of Psychoanalysis.* Translated by Donald Nicholson-Smith. New York: W. W. Norton, 1963.

Masson, Jeffrey Moussaieff. *Freud: The Assault on Truth: Freud's Suppression of the Seduction Theory.* London: Faber and Faber, 1984.

Nietzsche, Friedrich. *On the Genealogy of Morals.* Translated by Walter Kaufmann and R. J. Hollingdale. Together in one volume with *Ecce Homo.* Translated by Walter Kaufmann. New York: Random House, 1967.

————. *Thus Spoke Zarathustra.* Translated by Walter Kaufmann. New York: Viking Press, 1966.

Ricoeur, Paul. *Freud and Philosophy: An Essay on Interpretation.* Translated by Denis Savage. New Haven: Yale University Press, 1970.

Rokeach, Milton. *The Three Christs of Ypsilanti: A Psychological Study.* New York: Random House, 1964.

Sappenfeld, Bert R. *Personality Dynamics: An Integrative Psychology of Adjustment.* New York: Alfred A. Knopf, 1961.

Schatzman, Morton. *Soul Murder: Persecution in the Family.* New York: Random House, 1973.

Schreber, Daniel Paul. *Memoirs of My Nervous Illness.* Translated by Ida Macalpine and Richard A. Hunter. London: Dawson & Sons, 1955. Republished with the old pagination by Harvard University Press, 1988, with a new introduction by Samuel Weber.

Westphal, Merold. *God, Guilt, and Death: An Existential Phenomenology of Religion.* Bloomington, Indiana University Press, 1984.

Wollheim, Richard. Review of *Freud: A Life for Our Time,* by Peter Gay. *The New York Times Book Review,* April 24, 1988.

8   The Psychoanalytic Interpretation of St. Augustine's *Confessions:* An Assessment and New Probe

Don Browning

In the last four decades, there have been roughly a dozen published articles advancing a psychoanalytic interpretation of St. Augustine's *Confessions.* In these essays, one can in fact discern something of a history of the psychoanalytic interpretation of religion. Freud, psychoanalytic ego psychology, Erikson, and the self-psychology of Heinz Kohut have all been used to interpret the ways in which Augustine's childhood and adolescent experiences influenced his adult spirituality.

In recent years, scholars in the humanities have begun to take account of these studies, sometimes to refute them but often to build on them. A major symposium organized by Paul Pruyser and published in several issues of the *Journal of the Scientific Study of Religion* (1965–66) was followed twenty years later by another symposium assembled by the same journal. Although the first collection of essays was authored mainly by psychiatrists and psychologists, the 1985 articles were written chiefly by historians, theologians, or psychologists of religion functioning primarily within the context of religious studies. This alone may be a sign that the psychoanalytic study of religion is gaining in respect and popularity in the humanities and is now being primarily pursued under the sponsorship of these disciplines.

In spite of the many virtues of such studies, their number and the obvious disagreements among them suggest that their accumulative success is limited. There are four difficulties with these articles that limit their effectiveness as contributions to the humanities and religious studies.

First, there is insufficient attention to what the genre of autobiography means for the psychoanalytic interpretation of lives. The early

136

studies by Dodds (1927–28) and Kligerman (1957) did not address this issue nor did the authors of the 1965 symposium. Surprisingly, among the more recent studies only Capps (1983, 1985) and Gay (1985) have attended to the significance of genre for the psychoanalytic interpretation of the *Confessions.* Yet Olney (1972) in the humanities and Erikson (1975) and Cohler (1982) in psychology have convincingly argued that autobiography represents an attempt to order a person's life from the angle of vision of the issues in life being faced at the time that it is authored. Hence, it would seem reasonable that a psychoanalytic interpretation of a life, which seeks to trace the influence of early life events on later meanings, should also be concerned to take account of how later events and meanings work to reconstruct our understanding of early events and experiences.

Second, although each of these several essays discovers a somewhat different Augustine, basically two broad lines of interpretation have developed. There are those such as Kligerman, Dittes (1965), Bakan (1965), Woollcott (1966), Burrell (1970), and Rigby (1985), who have tended to interpret Augustine's childhood conflicts primarily in oedipal terms, that is, as a conflict between Augustine's mother and father, Monica and Patricius, that Monica won. And then there have been those such as Fredriksen (1978), Capps (1983, 1985), and Gay (1985), who have interpreted Augustine's childhood primarily in narcissistic terms, that is, as a problem in self-esteem, self-differentiation, and self-cohesion. No study to date has argued that even within the rubrics of Heinz Kohut's psychology of narcissism, liberally used by both Capps and Gay, there might be room to acknowledge the validity of both oedipal and narcissistic interpretations of what Paul Ricoeur would call Augustine's "archeology of the self" (Ricoeur 1970, 419–58).

Third, on the whole these studies have neglected to develop clear theses as to the claims being advanced for the usefulness of psychoanalytic interpretation. The studies have not reflected emerging advances in the philosophy of the social sciences and the theory of the relation of explanation and interpretation in the social and psychological disciplines. Burrell is an exception to this. While appreciating the insights of the earlier psychoanalytic interpretations of Augustine, he advanced certain philosophical and hermeneutical distinctions designed to challenge Dittes's earlier reductionistic interpretation of Augustine's dependency and argued for a higher dependency that resulted from Augustine's intellectual conversion to a more comprehensive neo-Platonist-Christian vision of God. Burrell's argument is not unlike Rigby's employment of Ricoeur's distinction between the archeology and teleology of the self.

Psychoanalytic interpretations can indeed, according to Ricoeur and Rigby, inform our understanding of the developmental archeology of the self that a person such as Augustine brings to a religious experience. But the teleological resolution of these conflicts, at least in some of the more creative religious experiences, must be understood with the help of a hermeneutical phenomenology that describes the restructuring of the self's archeology in light of the positive visions projected by commanding cultural personages—what Ricoeur calls, following Hegel, "figures of the spirit" (Ricoeur 1970, 462–68). But in the case of both Burrell and Rigby, the archeology that they assume and that they believe psychoanalytic interpretation can illuminate is basically oedipal. They have not caught how this archeology can be both narcissistic and oedipal, although, as I will argue, the narcissistic trends must be seen as the more profound. Nor have they fully investigated the question of the teleological transformation of this archeology, that is, its scope, nuances, and limitations.

And finally, these studies have not attended to the hermeneutical and philosophy-of-religion issues that they indirectly raise. They have not asked the question, what kind of enterprise is a psychoanalytically oriented psychology of religion? Is it genuinely a natural-science enterprise, or is it a dimension of a broader hermeneutical enterprise? Or is it a mixed discipline that combines hermeneutical and natural-science perspectives? If psychoanalysis is the last kind of discipline, as I believe, what does this mean for the matter of attempting a psychological evaluation of Augustine, something that most of these studies try to accomplish? I will end my remarks with some discussion of the question, what does a hermeneutically oriented psychoanalytical interpretation of Augustine have to contribute to the philosophy of religion? Or, to say it more simply, what does the psychoanalytic interpretation of religion have to contribute to the philosophical criticism of a religious expression?

Because of the limits set on the length of this article, the last two issues will be discussed quite sketchily; I will be content merely to outline issues that a satisfactory answer must address and point to some of the more promising directions.

Autobiography as Genre and the Psychoanalytic Interpretation of Religion

Volney Gay's Kohutian study of Augustine entitled "Augustine: The Reader as Selfobject" and Don Capps's "Parabolic Events in Augustine's Autobiography" are the only psychoanalytic interpretations of

Augustine that address the importance of the genre of autobiography as a form of self-presentation. Gay, using the terminology of Kohut, describes Augustine as a person whose weak father and smothering mother left him with narcissistic deficits in the form of a poor sense of self-regard and self-cohesion. The *Confessions,* Gay tells us, represents "a covert plea for selfobject relationships with an audience whose responses Augustine treasures deeply" (1985, 69). Augustine wants a consistency of recognition and a charity from his readers and God necessary for the support of his own fragmented, shameful, and guilty sense of self. Capps uses his reflections on autobiography to argue that shame rather than guilt is the fundamental preoccupation of Augustine. The *Confessions* is written as a mid-life autobiography and constitutes a monumental act of self-revelation before God, his friends, and the members of his congregation at Hippo. Rather than oedipal guilt being the primary preoccupation of Augustine (as Dittes, Pruyser, Bakan, and others have argued), Capps claims that the autobiographical context of Augustine's confessions suggests that shame over the experience of self-exposure before God and other humans is the primary concern.

Although Gay and Capps have made important contributions and are, I believe, generally correct in their views, there is still room for a more nuanced perspective on the importance of the autobiographical form for the psychoanalytic interpretation of Augustine. Erikson, in commenting on Gandhi's autobiography, asks how "does the aging man reconstruct his childhood to conform to the needs of his old age?" (1975, 128). This is what Gandhi appears to be doing when he tells the story of his childhood and youth to support his efforts to reconstruct his political and religious identity as the aging moral leader of his nation. Bertram Cohler has gone even further by suggesting that in both therapy and autobiography we fictionalize the narratives of our earlier lives to support the image of the self we feel compelled to present at the stage in life at which the autobiographical narrative is constructed. These perspectives should inspire us to look with more care than have earlier psychoanalytic studies at just what was happening in Augustine's life at the time of the writing of the confessions.

Peter Brown's majestic *Augustine of Hippo* may provide the clue. "Augustine wrote his *Confessions,*" he tells us, "at some time around 397, that is, only a few years after he had become a bishop in Africa" (Brown 1967, 161). Becoming a bishop, with all of the administrative and ecclesiastical responsibilities, was far from Augustine's life ambition. Even before Augustine's conversion experience in the garden toward the end of summer in 386, and immediately after during his philosophical retreat with friends at Cassiciacum, Augustine along with Alypius and Nibridius had dreamed of spending a lifetime in contemplative retirement pursuing the goals of wisdom and the good life so celebrated in both classical Greek and Christian culture (Brown 1967, 146). At the time of the writing of the *Confessions*, Augustine was painfully aware that the quest for the life of wisdom and perfection would be impossible for him. As Brown points out, his growing sense of the limitations of his own will was one source of his disillusionment, a theme well developed in chapter 8 of the *Confessions* (Brown 173; *Confessions*, 8.10; 8.19). But the responsibilities of being bishop, the obstinate wills of the people in his congregation, the assaults to his own sense of self-esteem resulting from the controversies and petty administrative squabbles that then plagued his life, and his growing isolation from his most intimate friends—all this and more left Augustine with an accentuated sense of emptiness and fragmentation and a growing fear that he was not going in the right direction with his life. The *Confessions* was written to convince himself that he was on the right course and that God's guiding hand was amidst all the details of his present life, as Augustine believed it had been so often in the past.

The psychoanalytically trained mind, however, is likely not only to notice Augustine's many references to the importance of his close friends and to his need for God's abiding recognition but also to interpret them as psychologically potent sources that he required to overcome his sense of scattered self. Brown points out that the *Confessions* was written for the *servi Dei*—a group of Augustine's friends dedicated to God but whose personal histories were very different and who were now largely separated from one another (162). But Augustine's need to reveal himself and gain a response went beyond the normal patterns of male friendships so ritualized among the intellectuals of his day. It was necessary to hold himself together against the onslaughts of the sense of derailment, impatience, and fragmentation that his position as bishop had brought about. It is not until Book 10 that Augustine begins to list his more serious reasons for writing the *Confessions*. He hopes to elicit a certain "charity" from those who hear his story, a "desire to rejoice with me" when he is close to God and to "pray" for him when he fails. He wishes to inspire a "brotherly mind which is glad for me when it sees good in me and sorry for me when it sees bad in me, because, whether it sees good or bad, it loves me" (10.3–4).

Toward the end of the same Book, Augustine discusses his propensity for the sins of lust, curiosity, and the vain need for the praise of others. His need for praise is particularly interesting. "Yet I wish it were not the case that when someone else praises me, my joy in whatever good quality I may have is increased. It is increased, however, I admit; not only that, but it is diminished by dispraise" (10.37). This sin, in contrast to the others, perplexes Augustine and leaves him "uncertain." In the same vein, we hear subdued complaints by the new bishop, who, as Brown tells us, "heartily resented" his bishop's task of keeping peace "within his 'family' by arbitrating in their lawsuits" (195). These arbitrations, and the disappointments and controversy that they inevitably engendered, must have been a source of part of the "dispraise" that Augustine laments.

It is also toward the end of Book 10 that Augustine reports the following remarkable thoughts about his "consultations" with God, thoughts so revealing of a harried and reluctant administrator whose needs for intimacy, praise, and self-cohesion were being systematically denied by his role in life.

> And in all these things over which I range as I am consulting you I find no secure place for my soul except in you, and in you I pray that what is scattered in me may be brought together. . . . And sometimes working within me you open for me a door into a state of feeling which is quite unlike anything to which I am used—a kind of sweet delight which, if I could only remain permanently in that state, would be something not of this world, not of this life. But my sad weight makes me fall back again. [10.40]

But if it is, in part, the hectic life of an administrator that fragmented a contemplative Augustine, the *Confessions* points to his attempt to resolve the problem. In Book 11, he admits once again that "my life is a kind of distraction and dispersal." But it is

> *through Him [that] I may apprehend in Whom I have been apprehended* and that I may be gathered up from my former days to follow the One, *forgetting what is behind,* not wasted and scattered on things which are to come and things which will pass away, but intent and *stretching forth to those things which are before*—no longer distracted, but concentrated as I *follow on for the praise of my heavenly calling,* which I may hear the voice of Thy praise, and contemplate Thy delight. [11.29]

These quotes together indicate that Augustine regularly consulted with God in prayer about the decisions of his life as bishop. During these sessions he was elevated into a kind of beatific vision. This vision would contain the dynamics of an interpersonal dialogue whereby Augustine's sense of scattered self was recollected and unified by virtue of coming to regard himself in the way in which he believed God regarded, praised, and delighted in him. In addition, it is clear that Augustine hopes to gain an analogous self-support from his friends.

The importance of the praise and delight of God in Augustine is a motif that runs throughout the *Confessions*. It suggests visions of a smiling and radiant countenance that shows forth prizing and affirmation. The *Confessions* is full of references to God's face, to God's presence filling Augustine, and to Augustine gaining self-cohesion in light of God's Oneness and unifying regard toward Augustine.

From the first pages of the *Confessions* we read, "When I pray to Him, I call Him into myself" (1.2). Not only must Augustine be filled by God but he also must see God's face. "Do not hide your face from me. Let me die, lest I should die indeed; only let me see your face" (1.5). In the opening paragraph of Book 2 he writes that he is confessing his sins before God in order to be "gathering myself together from the scattered fragments into which I was broken and dissipated during all that time when, being turned away from you, the One, I lost myself in the distractions of the Many" (1.2). With reference to the purpose of his philosophical retreat at Cassiciacum, Augustine writes, "I was longing for the peace and liberty in which I could sing to you from the depths of my being; *My heart hath said unto Thee, I have sought Thy face; Thy face, Lord, will I seek*" (9.3).

The psychoanalytic interpretation of the *Confessions* must begin by taking seriously the form and the occasion of the autobiographical genre as a mode of self-presentation. When this is done, we see that the *Confessions* is written against the background of Augustine's own concern about the direction of his life. It is written to gain a heightened sense of self-cohesion from the anticipated response of both friends and God. Later I will investigate the extent to which the writing of the *Confessions* and the deepened dialogue with God that it occasioned was successful, that is, actually contributed to his sense of cohesion. But it is precisely the promise of the psychoanalytic perspective to throw additional light on the sense of fragmentation that Augustine reports. The psychoanalytic perspective may give us a deeper perspective into what Paul Ricoeur calls the "archeology of the self," which in this instance would be the archeology of Augustine's sense of scatteredness, self-dispersion, and derailment. The debate among the psychoanalytic perspectives has been whether Augustine's feeling of fragmentation was primarily oedipal or narcissistic in origin. My view is that it was something of both.

The Archeology of the Augustinian Self: Oedipal or Narcissistic?

The issue from a psychoanalytic point of view is whether or not Augustine up to the time of his major conversion experience in the garden had *unusual* problems with self-cohesion and overdetermined needs to find self-consistency and self-recognition in the responses of friends and God. Psychoanalysis also would be interested in determining whether there is evidence that writing the *Confessions* as a religious act of dialogue with God contributed anything to Augustine's self-cohesion. By unusual and overdetermined needs for self-cohesion, I mean needs that exceed the common requirements that most humans seem to have for these interpersonal nourishments. If Augustine did have heightened needs for such sustenance, the psychoanalytic perspective is also interested in determining their developmental origins. Do these needs originate in oedipal conflict and guilt or in pre-oedipal deficiencies in self-regard and self-cohesion because of inadequate empathy from the parental figures in Augustine's life?

Although Peter Brown believes that the historian must avoid all psychoanalytic inquiries, it is obvious that his *Augustine of Hippo* reflects the sensitivities of a psychoanalytically oriented age. And on such issues as the developmental origins of Augustine's conflicts, Brown has subtle ways of communicating his own preferences. In one place he writes the following about the depth of Augustine's needs for praise in comparison to his problems with guilt and aggression.

> He faced this fact with exceptional honesty: he may no longer be vengeful when insulted, but love of praise, the need to feel admired and loved by others, still caused him to be "roasted daily in the oven of men's tongues." One feels that the tensions that sprang from his relations to others, his need to influence men, his immense sensitivity to their response to him, were far more deeply-rooted and insidious, than the more obvious temptations of greed and sexuality. His acute awareness of the motive-force of a "love of praise" in his ecclesiastical rivals, the Donatist bishops, and in the ancient pagan Romans, shows both how vividly he had experienced the emotion in himself, and how sternly he had repressed it: for "no one who has not declared war on this enemy can possibly know how strong it is." [205–6]

Brown has said more here than he realizes. Although he has presented no psychoanalytic reasons to support his judgment on the matter, he tells us here that Augustine had problems with both guilt and aggression *and* needs for affirming responses, but that the latter were the more profound.

On the whole, however, psychoanalytic writers have seen it differently; Augustine, to most of them, exhibited the classic features of oedipal guilt. It was an oedipal drama, however, that had a special twist: Augustine won the oedipal battle, was victorious over his father, Patricius, and indeed submitted to the psychological and sexual control of his mother, Monica.

James Dittes's "Continuities between the Life and Thought of Augustine" is considered the paradigmatic oedipal interpretation of Augustine's *Confessions*. His thesis is that both Augustine's adult personality and his religious thinking reflect his childhood oedipal conflicts and their final resolution by his submission to the will and God of his mother. Dittes depicts Monica as living an emotionally deprived life with her husband, as seeking a substitute "gratification" through her relation to Augustine, as sabotaging his wedding plans "at least twice," as moving in on Augustine's household in Milan, and as "sharing a mutual mystical experience in which it is difficult to avoid hearing erotic overtones" (133). After Augustine's various attempts to gain his autonomy from Monica—that is, his sexual rebellion, his experimentation with Manichaeanism, his stealing away to Rome on a ship in the middle of the night even though his mother expected to make the trip with him the next morning—Dittes interprets his conversion in the garden as a final submission to Monica. He writes,

> After years of the most vigorous assertion of his independence, Augustine submitted. . . . He abandoned those things which his father particularly endorsed and represented. He abandoned, in short, the effort to be a father. Instead he became an obedient son. [137]

But Dittes is not alone in seeing oedipal themes in the life of Augustine. Dodds, Kligerman, Woollcott, and Bakan all believed they had discovered oedipal themes in the *Confessions*. But Woollcott, and later Burrell and Rigby, although still functioning within an oedipal perspective on Augustine, emphasized a creativity and growth in Augustine's handling of his oedipal conflicts that are absent from the earlier articles. Rigby goes the furthest. He uses Ricoeur to emphasize the progressive resolution of these conflicts brought about by the restructuring of Augustine's childhood archeology with the images of God's paternal love to be found in the Christian neo-Platonism of his day.

Fredriksen, Capps, and Gay, on the other hand, advanced interpretations of Augustine's archeology that emphasize narcissistic in contrast to oedipal issues. Fredriksen, functioning as a historian, criticized these oedipal studies for their lack of historical sensitivity about Augustine and his times. It is only in light of a genuine understanding

of the historical options facing Augustine that we can assess the importance of psychological factors that tilted him one way or another. Rely-
ing heavily on Peter Brown, yet criticizing him for not coming clean
on his psychological assumptions, Fredriksen advances "the hypothesis that Augustine manifests the conflicts of the narcissistic personality" (1978, 219). Using the work of Margaret Mahler on separation
and individuation, Fredriksen argues that rather than having an in-
cestuous relation with Augustine, Monica is using him to prop up her
own sagging sense of self (220).

Although in his 1983 article Capps emphasizes the preoedipal aspects of Augustine's shame, he makes a much more explicit relationship between shame and narcissism in his 1985 response to Rigby,
titled "Augustine as Narcissist." Here he amplifies Fredriksen's interpretation with the theories of narcissism found in the work of the
late Heinz Kohut. He writes, "Episodes recounted in his *Confessions*
that are commonly viewed as admissions of guilt are, more deeply,
experiences involving profound shame owing to narcissistic injury"
(119–20).

Gay elaborates on the Kohutian theory of the relation of sexual tensions to narcissistic disturbances. In contrast to Augustine and Freud,
who both tended to see sexuality as a liquid drive, difficult to control,
that floods the self and needs the moral control of a strong ego and
conscience, Kohut understands such sexualization of experience as a
result of a fragmented self and deficits in self-selfobject relationships.
"Kohut," Gay tells us, "views sexualization as a product of prior, narcissistic injury. Sexualized and aggressivized images, as well as perverse
actions, are attempts to repair a wounded self" (73). Gay finds evidence
of empathic inadequacies toward the young Augustine in both Patricius
and Monica. He makes the additional passing point that Augustine's
need for an affirming response from Patricius may have been recapitu-
lated in his relationships with Faustus and later Ambrose (69).

But none of these readings points out the possible intimate relations
that can occur between narcissistic and oedipal problems. Furthermore, important evidence for the narcissistic reading of Augustine's
archeology is often overlooked. Some of this evidence is especially important for mapping the relation between the knowledge we have of
Augustine's childhood with what we learn about his psychological
needs from his use of the genre of autobiography.

As both Capps and Gay suggest, the psychoanalytic theories of
Heinz Kohut are a reliable guide to recent developments in the psychology of narcissism. His work on narcissism was built on new theoretical breakthroughs, first initiated by Heinz Hartmann, in the psycho-

analytic theory of the self. In 1950, Hartmann noted that "the opposite of object cathexis is not ego cathexis, but cathexis of one's own person." Accordingly he introduced the concept of the "self-cathexis" (and "self-representation" as opposed to "object representation") and defined narcissism "as the libidinal cathexis not of the ego but of the self" (127).

Building on this insight Kohut (1971, xiii) develops a much fuller psychoanalytic theory of the self. According to Kohut, when the infant's early symbiotic identification with the mother begins to break down under the impact of the normal differentiating forces of life, the child tries to compensate for the separation through two maneuvers. Kohut tells us that "the child replaces the previous perfection a) by establishing a grandiose and exhibitionistic image of the self: the *grandiose self*; and b) by giving over the previous perfection to an admired, omnipotent (transitional) self-object: *the idealized parent imago*" (1971, 25). The central project of the archaic grandiose self is to find significant people who will become self-objects and in their responses will both bestow and continuously confirm in the child a sense that "I am perfect." The central aim of the idealized self is to find significant and powerful people with whom to identify and gain the sense that "You are perfect, but I am part of you" (1971, 27). Optimal growth, according to Kohut, entails a twofold process in which parents and parental surrogates both convey a great deal of empathy in response to these maneuvers of the self and carefully modulate the failures in empathy that life inevitably brings.

Although in his first major book, *The Analysis of the Self*, Kohut formulated these theories in terms of the drive concepts of the traditional Freudian metapsychology, in his later books, *The Restoration of the Self* and *How Does Analysis Cure?*, he gradually developed an alternative metapsychology that provides for the growth of the self as an independent line of development. It is important for my argument here to note that in conceptualizing the self as an independent line of development, Kohut did not throw out completely the older Freudian metapsychology. He writes, "We must learn to think alternatingly, or even simultaneously, in terms of two theoretical frameworks. . . . a psychology in which the self is seen as the center of the psychological universe, and a psychology in which the self is seen as a content of the mental apparatus" (1977, xv). Kohut is telling us here that he plans to retain in his theory of narcissistic disturbances of the self a subordinate theory that can understand the reality of those sexual and aggressive conflicts that manifest themselves in the oedipal drama. What is unique about Kohut's perspective is his theory that undergirding

most if not all oedipal conflicts are earlier, preoedipal narcissistic deficiencies and injuries to the self. This point is highly relevant to the
debate over the psychoanalytic interpretation of Augustine.

Kohut admits that there are both aggressive and sexual impulses in
the human personality. But he distinguishes himself from the orthodox
Freudian theory in believing that neither is an isolated primordial tendency in the human personality. They manifest themselves in isolation
only when there is a breakdown in the more basic line of development
that establishes the coherence of the self. With regard to aggressive-
ness, he sees it "not as the manifestation of a primary drive . . . , but as
a disintegration product which, while it is primitive, is not psychologically primal" (1977, 114). The same is true of the sexual drives.

> The infantile sexual drive in isolation is not the primary psychological
> configuration—whether on the oral, anal, urethral, or phallic level. The
> primary psychological configuration (of which the drive is only a con-
> stituent) is the experience of the relation between the self and the em-
> pathic self-object. Drive manifestations in isolation establish themselves
> only after traumatic and/or prolonged failures in empathy from the side
> of the self-object environment. . . . If the self is seriously damaged, how-
> ever, or destroyed, then the drives become powerful constellations in
> their own right. In order to escape from depression, the child turns
> from the unempathic or absent self-object to oral, anal, and phallic sen-
> sations, which he experiences with great intensity. [1977, 122]

In light of these theoretical formulations, it is a respectable hypothesis
to hold that Augustine's archeology is really a fragmented and un-
cohesive self resulting from unempathic selfobjects; at the same time,
it is an archeology that manifests itself secondarily in both oedipal
symptoms and a relentless need for sexual gratification.

Kohut believes that problems with the coherence of the self and
oedipal problems can exist side by side but that the former are the
more profound simply because they are developmentally earlier. Although the classical view believes that the analyst has "arrived at the
deepest level when we have reached the patient's experience of his
impulses, wishes, and drives," the Kohutian view holds that the oedipal problem is likely to be "embedded" in a deeper "self-selfobject disturbance" and that "beneath lust and hostility there is a layer of depression and of diffuse narcissistic rage" (Kohut 1984, 5). This is what
may be the case with Augustine. And this is why the analyses by
Fredriksen, Capps, and Gay are the more penetrating. Yet, because it is
theoretically possible for narcissistic and oedipal problems to coexist,
these three authors may have gone further than they needed in reacting

against the oedipal interpretations. Both perspectives may be important even though the narcissistic interpretation is the more revealing.

We have already reviewed some of the evidence for the narcissistic interpretation of Augustine's archeology of the self. But is there more evidence that needs our attention? Can the narcissistic interpretation be extended to include aspects of the oedipal view of Augustine's early development? And finally, what difference does all of this delving into Augustine's archeology make for our understanding of the transformations that are traditionally believed to have occurred in his life?

In discussing the importance of the genre of autobiography for the psychoanalytic interpretation of religion, I hinted at the narcissistic vulnerability of Augustine. He wrote the *Confessions* to receive an affirming and self-supporting response from both the *servi Dei* and God. I also developed the tentative hypothesis that in the very act of writing the *Confessions* and contemplating the unity, beauty, and affirmation of his growing image of a neo-Platonic-Christian God, Augustine found both a deeper sense of self-cohesion and the conviction that God was guiding him in his responsibilities as a bishop and Christian statesman, just as he had guided him in the past. But the question remains, is Augustine's sense of fragmentation situationally induced, or is it grounded in early disturbances in self-selfobject relations?

Narcissistic injury can result from a variety of subtle factors. Certainly a failure of empathy from significant selfobjects is the central condition. But this can occur when a parent as a selfobject uses the child to support his or her own deficient sense of self. This may have been the major form in which Augustine received his narcissistic injuries, primarily from Monica but to some extent even from Patricius. The harpings of a middle-aged bishop about his insensitive teachers and parents and about his parents' misguided ambitions for him may tell us more about these old wounds than we might think at first glance. At school, Augustine was made to look "foolish" by being "beaten" when he failed to work hard (1.9). His parents told him school was important because it would provide him with a "reputation among men and with deceitful riches." His reaction was so serious that the young Augustine prayed to God for deliverance from the beatings, which seemed to be, he tells us, a source of "merriment among my elders and even among my parents." His "parents used to laugh at the torments with which we boys were afflicted by our masters," often for nothing more than a childhood fondness for play. And then the older Augustine, looking back across the years to his childhood pain, concludes, "And no one is sorry for children; no one is sorry for the older people; no one is sorry for both of them" (1.9). Are we not tempted to hear Augustine complain, in effect, that "no one was sorry for me then and no one is sorry for me now"? The trivial nature of the complaint makes one wonder what deeper message of failures in adult empathy for the young Augustine, and even the older Augustine, are being reported here.

In addition to Augustine's complaints about the insensitivity of the adults surrounding him, he also laments his parents' ambitions for him. Do we hear in this the complaints of one who felt that he was at times little more than an extension of his parents' ambitions, a selfobject for his parents' own fragmented self-regard and self-cohesion? In addition to telling Augustine that he should succeed in school to "get on in the world" and develop a reputation, his father sent him to Maduara and later to Carthage for his education, not because Patricius was rich but because he "had big ideas" and because he was interested more in Augustine's being "cultured" than in his being chaste or godly (2.3). Monica seemed to be equally ambitious for Augustine and opposed his early marriage, a pattern quite common at that time, so that he would not be derailed from her educational goals for him. In these hopes for his education, "both of my parents indulged too much" (2.3).

In Carthage, as a teenager, Augustine experienced simultaneously a need for self-control and a need for intimacy. On the one hand he can say, "I was given free play with no kind of severity to control me and was allowed to dissipate myself in all kinds of ways" (2.3), and yet on the other hand he attests that he was "in love with love" (3.1). Then, again, he reports feeling "emptier" yet finding it a sweet thing "both to love and to be loved, and more sweet still when I was able to enjoy the body of my lover" (3.1). Do we hear the recollections of the older Augustine, who is now able to acknowledge that in being sent to Carthage he felt both used and somewhat rejected and who found self-validation in being loved by another, a love that first of all provided an affirming selfobject and second a degree of sensual gratification?

Fredriksen may be correct in arguing that Monica is the principal source of Augustine's narcissistic wounds. Given at times to drinking too much wine yet highly intelligent, married by her parents to a warm but volatile middle-class civil servant who was not a Christian, Christian herself and ambitious that her favorite child become both a Christian and an intellectual, Monica may have projected many of her own disappointments and ambitions into her son. This has been the story well told by both the oedipal and the narcissistic interpretations of Augustine's developmental archeology. The same set of acts can yield to either interpretation depending upon the angle of vision of the interpreter.

It is my conviction that the narcissistic interpretation is the more fundamental even though it does not totally exclude the oedipal. There is little evidence of a genuinely erotic relation between Monica and Augustine, in spite of Dodds's mistranslation of *et illius carnale desiderium* (5.8) as "her carnal desire" (Fredriksen says "earthly affection" would be better). The famous "wooden ruler" dream of Monica's, which concludes with a voice telling her that "where she was, I was too," tells more about Monica's need for Augustine to support her self-cohesion than it does about any sexual fantasies either may have had for the other (3.11). Her incessant weeping over his move into Manichaeanism (3.11), her attempt to follow him to Rome (5.8), her decision eventually to join him in Milan (6.1), her arrangement of his engagement with an upper-class woman, and her banishment of his concubine (and mother of his child) back to Africa (6.15) all can be seen as acts designed to complete her own ambitions and confirm her own self needs rather than as simply or solely jealous oedipal behavior.

But there were ways in which Augustine stood in the middle of tensions between Monica and Patricius. Because of Monica's own self-selfobject needs and Patricius's paganism and infidelity, there were clearly ways in which Monica precipitated a strained and suspicious relation between Augustine and his father. This, plus Patricius's own tendency to use Augustine as a selfobject—through the prestige that Augustine's education would bring and through Patricius's hope for heirs that Augustine might some day father (2.3)—functioned to set up in Augustine a tremendous hunger for affirmation and intimacy with males, an observation that few interpreters, with the exception of Volney Gay, have chosen to emphasize. It is unfair to overemphasize Patricius's deficiencies. What is clear, however, is that Monica constituted a barrier between Augustine and his father. Oedipal reasons may have been a small part of this, but they were situated in a more basic matrix—Monica's own self needs to see her talented and promising Augustine as an extension of herself and to fashion his future on her terms and not on those of Patricius. Mother and father could agree on the importance of education, but little else. Although Patricius was eventually converted to Christianity, his early paganism and lusty morality were not what Monica wished for her favorite child. It is mainly within this context of meanings and struggles that we should interpret Augustine's telling statement "that she earnestly endeavored, my God, that you rather than he should be my father" (1.11).

There is evidence that Augustine tended to idealize most of the male figures in his life other than Patricius. Do we see here a need for a confirming male countenance that Patricius was either unable or, more likely, not permitted to bestow? I believe we do. From a Kohutian perspective, this amounted to a frustration of the development of the normal process of relating to an idealized parental imago. Kohut would call Augustine's complaints about being beaten and laughed at a reaction to an injury to his exhibitionistic grandiose self—that is, his need to gain stabilization of the self through admiration, prizing, and praise. Although he was permitted to idealize his mother, and clearly did, it is not clear that she permitted him to gain a sense of idealized self with reference to Patricius. He was not permitted to develop a sense that he was powerful and that they were one. But what is the evidence that he worked out this frustrated need with other men and the wisdom, truth, and power that they could convey?

Although it is typical of the young to have close friends, and although friendship between males was more stylized in the Greco-Roman world than it is today, Augustine's extensive mourning over the death of his youthful male friend and his comment that his "soul and my friend's had been one soul in two bodies" suggests an unusual need in Augustine to be mirrored and affirmed by other men (4.4).

Furthermore, there is a trail of references in the *Confessions* to men, mostly older, who were mediators of truth and enlightenment. People whose need for idealization has not been permitted to develop and to become gradually and nontraumatically moderate often bring unusually high expectations to idealizable figures only to be disappointed when they meet the flesh-and-blood persons themselves. It is as if they were saying to themselves, "You are not perfect and I cannot be perfect if I am like you." It is sometimes easier for narcissists to idealize individuals they have never met or to be moved by stories of people they do not actually know than it is to be touched or moved by those close at hand. Hence, in Book 4 Augustine tells of dedicating one of his writings to a famous rhetorician, Hierus, whom he had never met. He admits that he loved the "man more because of the love of those who praised him" (4.14). Augustine adds that it was important for him to have his works known by this famous orator. And "if he liked them, I should be all the more ardent about him; though if he thought little of them, then my vain heart, quite empty of your solidity, would be wounded" (4.14). Augustine looked forward with "boundless longing" to meeting Faustus, the great Manichaean, and to having all his questions answered about that faith (5.6). But when Augustine found him "ignorant of those subjects in which I had thought him to be so particularly learned," he writes of his disappointment with the words, "I began to lose hope in his being able to solve my perplexities and explain to me the questions that troubled me" (5.7).

Similar rhythms of idealization and disappointment can be found in his relation with Ambrose in Milan. Ambrose is seen as someone having a "worldwide reputation" whom Augustine immediately "began to love" because he was "kind and generous to me" (5.13). But then he soon found it difficult to get really close to Ambrose, to share his inner thoughts and to learn his thoughts and feelings. He complains, "I was prevented from having an intimate conversation with him by the crowds of people" who perpetually surrounded him (6.3). Nonetheless, he did listen to Ambrose's sermons, which did affect him; this raises one of the most important questions that the psychoanalytic interpretation of religion must face: the role of religious and philosophical ideas in the conversion process.

Ambrose's sermons deepened Augustine's understanding of neo-Platonism and its use in Christian thinking and helped begin an intellectual conversion process that culminated emotionally in the famous garden experience. They also helped him to put even further behind himself his Manichaean phase. But Ambrose's remoteness and unavailability meant that he was unable to help Augustine, with his needs for an affirming countenance and intimate sharing, to cross the final boundary keeping him from a full affirmation of the Christian faith. It took another series of older males and more stories of easily idealizable figures for that to happen. Simplicianus, Christian Platonist and spiritual adviser to Ambrose, told Augustine the story of the highly acclaimed Roman classicist and rhetorician Victorianus, who late in life converted to Christianity and even finally confessed this publicly before a Christian congregation (8.2). When Augustine heard the story of Victorianus, whom he had never met but with whom he could both identify and idealize, he "was on fire to be like him" (8.5). Shortly after this, the African Christian and imperial official Ponticianus paid Augustine and Alypius a visit. Learning that Augustine was reading Paul, Ponticianus was emboldened to tell him about the Egyptian monk Antony. The stories about these unknown men deeply moved Augustine, and he went immediately from this meeting into the garden where he had his famous conversion experience.

I find it important that the conversion that Monica wished for Augustine was actually mediated by a series of male figures, known and unknown, who included Ambrose, Simplicianus, Victorianus, Ponticianus, Antony, and still others. The complex dynamic here requires some differentiation between vision and mediators. The vision consisted of Christian neo-Platonism and its image of a perfectly self-sufficient God who was also *constant, unified, and unalterable.* Augustine also interpreted this God as *warm, responsive, listening, and affirming,* even though these two sets of values (God's unalterability and God's responsiveness) were difficult for Augustine to reconcile philosophically. The mediators of this vision (these "figures of the spirit," as Ricoeur calls them) were men whom Augustine both admired and idealized. Is it possible that Augustine was able to accept some variation of Monica's God only when it was permitted and confirmed by idealized father figures whose affirming (but somewhat untestable) countenances seemed to merge with the affirming and constant God to whom they gave witness? From this perspective, it is a decent hypothesis to hold that Augustine's conversion in the garden can be seen as reconciling and restructuring disturbances in his own self-selfobject relations. It helped reconcile the tension around a feeling of being unempathically used by both parents. It also helped alleviate a sense of being both used *and* smothered by his mother, and used and smothered in a way that kept him from developing a close relation with his father. The neo-Platonic image of God, as Augustine interpreted it, gave him a responsive, empathic, constant face with which to nourish his narcissistic needs and supply what he was unable to get satisfactorily from either of his parents. It also was mediated by a series of older men who, if not exactly father substitutes, could at least present this God as a man's God. In addition, it was important to Augustine, primarily because it was important to Monica, that his constant and affirming God also carried the name of "Christian."

This God was not the God he knew as a child or young man; it was a God he learned to know. It was a God taught to him by Christian philosophers and their texts and mediated to him by a long line of affirming Christian men. These men played a role with Augustine not unlike the role played by Staupitz with the young Luther (Erikson 1958, 14, 37). By virtue of the relative maturity of these men and the image of their God as *a se,* unneedful, and perfect, Augustine experienced this God's love as free, spontaneous, and gracious. These are qualities quite different from the needful love Augustine experienced from his two narcissistically preoccupied parents. Nonetheless, it was a God upon whom Augustine could project elements of his object relations with both his mother and his father. In return, this God-image both received these projections and, through successive testings by Augustine in the years and months before his garden experience, was perceived by Augustine as enduring in ways he never experienced with his own parents. Hence, in a highly condensed synthesis, the mature Augustine's personal appropriation of the Christian neo-Platonic God brought together many elements: it contained room for maleness and manhood that Monica's God could not include, a Christian identity that Augustine needed in order to be at ease with Monica, and a gracious constancy, affirmation, and positive regard that transcended anything he had experienced from either parent or any God-representation that could have been constructed out of his imagoes of them.

Implications for Psychoanalysis and the Humanities

This essay has concentrated primarily on the first two of my four issues—that is, the importance of the autobiographical genre and the possibility of interpreting Augustine's archeology in light of both narcissistic and oedipal perspectives. But I want to conclude with at least a few brief comments about the other two issues—the scope, logic, and limitations of the psychoanalytic interpretation of religion, and the possible contributions of psychoanalysis to the philosophy of religion.

First, the thrust of this essay suggests that the contributions of psychoanalysis to the interpretation of religion are primarily limited to the interpretation of the archeology of the self that is brought to the religious encounter. Psychoanalysis helps us to see the developmental history of the self (or selves) being studied. The self and its needs are admittedly projected into the religious experience. But the self archeology does not always dominate the meaning of the experience entirely, although in some cases it may. In Augustine's encounter with Christian neo-Platonism, we must imagine something more like a genuinely dialectical or two-way process. The constancy, dependability, pervasiveness, and responsiveness of this God gave him a selfobject that helped to restructure and unify the archeology of his self, just as it gave him an object into which to project his needs.

It is best to think that this God-image helped Augustine *begin* the process of self-integration; there is evidence that Augustine to some extent worked with his conflicts throughout his entire life. In the paragraphs above, I recounted how Augustine struggled with his narcissistic needs many years after his garden conversion even as he began writing the *Confessions* as a harried, middle-aged bishop. But as he moves toward the conclusion of the narrative sections and into the final and more peaceful theological sections of the *Confessions,* we observe Augustine writing, as we saw above, that he feels "apprehended" and "gathered up" by God and therefore is "no longer distracted" but able to concentrate anew on his "heavenly calling" (11.29).

We see that in the very act of writing the *Confessions* Augustine is struggling, with some success, to confirm, consolidate, and expand the earlier conversion process that began with the reading of Cicero, continued with his encounter with Ambrose, and climaxed with the visits from Simplicianus and Ponticianus shortly before his spiritual crisis in the garden. His self-assessment that God was helping reaffirm his "calling," his subsequent amazing literary output, and his hugely influential administrative career suggest a man of unusual energy and creativity and not a man whose power and initiative had been destroyed by submission to his mother, as Dittes and others have claimed.

Such a judgment may be sustainable even in light of his unbecoming resort to coercion during the Donatist controversy rather late in his life. Even here, love and persuasion were his first gestures. Sandra Dixon (1988) has perceptively demonstrated that his final use of coercion was primarily motivated by his need to protect the symbols and the church that had given him a heightened sense of self-cohesion, a self-cohesion that even as an older man he still felt he needed to protect. All these circumstances point to the truth that even genuine growth can be ambiguous if tested too severely by later circumstances.

This position implies that the psychoanalytic study of religion can proceed in the humanities best when, as Ricoeur has argued, the archeology and teleology of symbols are interpreted in dialectical relation to one another. The archeology of the self that helps create a symbol may not exhaust the total potential of the symbol. Manichaeanism, Monica's primitive African Christianity, and the neo-Platonism of Ambrose and Simplicianus all opened up different potential worlds of meaning (teleological horizons) for Augustine and helped him address the developmental tensions in his life in different ways. What Christian neo-Platonism did for Augustine can only partially be understood on psychoanalytic grounds. Augustine's Christian neo-Platonic God-image has to be understood with what Ricoeur would call a hermeneutic phenomenology—a careful description of the "mode of being-in-the-world" that the symbol opens up for the interpreter (Ricoeur 1981, 114–16). This Christian neo-Platonic God gave Augustine a sense of living trustingly before the empathic and constant face of the ground of all being. The psychoanalytic interpretation of religion must incorporate within it this descriptive moment in order to discern the prospective world of possibility (the teleology) that the symbol opens to those who confront it.

But to discern the full meaning of the religious symbol and experience requires the archeological interpretation of the conflict of the self brought to the symbol, which the symbol in some way addresses. Augustine's personal appropriation of the Christian neo-Platonic God-image functions as an integrating symbol for him not only because of the teleological world of trust, constancy, and responsiveness that it opens to him. It is a symbol also because of the archeology of narcissistic injury and oedipal jealousy that is both projected onto the symbol yet is to some extent transformed by it. As Ricoeur points out, symbols, in contrast to symptomatic signs, are growth producing precisely because of their double meaning and twofold movement—a backward-pointing archeology in tension with and to a degree transformed by a forward-moving teleology. Hermeneutic phenomenology is needed to describe the teleology; psychoanalysis is needed to account for the archeology. The full meaning of the symbol is grasped by a double interpretive movement that includes them both (Ricoeur 1970, 459–93).

This leads me to the final issue—the possible contribution of the psychoanalytic interpretation of religion to the philosophy of religion. By the philosophy of religion, I mean that reflective enterprise designed to test the truth and value of religious thought and practice. Much of the psychoanalytic interpretation of religion has entered too quickly and too incautiously into the province of the philosophy of religion—that is, philosophical reflection on what is true and good about a particular religious expression.

There are many approaches to the philosophy of religion. The psychoanalytic interpretation of religion has tended to gravitate, more or less unconsciously, toward what philosophers would call the pragmatic evaluation of religion, an approach to religion that was best articulated by the American pragmatists William James (1902) and John Dewey (1934). That is to say that the psychoanalytic interpretation asks about the value or the good of religion, generally with regard to some quality seen as essential to mental health. Because of the obvious projective element in most religious ideation, some psychoanalytic approaches, particularly Freud's, have also advanced questions about the truth of religion—that is, whether religious symbols refer to anything beyond the subjective feelings and conflicts of religious people (Freud, *S.E.* 21:22–24). But most philosophically sophisticated psychoanalytic interpretations of religion today are willing to admit that psychoanalysis, as a form of psychology, cannot on its own grounds make and sustain the metaphysical judgment that all symbolizations of religion have no referent other than subjective needs. Hence, most psychoanalytic interpretations of religion are more like the majority of the studies cited in this chapter; they attempt to determine the consequences of religious expression for some condition, such as mental health, into which psychoanalysis is presumed to have some special insight.

The argument thus usually follows the rough contours of the pragmatic approach to the philosophy of religion. However, the issue at stake then becomes the assumptions made about the health values that are used to judge the religious phenomena. James and Dewey had both health values and moral values in mind when they evaluated religion. But psychoanalysis tends to restrict itself to some model of psychological health and to this extent should be seen as a somewhat narrow form of the pragmatic argument.

Here the plot thickens; even within the psychoanalytic tradition considerably different models of health are implicit or explicit in the different schools. With the introduction of self-psychology into psychoanalytic thinking (and to a considerable extent my point applies to the introduction of object-relations theory as well) self-cohesion and relational values now become more central to health than values pertaining to control and autonomous initiative, thought by some to be more typical of qualities valued by orthodox psychoanalysis (Kohut 1977, 206–8, 224–25). Hence, the later developments present a somewhat different, and perhaps broader, view of health—one that may help us see value dimensions that we formerly overlooked in certain religious expressions. Recent developments in psychoanalysis cannot tell us whether the God that Augustine learned to worship actually exists, but they can help us to see more favorably the possible human modes of being-in-the-world implied by this God. They further encourage us to entertain hypotheses about what it might be like to live in a world where such a God was indeed thought to exist. Looking at Augustine from this perspective helps us to see new similarities between Augustine's life and our own lives and also invites us to imagine whether his vision has relevance for the narcissistic wounds of the modern era.

At this point, the psychoanalytic interpretation of Augustine turns into a hermeneutic conversation of a kind suggested by Hans-Georg Gadamer (1982, 235–344). But now the conversation is not simply between the prospective and teleological dimensions of various modern visions in comparison to the prospective and teleological vision in certain classic texts. The conversation now ranges between modern archeologies and teleologies in comparison to the archeology and the teleology of Augustine's classic text. Augustine's *Confessions* lends itself particularly well to such a multidimensional conversation and helps us imagine possibilities for life that the modern world is inclined to forget.

References

Augustine, St. *The Confessions of St. Augustine.* Translated by Rex Warner. New York: New American Library, 1963.

Bakan, David. "Some Thoughts on Reading Augustine's *Confessions.*" *Journal for the Scientific Study of Religion* 5 (1965):149–52.

Brown, Peter. *Augustine of Hippo.* Berkeley: University of California Press, 1967.

Burrell, David. "Reading *The Confessions* of Augustine: An Exercise in Theological Understanding." *Journal of Religion* 50 (1970):327–51.

Capps, Don. "Parabolic Events in Augustine's Autobiography." *Theology Today* 40 (1983):260–72.

———. "Augustine as Narcissist." *Journal of the American Academy of Religion* 53 (1985):115–27.

Cohler, Bertram. "Personal Narrative and Life Courses." In *Life Span Development and Behavior,* edited by P. Baltes and O. Brim, Jr. New York: Academic Press, 1982.

Dewey, John. *A Common Faith* (1934). New Haven: Yale University Press, 1960.

Dittes, James. "Continuities Between the Life and Thought of Augustine." *Journal for the Scientific Study of Religion* 5 (1965):130–40.

Dixon, Sandra. "The Many Layers of Meaning in Moral Arguments: A Self-Psychological Case Study of Augustine's Arguments for Coercion." Unpublished manuscript. Divinity School, University of Chicago, 1988.

Dodds, E. R. "Augustine's Confessions: A Study of Spiritual Maladjustment." *The Hibbert Journal* 26 (1927–28):459–73.

Erikson, Erik. *Young Man Luther.* New York: W. W. Norton, 1958.

———. *Life, History and the Historical Moment.* New York: W. W. Norton, 1975.

Fredriksen, Paula. "Augustine and His Analysts: The Possibility of a Psychohistory." *Soundings* 61 (1978):206–27.

Freud, Sigmund. *The Future of an Illusion* (1927). *Standard Edition of the Complete Psychological Works of Sigmund Freud,* vol. 21. Edited and translated by James Strachey. London: Hogarth Press, 1961.

Gadamer, Hans-Georg. *Truth and Method.* New York: Crossroad, 1982.

Gay, Volney. "Augustine: The Reader as Selfobject." *Journal for the Scientific Study of Religion* 25 (1985):64–75.

Hartmann, Heinz. *Essays on Ego Psychology.* New York: International Universities Press, 1950.

James, William. *The Varieties of Religious Experience* (1902). New York: Doubleday, 1978.

Kligerman, Charles. "A Psychoanalytic Study of the Confessions of St. Augustine." *Journal of the American Psychoanalytic Association* 5 (1957):469–84.

Kohut, Heinz. *The Analysis of the Self.* New York: International Universities Press, 1971.

———. *The Restoration of the Self.* New York: International Universities Press, 1977.

———. *How Does Analysis Cure?* Chicago: University of Chicago Press, 1984.

Olney, James. *Metaphors of Self.* Princeton: Princeton University Press, 1972.

Ricoeur, Paul. *Freud and Philosophy.* New Haven: Yale University Press, 1970.

———. *Hermeneutics and the Human Sciences.* Cambridge: Cambridge University Press, 1981.

Rigby, Paul. "Paul Ricoeur, Freudianism, and Augustine's *Confessions.*" *Journal of the American Academy of Religion* 53 (1985):93–114.

Woollcott, Philip. "Some Considerations of Creativity and Religious Experience in St. Augustine of Hippo." *Journal for the Scientific Study of Religion* 5 (1966):273–83.

9 Psychoanalysis and Religion: Current Status of a Historical Antagonism

Ernest Wallwork and Anne Shere Wallwork

The opposition between psychoanalysis and religion has modified considerably since Freud's iconoclastic attack on theism in *The Future of an Illusion* (1927). Psychoanalysts today are far less inclined than Freud and his immediate followers to assume that psychoanalysis either undermines the validity of religious beliefs or shows religious convictions and practices to be necessarily psychopathological.[1] Nevertheless, if the historical antagonism between psychoanalysis and religion is no longer as acute as it once was, tension continues to exist between these two contrasting visions of the human being's place in the world. Although there has been a gradual parting of the ways with Freud's expressly hostile attitude, psychoanalysts continue to favor secular alternatives to traditional religious beliefs and practices. The present chapter seeks briefly to set forth the prevailing contemporary psychoanalytic views of religion and to explore the reasons why, despite their greater tolerance for and appreciation of the religious worldview, psychoanalysts tend to remain fundamentally areligious in their basic outlook.

Theoretical Advance and the Lessening of Psychoanalytic Hostility toward Religion

One reason Freud's outright hostility toward religion no longer holds such sway among today's psychoanalysts is that the founder's faith in empirical science as the sole legitimate mode of access to truth and reality has been softened. In responding to such scientific detractors of their own discipline as Karl Popper (1962) and Adolf Grünbaum

(1984), psychoanalysts have found it necessary to acknowledge that much in psychoanalysis itself goes beyond the empirically verifiable. This is true not only in terms of the general philosophy-of-science proposition that a scientific theory *always* goes beyond the facts that support it, in that facts do not exist except as defined within the context of some theory, but also because the unique endeavor that is psychoanalysis depends in part upon modes of knowing or insights that are not empirically demonstrable—or at least not in the manner of the hard sciences. Thus, it is now commonplace for defenders of psychoanalysis to cite hermeneuticists such as Paul Ricoeur (1970, 1981) and Jürgen Habermas (1971) to the effect that we know human beings and the world in which they live to a significant degree by interpreting discourse and texts—that is, through the modes of knowing that involve the empathic understanding (*Verstehen*) traditionally employed in the humanities, including religious studies.[2]

This is not to deny that some psychoanalytic propositions, such as the theory of child development and the etiology of the major characterological disorders, are capable of being empirically proven or disproven. But it is to acknowledge the limits of psychoanalysis's empirical supports—and this realization tends to legitimate nonempirical modes of knowing that are sometimes invoked in defense of religion. Appreciation of the interpretative or hermeneutical aspects of psychoanalysis evokes in the psychoanalyst an epistemological humility, insofar as psychoanalytic knowledge is seen as existing alongside other ways of knowing not only in allied sciences such as biology, neurology, and sociology, but also in such humanistic fields as literary criticism, aesthetics, philosophy, and even religious studies.

The shift in focus from the oedipal to the preoedipal origins of some religious beliefs and practices, which has come about as a consequence of the insights of psychoanalytic ego psychology, object-relations theory, post-Lacanian French psychoanalysis, and Kohutian self-psychology, has also led psychoanalysts today to be more open to the positive functions of religion and to recognize that Freud's criticism of immature and defensive forms of religiosity does not necessarily apply to all forms of religious faith and practice. Freud stressed that religious beliefs and practices suppress instinctual drives and encourage infantile substitutes for mature behavior. Contemporary analysts, while still keeping sight of the ways in which traditional religion can tap and, indeed, exploit unconscious motivations stemming from infancy, do not discount that, at its best, religion can reinforce such essential ego strengths as trust and the capacity for intimacy, play, and care. Even the regression that religions trigger, which Freud depicted as invariably corroding rationality and mature adaptability, is now often viewed as potentially positive when such regression is, like creative art, "in the service of the ego" and mature character strengths (Kris 1952).

Psychoanalyst Erik Erikson goes so far as to argue that no mature person can function adequately without some sort of ideological support for the trust, hope, and capacity for intimacy that infants first learn in relating to their mothers. Erikson implies that a secular ideology, such as humanism, may function as well as or better than a theistic orientation in reaffirming these vital ego strengths. However, the point is not the relative advantages of secular versus religious ideologies, but the fact that Freud's claim that religion is necessarily psychically dysfunctional because of its ties to developmentally early motivations and modes of thought has been turned on its head by such prominent psychoanalysts as Erikson (1964), Pruyser (1983), and Meissner (1984).[3] From this perspective, religion is viewed as sometimes providing ideological support for bedrock psychic strengths, precisely because of its origins and continued involvement in the earliest psychological tasks.

Of course, there remain those who dismiss the possibility of more mature, less defensive modes of religiosity and hold that a fully analyzed patient must necessarily end up being irreligious. But many, even though holding with Julia Kristeva that "the experience of psychoanalysis can lead to renunciation of faith with clear understanding" (1987, 26), would refrain from judging all religious belief and practice as necessarily immature, pathological, or defensive. This is based on the analyst's ethical stance of respect for the patient's right to form his or her own opinion, independent of authoritarian dictates. Intolerance of difference in worldviews would be at odds with the spirit of psychoanalytic inquiry. It is not self-evident that a successful analysis must necessarily produce an atheist. Indeed, as Kristeva has suggested (1987, 26), atheism itself might be the product of repression that a successful analysis would have to uncover before a move toward either faith or renunciation of faith could be made. All of this suggests that although what psychoanalysts learn from their patients may highlight the ways in which traditional religion exploits unconscious infantile motivations, evidence from the couch does not preclude the possibility of more mature, less defensive modes of religiosity. At least theoretically, there appears to be no reason why in some cases a successful analysis might not lead a believer to drop defensive and infantile modes of religiosity in favor of more mature and adaptive religious beliefs and practices.

The Continuing Tension: Psychoanalytic and Religious Worldviews

Although analysts have become both less dogmatic about the claims of their discipline and more appreciative of the possibilities of mature religion, the rapprochement between psychoanalysis and religion is definitely a limited one. Most psychoanalysts themselves are non-believers, and while they may take a more hands-off position about where their patients end up, they often presume for themselves a fundamental tension between psychoanalysis and traditional religion.

One obvious source of this tension is the blatantly antireligious content of Freud's own work. *Totem and Taboo, Group Psychology and the Analysis of the Ego, The Future of an Illusion, Civilization and Its Discontents,* and *Moses and Monotheism* all contain powerful indictments of religion that are read by every analyst-in-training, with the result that formative attention continues to be directed to the immature and defensive aspects of religion, whether or not the more positive functional aspects brought forth by post-Freudian theoretical developments are also highlighted.

A more fundamental ground for the opposition between psychoanalysis and religion resides in the deep chasm that separates the psychoanalytic worldview[4] from that of traditional religion. The most salient characteristic of the psychoanalytic worldview is its thoroughly naturalistic, this-worldly orientation. Psychoanalysts treat the "out of the ordinary" phenomena that religious persons take as signs of a transcendent or spiritual realm as perfectly natural occurrences. Thus, the psychoanalyst specializes in looking for the unacknowledged but natural instinctual, developmental, and conflictual origins of those uncanny or mysterious experiences that magicians, soothsayers, miracle workers, priests, and ministers have traditionally used as evidence of the work of unseen spiritual powers, gods or God.[5] What cannot be explained psychologically is thought to be explicable in terms of such other behaviorial sciences as sociology and anthropology or by an interdisciplinary combination of insights drawn from several of the human sciences.

It is this naturalistic aspect that most clearly distinguishes the psychoanalytic worldview from the religious one. But the other characteristics of psychoanalysis that Freud stressed—namely, its openness to continuing self-criticism and to change—also provide realistic points of difference that once led to antagonism and now undergird indifference. For example, Freud thought that religions always postulate closed worldviews that solve "all the problems of our existence uniformly on the basis of one overriding hypothesis" and leave "no question unanswered" (*S.E.* 22:158). He recognized somewhat pejoratively, as something soothing to be surrendered with mature adherence to the reality principle, that "the possession of a *Weltanschauung* of this kind is among the ideal wishes of human beings," because "believing in it one can feel secure in life, one can know what to strive for, and how one can deal most expediently with one's emotions and interests" (*S.E.* 22:158).

In contrast, science for Freud was always nondogmatic and self-critical. He wrote that the scientific *Weltanschauung*

> scarcely deserves such a grandiloquent title, for it is not all-comprehensive, it is too incomplete and makes no claim to being self-contained and to the construction of systems. Scientific thought is still very young among human beings; there are too many of the great problems which it has not yet been able to solve. A *Weltanschauung* erected upon science has, apart from its emphasis on the real external world, mainly negative traits, such as submission to the truth and rejection of illusions. [*S.E.* 22:181–82]

The comparison of religion and science posed by Freud is not entirely fair, of course. There are "fundamentalist" scientists who are just as "literal" about their findings and dogmatic about their theories as orthodox religious believers, and there are believers who are as open to continuing dialogue about their faith as Freud's archetypical scientist. Moreover, sophisticated versions of traditional religions—for example, those espoused by theologians such as David Tracy (1987)—can seek to locate man in the cosmos without necessarily providing a closed system. But as a broad typology, Freud's contention does have some basis and hits a responsive chord with analysts' self-understanding and their understanding of traditional religion.

It is worth noting that when Freud identified psychoanalysis with "the scientific worldview," he had in mind something that is considerably richer than what is conveyed by the English word "science."[6] The German term Freud uses, *Wissenschaft,* points toward a "this-worldly" rationalism, in that it includes such rationalistic disciplines as ethics and law as well as such interpretative disciplines in the humanities as history and clinical psychotherapy. As Freud says of his perspective, it involves "the intellectual working-over" of carefully scrutinized observations, but these may be gleaned from a variety of sources, many of them previously suspect, such as dreams and fantasies.

There is thus within psychoanalysis itself an interesting tension that parallels the conflict between psychoanalysis and religion. Although a rationalistic secular orientation leads Freud and most of his followers to reject as patently absurd and spurious claims about a supersensual or transcendent realm derived from "revelation, intuition or divination" (*S.E.* 22:159), psychoanalysis itself recognizes the importance of fantasy and imagination in understanding. Indeed, these are the very tools of analysis, for both the analysand's free association and the analyst's evenly suspended judgment make use of the free play of emotionally laden associations in probing for the truth.

Even at the level of metatheory, Freud acknowledges the imaginative and mythological nature of his hypotheses and speculations. (See, e.g., *S.E.* 14:77; *S.E.* 22:211.)[7] What psychoanalysis opposes is not illusion per se but lack of reflection about the unconscious wishes that enter into the creation of illusions and defensive opposition to critical examination of the works of the imagination with respect to their truthfulness. Freud's disparagement of religious illusion thus by no means entails a similar disparagement of illusion in other spheres of life.[8] As Freud puts it, illusions may be valued as long as they "are recognized as such" (*S.E.* 21:80).

Current Views of Illusion

There is thus something fundamentally uncharitable, to say the least, about the current vogue of using Winnicott's theories of illusion to attack Freud on the grounds that he wished to rule out illusion per se. (See, e.g., Meissner 1984, 177.) The psychoanalytic proponents of religion who make this claim argue that Freud's worldview seems too "sterile" and "harsh, without color or variety, without the continual enrichment of man's creative capacities" (Meissner 1984, 177). But this is certainly a misreading, born of a wish to highlight the richness of religious experience by comparing it with the allegedly cold, scientific world offered up by Freud.

Be that as it may, the use that Meissner and a number of other psychoanalytically informed scholars have made of Winnicott's theory of how illusion functions in the realm of transitional reality has certainly augmented the depth-psychological understanding of religion. Rizzuto, for instance, has taken Winnicott's theories about the importance of transitional objects for mediating the individual's relationship to his or her environment in childhood and throughout life and applied them to the "God-representation," which Rizzuto presents as performing a similarly crucial function. Like the child's teddy bear or blanket, the God-representation stands at the border between inside and outside, between subject-reality and external-reality. Unlike the teddy bear, however, the God-representation evolves as the person matures in accordance with developmental criteria and can therefore provide the growing person with crucial psychic support throughout the life stages. According to Rizzuto, this means that

> reality and illusion are not contradictory terms. Psychic reality—whose depths Freud so brilliantly unveiled—cannot occur without that specifically human transitional space for play and illusion. To ask a man to renounce a God he believes in may be as cruel and as meaningless as wrenching a child from his teddy bear so that he can grow up. We know nowadays that teddy bears are not toys for spoiled children but part of the illusory substance of growing up. Each developmental stage has transitional objects appropriate for the age and level of maturity of the individual. After the oedipal resolution God is a potentially suitable object, and if updated during each crisis of development, may remain so through maturity and the rest of life. Asking a mature, functioning individual to renounce his God would be like asking Freud to renounce his own creation, psychoanalysis, and the "illusion" promise of what scientific knowledge can do. This is, in fact, the point. Men cannot be men without illusions. The type of illusion we select—science, religion, or something else—reveals our personal history and the transitional space each of us has created between his objects and himself to find "a resting place" to live in. [Rizzuto 1979, 209]

Freud would turn over in his grave at this characterization of science as just one more illusion, the choice of which depends entirely on one's personal taste. But Rizzuto's suggestive application of Winnicott's ideas to religion has led at least one psychoanalyst, Jesuit William Meissner, to assert that "psychoanalysis has moved to the position of staking a claim for illusion as the repository of human creativity and the realm in which man's potentiality may find its greatest expression" (Meissner 1984, 183). Where for Winnicott, the area of illusory experience has to do with support for basic trust, Meissner wants illusion to support a faith that "carries with it a transcendent element . . . [that] is not merely a reassertion of basic trust . . . [but], rather, a creative assertion of something beyond trust"—a true religiosity (Meissner 1984, 183).

Few other psychoanalysts have followed Meissner's move into the domain of traditional religion from Winnicott's concept of the transitional object. This is probably because of belief based on their own work with persons at all stages of development that there are effective nonreligious ways of handling developmental crises and that the religious route carries with it a unique tendency either to trigger regression or lend itself to autistic use in regression triggered by other events. This association of religion with dysfunctional episodic regressions is acknowledged by even psychologically informed advocates of religion, such as Erikson, Pruyser, and Meissner. Thus, in the middle of his defense of an illusionist approach to religion, Paul Pruyser (1983, 173) observes that "among man's illusionistic pursuits religion is probably the most prone to autistic distortion." The reasons for this are several. As Freud saw so clearly and as contemporary analysts continue to appreciate, religion is tied to primitive wishes for parental nurture that can lead to dysfunctional regression. Religious symbols and myths invite fantasies of infantilizing kinship: God is like a mighty parent; people are children of God; God is love. Indeed, some rituals, such as the Eucharist, encourage in the most concrete terms the internalization of God by means of the primitive mode of incorporation (Pruyser 1983, 173–74).

Life, Death, and Interpretation

What is often not so clearly articulated are the many ways in which psychoanalysis handles the existential problems of affirming the meaningfulness of life in the face of such threats as death, injustice, and anomie, independently of and to some extent in competition with traditional religion. For example, psychoanalysis provides an opportunity for the patient to mourn the losses of a lifetime by reexperiencing painful affects on the couch. Religious ritual at its best functions similarly in funerals, memorial services, and rites of passage. But most psychoanalysts believe that psychoanalysis goes beyond religious ritual by providing the analysand with permanently augmented ego strengths as well as a wider range of behavioral options that enable the patient to handle new losses as they occur, beginning with the anticipated loss of the analyst with termination and extending to the eventual loss of loved ones and even of one's own life. It is also widely believed that psychoanalysis goes beyond religious ritual in expanding the patient's ego to include a self-analytic function (Schlessinger and Robbins 1983, 37–40) that enables the patient to face and work through new conflicts and crises as they arise.

Similarly, the psychoanalytic theory of instincts provides a kind of alternative naturalistic cosmology, in that it acknowledges forces at work in the world and within the individual that are a priori and not immediately or ever completely subject to rational control. Within the individual and the social aggregate, both Eros and aggression are understood to shape human experience and to provide the impetus for events in ways that parallel religious concepts of good and evil and of divine power. Like traditional religion, the psyche or soul is viewed by

Freud as shaped by forces that originate beyond itself. The difference is that in Freud's view, these life-sustaining forces are immanent in the natural world.[9]

Some recent students of religion have sought to defuse the power of psychoanalytic naturalism by arguing that even Freud was forced to acknowledge the mystery of the Unknown. In claiming that Freud was implicitly religious, they cite the following passage from *The Interpretation of Dreams*:

> There is at least one spot in every dream at which it is unplumbable—a navel, as it were, that is its point of contact with the unknown. [*S.E.* 4:111, n.1]

However, Freud is not referring here to the Unknown with a capital U, but to aspects of this world and subjective reactions to them that are not yet known. For Freud, that which is not yet known is not beyond this world. In a later passage, he returns to the navel metaphor:

> The dream-thoughts to which we are led by interpretation cannot, from the nature of things, have any definite endings; they are bound to branch out in every direction into the intricate network of our world of thought. It is at some point where this meshwork is particularly close that the dream-wish grows up, like a mushroom out of its mycelium. [*S.E.* 5:525]

It is the inexhaustiveness of the interpretability of dreams that makes them in a sense unknowable, not a transcendent reality.

It is noteworthy, however, that despite his naturalism, Freud remained profoundly aware of the degree to which we live in the world darkly. In his perspective, human beings are capable of continual self-transcendence. Our truths are always partial, though we can, if we take proper steps, know more today than yesterday and more tomorrow than today. Freud's appreciation of our partial grasp of truth contrasts strikingly with the dogmatic and monolithic naturalism of nineteenth-century materialism and led him to describe his own, ever-evolving theories repeatedly as "myths" and "scaffolding." Freud's position is thus close to what Harvard Divinity School Professor Wilfred Cantwell Smith (1988) describes as "positive secularism," which retains a sense of mystery yet to be explored as a part of secularism, as opposed to "negative secularism," which denies the existence of any such mysteries.

It is part of the fascination of Freud's critique of the religious *Weltanschauung* that he accuses it of having lost touch with the sense of reality as an unfolding process and our creative involvement in that

process. The problem with the religious worldview for Freud is that it
professes to solve too many problems simplistically (*S.E.* 22:158). In
contrast, the virtue of scientific thought, in Freud's opinion, is that it
keeps us in touch with the mysteries of life that remain to be addressed. Science, he writes,

> is still very young among human beings; there are . . . many of the great
> problems which it has not yet been able to solve. A *Weltanschauung*
> erected upon science has, apart from its emphasis on the real external
> world, mainly negative traits, such as submission to the truth and rejec-
> tion of illusions. [*S.E.* 22:182]

Freud's ideal of the truth is indebted to the Greco-Roman tradition.
Truth is elusive, yet not completely beyond our grasp, and there is a
strong moral imperative pushing us to grasp what of it we can while
recognizing that it always remains partially beyond our reach. It is in-
cumbent upon us to search for truth and to live in terms of what we
have learned. This sense of Truth with a capital T is even proclaimed
by Freud as "Gott Logos," as the only transcendent ideal to which the
individual and humanity can attach their hopes for the future. Thus, in
Future of an Illusion, Freud writes:

> The primacy of the intellect lies, it is true, in a distant . . . future, but
> probably not in an *infinitely* distant one. It will presumably set itself the
> same aims as those whose realization you expect from your God . . . ,
> namely, the love of man and the decrease of suffering. . . . Our God,
> *Logos,* will fulfil whichever of these wishes nature outside us allows, but
> he will do it very gradually, only in the unforeseeable future, and for a
> new generation of men. [*S.E.* 21:53–54]

As for those who falsely insist that religion in some form is necessary to morality, it is especially interesting to note that Freud's depic-
tion of the psychoanalytic worldview explicitly commits its devotée
to such moral values as "the love of man and the decrease of suffering." [10] In fact, Freud argues that the *Weltanschauung* underlying psychoanalysis calls for greater self-sacrifice than that enjoined by the
Judeo-Christian tradition:

> We desire the same thing [the love of man and the decrease of suffer-
> ing], but you [the religious believer] are more impatient, more exacting,
> and—why should I not say it?—more self-seeking than I and those on
> my side. You would have the state of bliss begin directly after death; you
> expect the impossible from it and you will not surrender the claims of
> the individual. [*S.E.* 21:54]

Notes

1. For an analysis of Freud's critical writings on religion, see Wallwork (1973).

2. Paul Ricoeur and Jürgen Habermas are concerned with defending the clinical enterprise as an *interpretative* process that centers on the patient's narrative as a means of understanding motivating beliefs and desires. The focus is on psychoanalytic procedure as a method of semantic explanation that depicts the agent's behavior in terms of motives (i.e., wishes, desires, reasons, purposes, intentions, etc.), not as an empirical method aimed at elucidating antecedent causes. Their hermeneutic defense of psychoanalysis is convincingly predicated on the notion that human behavior cannot be fully explained without taking account of the meanings and motivations of human subjects as these are expressed in the signs and symbols by which human beings communicate the meaning of what they are about. The hermeneuticists take very seriously the issue of the proof and validity of psychoanalytic interpretations and offer such criteria as narrative coherence, praxis, the verification of hypothetical predictions, and the correlation between fact and theory.

3. For further discussion of Erikson's work on religion, see Wallwork (1973b).

4. Freud is sometimes interpreted as having disputed the assumption that everyone needs such a comprehensive framework and value orientation, on the basis of a statement in *New Introductory Lectures* that psychoanalysis does not give rise to a *Weltanschauung* (*S.E.* 22:158–82). But Freud is not here disputing the need for a worldview or even psychoanalysis's acceptance of one. His point is rather that psychoanalysis does not need to construct a worldview of its own because it already relies on the scientific one.

5. For example, from the psychoanalytic perspective, the experience of religious faith and of transforming, transcendent power from beyond the self can be understood as a repetition of the infant's core identity-forming experiences, which originate within a symbiotically structured relationship with the mother. In this earliest relation, there is not yet a differentiation between an I and a not-I. According to Heinz Lichtenstein (1961) the primal mother corresponds to what is later understood to be the surrounding universe and the infant to an organ within this totality. "Just as an organ within an organism is both 'separate' and 'symbiotic,' the infant is one with the mother, but simultaneously there is a primary relatedness of a part to a whole" (Lichtenstein 1961, 202). In later life, religious faith and experiences of "the holy" recapture the nucleus of the infant's experience in relating to the primal mother.

Christopher Bollas's work on the mother as "the transformational object" elaborates on this account of adult religiosity. Bollas observes that the infant initially experiences the mother not as an object but as "a process of transformation"—as "enviro-somatic transformer of the subject." Bollas argues that preverbal memory of this identification explains the religious desire to surrender to a transcendent process that alters the self. He writes:

In many religious faiths . . . the subject believes in the deity's actual potential to transform the total environment, thus sustaining the terms of the earliest object tie within a mythic structure—where knowledge remains symbiotic (i.e., the wisdom of faith). . . . [The] uncanny quality [of many religious experiences is due to] . . . being reminded of something never cognitively apprehended, but existentially known, the memory of the ontogenetic process, rather than thought or fantasies that occur once self is established. . . . This anticipation of being transformed by an object . . . inspires the subject with a reverential attitude toward the object, so that . . . the adult subject tends to nominate the object as sacred. [1979, 98–99]

6. The German philosopher Wilhelm Windelband compares *Wissenschaft* to the Greek *philosophia,* pointing out that it "includes much more than the English and French *science."* Wilhelm Windelband, *Präludien,* quoted in Ringer (1969, 103).

7. Freud wrote Einstein in 1932: "It may perhaps seem to you as though our theories are a kind of mythology. . . . But does not every science come in the end to a kind of mythology like this? Cannot the same be said to-day of your own Physics?" (*S.E.* 22:211).

8. For instance, Freud's attitude toward illusion in art was very different from his attitude toward religion. This is because, from a naturalistic perspective, the acknowledged illusion involved in art represents an acceptable way of obtaining satisfaction from life in this world, whereas religion, insofar as it denies its illusory character, poses a positive threat to the unflinching truthfulness that lies at the heart of psychoanalytic inquiry.

9. *Beyond the Pleasure Principle,* Freud's most manifestly religious work, expanded on the concepts of drives to postulate both the life instincts (Eros) and the death instinct (Thanatos) as the constructive and destructive forces, respectively, at work in the universe. The life instincts are defined by Freud as the constructive or assimilative forces at work in the universe that aim "to establish ever greater unities and to preserve them" (*S.E.* 18:49; 23:148). They struggle against the death instinct, which undoes connections and pushes for destruction, for as long as life exists. This naturalistic cosmic orientation of Freud's goes well beyond the clinical theory that most analysts accept, but the fact that Freud could engage in this kind of metathought points to the potential richness of the psychoanalytic perspective and contradicts the religionists' characterization of psychoanalysis as too narrow to deal with the larger questions of life and meaning.

10. For a discussion of the foundation of morals in Freudian theory and some of its consequences for ethics, see Wallwork 1982 and 1986.

References

Bollas, Christopher. "The Transformational Object." *International Journal of Psycho-Analysis* 60 (1979):97–107.
Erikson, Erik. *Young Man Luther.* New York: W. W. Norton, 1964.

Freud, Sigmund. *The Standard Edition of the Complete Psychological Works of Sigmund Freud.* Edited and translated by James Strachey. 24 vols. London: Hogarth, 1953–74.
  The Interpretation of Dreams (1900), vols. 4–5.
  Totem and Taboo (1913), vol 13.
  "On Narcissism" (1914), vol. 14.
  Beyond the Pleasure Principle (1920), vol. 18.
  Group Psychology and the Analysis of the Ego (1921), vol. 18.
  The Future of an Illusion (1927), vol. 21.
  Civilization and Its Discontents (1930), vol. 21.
  New Introductory Lectures (1933), vol. 22
  "Why War?" (1933), vol. 22.
  Moses and Monotheism (1939), vol. 23.
  An Outline of Psycho-Analysis (1940), vol. 23.
Grünbaum, Adolf. *The Foundations of Psychoanalysis.* Berkeley: University of California Press, 1984.
Habermas, Jürgen. *Knowledge and Human Interests.* Boston: Beacon Press, 1971.
Kris, Ernst. *Psychoanalytic Explorations in Art.* New York: International Universities Press, 1952.
Kristeva, Julia. *In the Beginning Was Love: Psychoanalysis and Faith.* Translated by Arthur Goldhammer. New York: Columbia University Press, 1987.
Lichtenstein, Heinz. "Identity and Sexuality: A Study of the Interrelationship in Man." *Journal of the American Psychoanalytic Association* 9 (1961): 179–260.
Meissner, William W. *Psychoanalysis and Religious Experience.* New Haven: Yale University Press, 1984.
Popper, Karl R. *Conjectures and Refutations.* New York: Basic Books, 1962.
Pruyser, Paul. *The Play of the Imagination: Toward a Psychoanalysis of Culture.* New York: International Universities Press, 1983.
Ricoeur, Paul. *Freud and Philosophy: An Essay on Interpretation.* New Haven: Yale University Press, 1970.
———. "The Question of Proof in Freud's Psychoanalytic Writings." In *Paul Ricoeur: Hermeneutics and the Human Sciences,* edited by John B. Thompson. New York: Cambridge University Press, 1981.
Ringer, Fritz K. *The Decline of the German Mandarins: The German Academic Community, 1890–1933.* Cambridge, Mass.: Harvard University Press, 1969.
Rizzuto, Ana-Maria. *The Birth of the Living God.* Chicago: University of Chicago Press, 1979.
Schlessinger, Nathan, and Robbins, Fred P. *A Developmental View of the Psychoanalytic Process: Follow-up Studies and Their Consequences.* New York: International Universities Press, 1983.
Smith, Wilfred Cantwell. "Transcendence." *Harvard Divinity Bulletin* 18 (1988): 10–15.

Tillich, Paul. *The Courage To Be.* New Haven: Yale University Press, 1952.

Tracy, David. *Plurality and Ambiguity: Hermeneutics, Religion, Hope.* New York: Harper & Row, 1987.

Wallwork, Ernest. "Sigmund Freud: The Psychoanalytic Diagnosis—Infantile Illusion." (a) "Erik H. Erikson: Psychosocial Resources for Faith." (b) In *Critical Issues in Modern Religion,* edited by Roger Johnson, Ernest Wallwork, et al. Englewood Cliffs, N.J.: Prentice-Hall, 1973.

————. "Thou Shalt Love Thy Neighbor as Thyself: The Freudian Critique." *Journal of Religious Ethics* 10 (1982):264–319.

————. "A Constructive Freudian Alternative to Psychotherapeutic Egoism." *Soundings* 69 (1986):145–64.

10   Sparks from God: A Phenomenological Sketch of Symbol

Graham M. Schweig

Psychoanalysis and the study of religion are both sciences involved in the interpretation of human thought, feeling, and action. Both aim to integrate humans with their worlds. Psychoanalysts seek to decipher and interpret the data of the psychic world in order to reveal the meaningful messages of the unconscious to human awareness. Scholars of religion seek to interpret the data of the sacred world in order to reveal the nature of divinity to persons in various cultures.

As interpreters of different worlds, students of both religion and psychoanalysis strive for methodological accuracy and hermeneutical integrity in their respective approaches. Although psychoanalytic theorists and scholars of religion recognize procedures unique to their specific disciplines, each group, as scientists in their own right, systematizes the results of their work to reflect the nature of psychological and religious phenomena. Indeed, there are many parallels between these diverse fields. But more important, they share the common task and challenge of interpreting a basic, universal structure of the way in which meaning, psychic or sacred, comes into being—the structure of *symbol.*

The purpose of this essay is to reflect on the challenges of interpreting meaning. The discussion of the meaning of symbol (and sign, a term often interchangeable with symbol) goes back far in the history of Western thought. However, I will not here focus on this long and rich history of symbol, nor dwell upon particular religious symbols, nor present a general typology of symbols. Rather, in this essay, from the perspective of one in the field of the study of religion, I will analyze symbolic being and experience, or symbol as a dimension of human reality. To this end, I will first review tensions in interpretation within the field of the study of religion, and then provide a phenomenological sketch of symbol. I will discuss subjective-existential dimensions of symbol, the structural elements within symbolization, the varieties of contexts, and the ontological dimensions of symbol. I will attempt to demonstrate how meaning comes into being by symbolic mediation, the essential structural dynamic of which consists of existentially and ontologically charged polarities, between the human and a world. Furthermore, I will suggest that the dynamic structure of symbol itself is a possible key to understanding the nature of metaphysical reality.

In dealing with data of symbol in any discipline of the human and social sciences, there is a tension between fulfilling the expectations of a rational and systematic science and fulfilling the requirements of depth analysis that does justice to the individual phenomenon. If the former is lacking, then the latter will appear unobjective and uninformed; if the latter is lacking, then the former will appear reductionistic and impersonal. In both cases, interpretation will be distorted. Emphasis of the former to the exclusion of the latter does not account for the uniquenesses in all human phenomena; emphasis of the latter to the exclusion of the former overlooks the universal qualities that exist. These hermeneutical imbalances are themselves symptoms of an incomplete understanding of the nature of symbol, and every interpreter of symbol must achieve a balance of these emphases. A healthy hermeneutical tension between both levels of emphases is necessary because the symbol itself, I will attempt to show, manifests this tension in its very structure. It is in such a hermeneutical tension that an interpreter may discover realms of meaning otherwise inaccessible. Differences of approach within the study of religion are worth briefly reviewing because of the way these differences anticipate the structure of symbol.

Two Approaches of Interpretation in the Study of Religion

The interpretation of symbol by scholars of religion, without a full appreciation of the existential and ontological polarities within the structure of symbol, has led in turn to different approaches within the field itself. To understand a symbol in all its uniqueness and particularity and at the same time understand a symbol as relatable to all other similar symbols in its class, each possessing universally recognized attributes, is the desirable hermeneutic balance to be achieved. No symbol can be so unique and exclusive that it becomes absolutely unrelatable and irrelevant; no symbol can be so uniform and exactly similar in content and context that it becomes possible to predict fully or precisely how meaning itself will unfold. Interpretation of symbolic phenomena must hold this hermeneutic tension, which—taking into consideration the existential and metaphysical levels of interaction—transcends the purely subjectivistic and objectivistic approaches.

The study of religion can encompass a broad spectrum of human inquiry. That the study of religion is also known as the history of religions, comparative religion, the science of religions, phenomenology of religion, religious studies, and so forth, attests to this breadth of disciplinary focus. Ninian Smart states that the study of religion should include an analysis of *all* ideological systems, which he calls "worldviews." According to Smart, explicitly "religious" phenomena do not comprise the total domain of religious study, but such study should extend to all "systems of belief which, through symbols and actions, mobilize the feelings and wills of human beings" (1983, 1). Wilfred Cantwell Smith, a historian of religion, takes this one step further when he states that "in comparative religion man is studying himself" (1976, 154). Thus the study of religion is necessarily polymethodic since it comprises such breadth of inquiry. Disciplines of other fields—such as anthropology, psychology, archeology, linguistics, and history—are often consulted or employed.

However, the study of religion also possesses its own discipline and set of procedures. Mircea Eliade states that "the historian of religions is preoccupied uniquely with *religious* symbols, that is, with those that are bound up with a religious experience or a religious conception of the world" (1959, 88). Eliade goes on to say that "while the research on symbols in general and religious symbolism in particular by specialists in other disciplines deserves his consideration, the historian of religions is obliged in the final analysis, to approach the subject with his own means of investigation and in his proper perspective" (89). Thus there is a tension within the field of the study of religion between those who emphasize the historical particularity and uniqueness of the religious dimension of human existence while promoting an all-encompassing discipline and those who emphasize the systematic classification of specifically "religious" phenomena while promoting particular methods of depth-analysis of the discipline. This tension is well expressed by Wilfred Smith when he comments upon Jung and Eliade in the following words:

> My studies have led me to the view that a symbol in principle never means exactly the same thing to any two persons (nor even necessarily

to any one person at different times), although on this both Carl Jung and Mircea Eliade, two of the greatest twentieth-century scholars in this realm, have tended to presume otherwise, without, I feel, having thought the matter through. [168]

There is a tension between approaches within the field of religion; Eliade states that in the final analysis the scholar of religion has techniques of investigation that allow for the systematic classification of religious phenomena, and Smith, with a view of the study of religion that is close to all-encompassing, insists upon the particularity of religious phenomena. This tension, however, is not altogether unhealthy; in the analysis of phenomena of the religious world or, for that matter, of the psychic world, uniquenesses and commonalities among phenomena must be observed simultaneously, because, as we shall see, meaning itself has incorporated these aspects of the data.

Subjective Dimensions of Symbol

The philosopher Susanne Langer states that in all scientific as well as artistic and religious pursuits humans are fundamentally symbol-making creatures (1982, 26–52). Mirroring thinkers such as Ernst Cassirer and Langer, Smart says that "once we look around us we find that our life is drenched in meanings, and everything has its symbolic sense, often changing, differing in one culture and time from others. The crosscultural exploration of religious and symbolic themes is a way we can understand this world of meanings" (33).

Wilfred Smith explains that the notion of symbol in general is a human concept, stating that "no building is objectively a temple. No space is objectively sacred. No object is objectively a symbol, in and of itself: an object becomes a symbol in the consciousness of certain persons" (167). Langer develops this idea that symbolizing is the process of mind, writing that "the material furnished by the senses is constantly wrought into *symbols,* which are our elementary ideas" (42). The experiential data received through the organs of sense undergo a process of symbolic transformation, a change of character, by being "sucked into the stream of symbols which constitutes the human mind" (42). This function of symbolic transformation within the mind is more essential than either the receiving or transmitting of symbols. It is in itself a primary human activity that goes on in conversation, dreaming, perceiving, and so forth. Indeed, Langer claims that symbolization is not merely an act of thought but an act prior to and essential to thought itself (41).

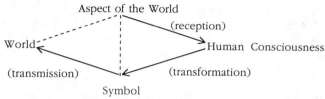

Figure 1

These symbolic transformations become our elementary ideas, and they are ordered and manipulated into functions of what we call reasoning, or discursive thought (Langer's first general category of symbolic types). Other symbolic transformations lend themselves not to discursive thinking as do science, mathematics, physics, and the like, but rather to presentational symbolization.[1]

Langer's ideas represented diagrammatically might look like Figure 1. Human consciousness receives an aspect of the world and transforms it into the stream of symbols, thereby creating a symbol of this aspect of world, and then transmits this symbol back into the world. In this diagram of Langer's process of symbol creation and function, the basic relationships among the components of the process can be seen. Symbol is related to the transformational process of mind as it interacts with an aspect of the world. What becomes noticeable when one scrutinizes this diagram is that some of the possible relationships among components (indicated by dotted lines) have not been explored by Langer. For example, the relationship between the symbol and the aspect of the world is not analyzed.

Although Langer shows us that the mind is a symbol creator, and Smith claims that a symbol should be understood not objectively but rather as a personal, subjective phenomenon, the subjective origin of symbol does not negate the power of the symbol. Once symbols are hurled back into the world for others to experience, they take on a life all their own.

The Structure of Symbol

In attempting to understand the structure of symbol, I will utilize ancient Indian poetics, hermeneutic philosophy, and the history-of-religions discipline. According to Indian poetics,[2] a symbol can be analyzed as having three moments: the literal, the connotative, and the suggestive. All symbols have a literal denotative dimension, which is established by convention or direct empirical experience. For example, the phrase "stars and stripes" conveys literally a mixture of two geometrical shapes: those of stars and stripes, nothing more, nothing less. However, the image of stars and stripes carries with it, unavoidably, the immediate connotation of an American flag, the established context within which the image of stars and stripes is known to all Americans. The third moment of the symbol of stars and stripes is the deeper meaning that the image suggests.[3] The image of stars and stripes could suggest innumerable things—say, freedom, or perhaps power and victory; or it could suggest the courage and sadness associated with the death of brave Americans. Thus the symbol stars and stripes can open up the whole patriotic world of meaning. In the Sanskrit *dhvani*, according to Indian poetic theory, the third moment of the symbol as "suggestion" is what gives poetic symbolism and imagery its power and poignant meaning. Since symbolic meaning is multivalent, the ability of the recipient of a symbol to understand specific symbolic meanings is dependent upon experiencing their corresponding contexts.

Contexts of Symbol

A symbol is not just the subjectively created and maintained representation of a mind; immediate contexts such as mythic narrative, greater contexts such as a symbol system or a historical tradition, and even wider contexts such as the culture within which a tradition thrives or metaphysical contexts (the universe or a sacred world) are all possible environments that breathe life into a symbol.

The interpreter of symbol must be able to identify the various contexts within which it functions. A context can be defined simply as the immediate environment within which a symbol receives its support and sustenance. Each context fits within a total ecology of contextual environments that make up a whole world which is mediated by symbol.

Any one symbol may possess more than one context, thus mediating more than one world or meaning to more than one person, or even the same person. It is not possible to analyze here all the categories of contexts that could be identified, but the enormous range of different possible contexts includes such examples as dreams, myths, specific episodes in one's life, a religious tradition, a political state, an economic system, a cultural practice, and so forth, depending on the extent of function of a particular symbol.

Wilfred Smith recognizes that symbol must mediate between humans and contexts of existence far greater than culture:

> it is not simply what the symbol itself means to persons, but what life means, what the universe means, in the light of that symbol. . . . there is no dispute that the meaning of things in human history lies in their relation to persons, in the interaction of human beings with them, and not in themselves as objects. [1976, 168]

Smith confirms here the necessity of an existential relation between human and symbol and the ontological function of symbol mediating cosmic meaning to humans, which I will discuss below. But the medial role of symbol possesses contexts more immediate than "universe," as Smith suggests. Every symbol, as Eliade explains, has a history, and the interpreter is obligated to restore all the meanings it has had throughout the course of its life as a symbol (1959, 105). In addition to the various contexts one may find throughout history, symbols often have similar counterparts (in either form or content) in other cultures. The delicate process of comparative analysis is required for examining this cross-cultural context.

Fundamentally, all symbols have at least a double context to consider, according to the literal form of symbol and its suggestive content. In Figure 2, the parallel contexts and worlds are illustrated. This structure is further complicated when there is more than one symbolic meaning; accordingly, there can be that many more contexts and worlds of meaning working through the same symbol. For example, the swastika is a symbol of geometric form, its literal moment. It is an ancient symbol that has appeared in many cultures.[4] To a Jew the swastika symbolizes the Holocaust and everything that the tragedy of Hitler's regime means. However, to a Hindu the swastika symbolizes auspiciousness. The word "swastika" itself is a Sanskrit word meaning "well-being." As the Jew and the Hindu gaze at the swastika symbol, something of the religious world is opened up for each of them. Thus the symbol can carry the meaning of catastrophic death (context[2]) and all-auspiciousness (context[3]), two very different meanings, at one and the same time.

Understanding the complexity of context in symbol is crucial to a discussion of the religious and psychoanalytic interpretation of symbol. As interpreters of symbol, the different fields of knowledge—such as theology, psychology, and anthropology—often constitute the various contexts within which one observes symbol at work. For example, the anthropologist Clifford Geertz defines religion based on the greater sociocultural context of symbol.[5] Moreover, Sigmund Freud provides psychological contexts for understanding religion in terms of a universal obsessional neurosis, or a form of human wish fulfillment, or as a

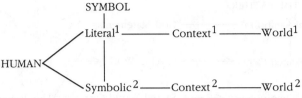

Figure 2

"consolation of life" without which one could not bear the "cruelties of reality" (*S.E.* 21:49). The interpretations of religious symbolism from the contexts of various fields of knowledge are valid so far as they fulfill the methodological and scientific requirements imposed from within their fields. The danger, however, of interpreting religion or religious symbolism from, for example, the psychoanalytic or anthropological perspective is that some scholars overextend the boundaries of their fields, as if they possessed larger or more numerous contexts for symbolic analysis than what actually is epistemologically appropriate. Such overextension of a field of knowledge can lead some scholars within that field to believe that they have a complete explanation or interpretation and to ignore any other possible explanations that may exist. On the other hand, theologians and historians of religion, who are perhaps most appropriately positioned to deal with the sine qua non of religion, fail to extend the boundaries of their fields enough to be able to account scientifically for their knowledge of divinity.

Let us take the example of the God-as-Father symbol. Freud, with the motive of determining its psychical origins, understands this religious symbol as being a result of a primordial longing for the father in the psychic world of humans; God, then, is an exalted father. Does this interpretation of God as Father necessarily deny the existence of God, or deny other relationships with the divinity that have nothing to do with father symbolism? No, not only because of the structure of symbol and its multivalency, which accommodates many layers of interpretive significance, including Freud's interpretation, but also because of the metaphysical significance of symbol itself. In Figure 3 (indicated by the dotted lines), the relationship between the two convening worlds, psychic and sacred, is neglected, as is the relationship between the interpreters of these worlds.

The twofold symbolic or suggestive meanings of the God-the-Father symbol are indicated in Figure 3, with their individually corresponding context-worlds and interpreters. The psychic world generates the

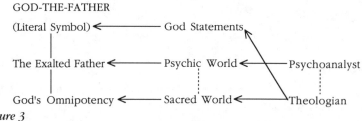

Figure 3

idea of the exalted father as the suggestive meaning, which Freud suggests is what is really meant by (to use his phrase) the "symbolic clothing" of the image of God-the-Father. Here there is an attempt to strip or deconstruct the symbol, to desymbolize if you will, while the literalness of the symbol is called into question. In contrast to this, the sacred world generates the idea of God's omnipotence, such that God possesses the capacity to relate personally with humans in this world as a father. Interpreters of religion or psychology understand the sacred or psychical origins of this God from their respective disciplines: The anthropocentric orientation of psychology identifies the origin of its God in the human mind. The theocentric orientation of theology identifies the origin of its God in the divine realm, a God who is experienced, revealed, and rationally understood. Although both of these orientations are valid, and both inform the symbol and give it meaning, they must participate in a greater hermeneutic openness whereby each informs the other, revealing even more of the symbol than is possible from the orientation of each discipline individually. This greater hermeneutic orientation will open up worlds of richness in the symbol.

Ontological Dimensions of Symbolic Meaning

A greater hermeneutic openness is possible when the subtleties of the dynamic structure of symbol are appreciated. There are paradoxical elements in the structure of symbol. Symbols possess an opacity that binds the literal and suggestive, or symbolic, moments together, and symbols possess a transparency that binds reality to the symbolic. Paul Ricoeur explains that symbols have the power to reveal and conceal (1978, 36). Symbols have an intentional structure similar to that of signs; they intend something beyond and they stand for this something. Aimed through the first, literal meaning of a symbol is a pointing beyond itself. Ricoeur states that unlike signs, which are *only* transparent in their ability to point, "symbolic signs are opaque: the first, literal, patent meaning analogously intends a second meaning which is not given otherwise than in the first. This opaqueness is the symbol's very profundity, an inexhaustible depth" (1978, 38).

An etymological analysis of symbol indicates the ontological relationality of symbol. The word "symbol," from the Greek verb *symballein,* means "to put together," "to throw together," "to compare," or "to contribute." A symbol involves putting one thing together with another, or comparing one thing with another, or contributing something to another. We have already seen that symbol connects human consciousness with a particular world of meaning, and as we shall see, symbol is an existential phenomenon through which human beings relate to the world. However, it is also true that world "contributes" a portion of itself to the appropriate symbolic form that can re-present it. The symbol is saturated with the presence of the symbolized, and the mind experiences this symbolic presence.

The symbol shares in the being of that which it *re*-presents; indeed, it is the ontological function of the symbol to extend the presence of that which is absent. This dimension of transparency is in an analogical form. The definition of symbol "to compare" implies analogy. Ricoeur points out that there is an "analogous bond" between symbol and symbolized, and he skillfully describes the ontological function of the symbol: it *gives* the symbolized to humans in an accessible way:

> In symbol I cannot objectivize the analogous relation that binds the second meaning to the first. By living in the first meaning I am drawn by it beyond itself: the symbolic meaning is constituted in and through the literal meaning, which brings about the analogy by giving the analogue. Unlike a comparison that we *look at* from the outside, symbol is the very movement of the primary meaning that makes us share in the latent meaning and thereby assimilates us to the symbolized, without our being able intellectually to dominate the similarity. This is the sense in which symbol "gives"; it gives because it is a primary intentionality that gives the second meaning. [1978, 38–39]

In Hans-Georg Gadamer's work *Truth and Method,* aesthetic language takes on special significance for understanding how consciousness interacts with the world, further revealing for us some of the paradoxical qualities of symbol. By examining aesthetic experience, Gadamer indicates what is involved in the phenomenon of meaning and illuminates the subtle ontological dimensions of the symbolic.

> The aesthetic experience is not just one kind of experience among others, but represents the essence of experience itself. . . . The work of art is understood as the perfecting of the symbolic representation of life, toward which every experience tends. [1975, 63]

Gadamer illustrates the paradoxical ontology of meaning coming into being by the example of "picture." A picture possesses an essential relation between that which is represented in the picture and the picture itself. A picture does not function as only a copy, like the reflection in a mirror, nor as the mere indication of a sign, nor as the pure standing-for representation of what is normally thought of as a symbol (135). The importance of the concept of picture is that it demonstrates how the being of that which is represented in the picture is transformed into the structure of a picture, by virtue of the fact that it takes on an "autonomous" reality and becomes an independent world unto itself. It also shows how the represented object in the picture still participates in and is "continuous" with the being of the original. The picture extends the being of that which is represented, illustrating the "transparency" of symbol, and in the process, it increases the very being of the symbolized. Concomitantly, the picture becomes an autonomous whole, illustrating the "opacity" of symbol, independent not only from what it represents but also from all reality. When that which is represented becomes transformed in the process of being represented, it takes on the quality of a structure in the sense of its exclusivity. Gadamer means here by structure that it has

> found its measure in itself and measures itself by nothing outside it. . . . It no longer permits of any comparison with reality as the secret measure of all copied similarity. It is raised above all such comparisons— and hence also above the question whether it is all real—because a superior truth speaks from it. [101]

This process encapsulates the way by which all meaning comes into being. Gadamer calls it "the transformation into structure" (99). Symbolic meaning is transmitted by the symbol, which is the transformation of an image of this world into a form that conveys another world, a structure that is continuous with and yet autonomous from both.

Polarities within the Structure of Symbol

The paradoxical dynamic within the structure of symbol, I propose, must be resolved by understanding it in terms of the nature of polarity.[6] These paradoxical elements found in the structure of symbol, which should not be thought of euphemistically as rationalized contradictions, I will refer to herein as "polarities." To explain what is meant by polarity I will contrast the ideas of "contradiction," "paradox," and "polarity."

Contradiction does not adequately describe the nature of these paradoxes because it contains two juxtaposed opposite elements that are seen, in rational terms, as irreconcilable on all levels. In a paradox, two opposing elements are juxtaposed and not reconciled, yet are accepted in a relation. Many scholars have said that theological language involves the inescapable element of paradox. John Macquarrie states that

> the paradox cannot be dissolved; it is inherent in the attempt by finite minds to reflect on ultimate issues. But even so we have a duty to reflect as deeply as possible and to show, so far as we can, that the paradox is a dialectical conjunction of opposites and not sheer nonsense or irreconcilable contradiction. [1966, 306]

While theology necessarily involves paradoxical language, it is important, as Macquarrie urges, to articulate what this "dialectical conjunction" of opposing elements is, and not to abandon rational explanation by resorting to mere paradoxical explanation.

Polarity, as I shall define it here, is certainly not contradiction, nor is it mere paradox. The word "polarity" implies more than just the mere juxtaposition of opposing qualities or states of being, as is found in paradox. Polarity implies an axial differentiation of a whole within which the poles are distinguished. The term further implies that those qualities placed in opposition within a greater whole, even if endowed with mutually exclusive existences and opposite tendencies from each other, are nevertheless bound or unified by a deeper underlying structure within which they are intrinsically related and connected. If two opposing elements that under some circumstances might be thought of as mere paradox can truly be shown to be related to each other as poles of a greater whole, then they could more appropriately be called a polarity. A polarity, however, does not always involve two mutually exclusive and totally independent elements and therefore does not always involve paradox. Paradox does not involve the reconciliation or resolution factor—that is, the connectedness between two opposing elements—that a polarity must demonstrate. The greater context that is required for resolving or rationally explaining the paradox, thereby raising it to the status of polarity, implies a deeper level of inquiry and analysis which I call "axiological" analysis.[7]

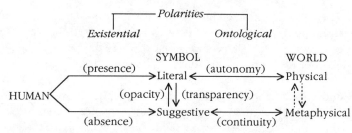

Figure 4

The word "axiology" is normally used in the philosophy of ethics, but it is also associated with the fields of aesthetics, religion, and economics. In general, the word refers to the "existence, nature, and criteria of value,"[8] and this is precisely what is involved in the interpretation of symbol. Axiological analysis of symbol must define the various polarities according to the existential-ontological context in which they are interrelated and must function within a greater system or arrangement of symbols.

The symbolic includes existential and ontological polarities, some of which I have tried to indicate in Figure 4. The experience of simultaneous presence and absence of the symbolized is the existential polarity. The tension between opacity and transparency of literal and symbolic moments of symbol, the power of symbol simultaneously to reveal a heightened sense of a world and yet to conceal that world, the autonomy of symbol as expressed in its ability to stand independently as a whole world unto itself, and yet the continuity of symbol in its simultaneous dependence upon a whole other world for its very existence—these are some of the ontological polarities of symbol.

When the interpreter of symbol observes and translates the ontological and existential polarities within the structure of a particular symbol, only then can such a symbol be understood in relation to other symbols similar in form, and not necessarily in meaning. The polarities within symbol are dependent upon a greater whole within which their dialectical conjunction makes rational sense, and this is precisely what must be understood before any individual symbolic phenomenon can be placed within the classification of a scientific system. I am suggesting here that, as far as possible, the total structure of meaning of a given symbol, along with the layered contexts it may possess, must be analyzed in order to avoid the reductionistic tendencies of typological analysis.

The Theologian as Interpreter

As a psychotherapist reveals the messages of the unconscious mind to the patient, a theologian reveals the messages of ancient scripture to the contemporary mind. As dreams are a primary source of information for the psychotherapist, myths are a primary source of information for the theologian. Myth is found in all cultures at all times in all religions. As a mode of human knowledge, myth can be understood to reveal different meanings as well as different aspects of reality. In those religious traditions that possess divine revelation and grace it is through the form of "myth" that aspects of supreme being are revealed. Myth is story that is thought to have no empirical basis in reality, and yet it is also understood as story that is more real than what is ordinarily considered as reality.

As mentioned earlier, myth forms a context within which symbols are functioning. Myth, according to Ernst Cassirer, along with art, language, and science, is a force "which produces and posits a world of its own" (1946, 8). As a symbolic form, myth is an organ of reality. Cassirer states that

> for the mind, only that can be visible which has some definite form; but every form of existence has its source in some peculiar way of seeing, some intellectual formulation and intuition of meaning. [8]

Myth, Cassirer goes on to say, has a definite structure:

> Mythic ideas . . . have their own inner lawfulness; they do not arise from a boundless caprice of the imagination, but move in definite avenues of feeling and creative thought. This intrinsic law is what mythology seeks to establish. Mythology is the science . . . of myth, or the science of the forms of religious conception. [15]

More specifically, myth is story that, as Langer describes,[9] is not mere fantasy, ordinary dreaming, or fairy tale; rather, it is

> recognition of natural conflicts, of human desire frustrated by non-human powers, hostile oppression, or contrary desires; it is a story of the birth, passion, and defeat by death which is man's common fate. Its ultimate end is not wishful distortion of the world, but serious envisagement of its fundamental truths; moral orientation, not escape. [Langer 1982, 176]

The twentieth-century Protestant theologian Rudolf Bultmann, in his *Theology of the New Testament,* states that the task of Christian theology is to explicate the theological thoughts of the New Testament in terms of human existence. Bultmann claims that in the New Testament itself there lies a meaningful message for humans in the modern world. This message is available to persons whose "believing self-understanding" is opened up by the kerygma[10] that is buried in the mythological language of the New Testament.

The challenge of interpreting the ancient revelational texts that are mythic in form is to recognize the differences between contemporary mythic language and world and the often starkly contrasting mythic language and world of the ancient tradition. In making such a comparison one is immediately confronted by a clashing of worldviews. Indeed, this challenge of interpreting the ancient religious text has been acutely felt by Bultmann; in his theology, he has depended upon an existential hermeneutic in order to create a meaningful and relevant interpretation of the New Testament for persons living in modern times. Bultmann observes that "the contrast between the ancient worldview of the Bible and the modern worldview is the contrast between two ways of thinking, the mythological and scientific" (1958, 38). For Bultmann there is an irreconcilable clash between the mythic worldview of the New Testament and the worldview of modern science. He claims that because the "mythic" descriptions of the various miraculous events in the New Testament do not conform to the modern scientific or historical worldviews, modern peoples simply cannot accept the message of the Bible as it is presented in the New Testament. Moreover, for Bultmann mythological thinking is a shortcoming. Bultmann claims that mythic thinking is not "capable of forming the abstract idea of transcendence [which] expresses its intention in the category of space" (20). Because ancient peoples cannot express abstract ideas, they are driven to the use of mythic representation. Therefore Bultmann devises a method that he calls "demythologization," which he claims recovers the deeper meaning behind mythological presentations. The aim of Bultmann's hermeneutic method is to separate the proclamation, or kerygma, from the mythology of the New Testament in order to reveal for modern people the essential Christian message.

Bultmann's demythologization raises the important question of the task of the interpreter. The method of demythologizing myth ignores the essential structure of symbol: the meaning of symbol holds the literal mythic text together with the kerygmatic content.[11] To ignore the bond between the literal and suggestive moments of symbolic expression is to misinterpret, to create something else, perhaps another myth. Bultmann is strongly influenced by the expectations of modern science; I believe that fewer demands would be made on him by an axiological analysis, which would include a new appreciation, a new translation of myth that would preserve it and yet make it relevant. Such an analysis would demand that the interpreter learn a new way of seeing; to ignore myth results in the creation of a new one, or to accept myth while excluding the information from other disciplines results in a fundamentalistic clinging onto the old one. As mentioned earlier, theologians generally do not extend their knowledge of divinity beyond their own tradition. Thus they are unable to create a true science of divinity.[12] Instead of allowing himself to be so influenced by the natural sciences, Bultmann could have used the support of a science that examines and analyzes all statements on the nature of divinity from all traditions that have a claim to knowledge of God, in order to translate and preserve the mythological ideas in the New Testament.

The interpreter must be a transparent medium: he or she must transmit a myth's meaning and yet be able to add his or her realization without compromising or distorting the original. The interpreter must allow the original to address us. He must fulfill the purpose of the original, and yet he has to enhance it by nurturing the original as he presents it. He can be compared to a conductor of symphonic music. The interpreter of the psychic world is a conductor who performs and presents the symphony of the unconscious world to the audience— the patient. He does not rewrite the piece, nor does he give an exact literal sterile replication of the work; instead he is sensitive to the subtleties and nuances of the music and also to the receptivity and capacity of the audience.

Concluding Remarks

The symbol is subjective; it is completely personal, efficacious through the consciousness of humans. Yet, symbol is objective; it imposes itself from its greater contexts, manifesting meaning through its very image. Although symbol and symbolic meaning are personal, individual, and subjective experiences, symbols are constantly being passed down to us from the traditions of this world to connect us with other worlds of meaning. It is evident that symbols have an objective existence.[13] When Wilfred Smith says that "religion is something that links the present moment to eternity" (1976, 67), he is referring to religion's ability to mediate between the worlds of humans and the sacred. This mediation is the function of symbol. Experience itself always functions symbolically; different worlds are speaking to us at different levels, and we are speaking back to them through various symbolic forms.

Symbol is the confluence of worlds of meaning. The structure of any given symbol can convey many meanings to many persons, and I have attempted to describe this in the discussion of symbolic contexts. But it is the complex structure of dialectical tensions, which I characterized as polarities, that forms the intersection of this confluence. The analogous bond between the literal and the symbolic is the very structural core of symbol itself. From this core, the existential polarity of the dialectical tension between the presence and absence of the symbolized is experienced by the human mind and heart; the ontological polarity of the symbol's dialectical autonomy from and continuity with the symbolized, informing the core structure of symbol with its qualities of opacity and transparency, respectively, breathes life into the symbol. Finally, it is in what I propose as axiological analysis that the structure of all polarities operative in symbol can be revealed; to interpret some polarities while ignoring others, or not to recognize polarities and simply to interpret isolated components of symbol, is to lose the fullness of symbolic expression, which thus results in a distorted interpretation.

That the symbol possesses a capacity to inform human consciousness of meaning from diverse worlds indicates that the structure of symbol itself is a deeper symbolization of an ultimate and interrelational unity in all existence. In order for symbol to function, reality must consist of strata of worlds, layered against one another, possessing paralleled phenomena, each one having the capacity to reflect and inform one world from another.

The following verse from the ancient Sanskrit text of the Bhagavad Gita symbolizes the capacity of the metaphysical world to inform our everyday manifest world:

> Know that all powerful, beautiful, and glorious
>   creations spring from but a spark of my splendor.
>
> Bhagavad-Gita, 10.41[14]

According to the Bhagavad Gita, the everyday world reflects the sacred world, and a short exegesis of the text might prove illuminating. The verse demonstrates the ontological connectedness between three elements in symbol: "God's splendor" as a whole world, "a spark" as an aspect of a whole world, and "creation" as a symbolic representation of an aspect of a whole world. The "splendor" of God is the sacred world, and it is from a tiny "spark" of that world that all superlative "creations" of the everyday world "spring." The superlatives of the manifest world have become identified as comparatives of the sacred world, symbolically relating the two worlds. Furthermore, our world both reveals and conceals the splendor of God's world. As a spark is a dependent part of the splendor of fire, this manifest world reveals the splendor of God's world. As a spark is an autonomous whole apart from the splendor of fire, this manifest world conceals God's world.

Perhaps more of a metaphysical system is implied by the nature of symbol than that of which we are aware. The structure of symbol invites us to an ever greater hermeneutical openness that extends to us a heightened sensitivity beyond our own fields of inquiry.

Notes

1. Langer contrasts discursive and presentational symbolism:

> The meanings given through language are successively understood, and gathered into a whole by the process called discourse; the meanings of all other symbolic elements that compose a larger, articulate symbol are understood only through the meaning of the whole, through their relations within the total structure. Their very functioning as symbols depends on the fact that they are involved in a simultaneous, integral presentation. This kind of semantic may be called "presentational symbolism," to characterize its essential distinction from discursive symbolism, or "language" proper. [1982, 8]

2. Daniel H. H. Ingalls discusses and summarizes in his General Introduction, "Sanskrit Poetry and Sanskrit Poetics," from *Sanskrit Poetry from Vidyakara's 'Treasury,'* some of the essential features of Sanskrit poetics from which I will draw here.

3. Later in this essay, I refer to the third moment also as the "symbolic." The second connotative moment is collapsed into the third suggestive moment, leaving only two fundamental moments: the literal and the symbolic. For purposes of analysis, Indian poetics is helpful in isolating the literal and its immediately associated connotative meanings from the symbolic or suggestive meanings.

4. The swastika is an equilateral cross with its arms bent at right angles, appearing to rotate in the same direction. There are in fact two swastikas, which can be easily mistaken for each other: the right-handed with arms rotating in a clockwise motion, and the left-handed with arms rotating in a counterclockwise motion. Swastikas are also found in different colors: the Hindu and Jaina use of swastika as light and auspiciousness is usually found in red; the Nazi swastika is found in black.

5. "*Religion* is: (1) a system of symbols which acts to (2) establish powerful, pervasive, and long-lasting moods and motivations in men by (3) formulat-

ing conceptions of a general order of existence and (4) clothing these conceptions with such an aura of factuality that (5) the mood and motivations seem uniquely realistic" (Geertz 1958, 90).

6. I owe the idea of analyzing "polarities" in religious thought to Professor John B. Carman of Harvard University. In recent years, he has explored the nature and usefulness of the concept, as in a seminar that I attended, "Divine Polarities in a Hindu Theology" (Fall 1984).

7. Axiological analysis is a procedure I attempt to explore and demonstrate in my Th.M. thesis, submitted to Harvard University.

8. *Webster's Third New International Dictionary* defines axiology as: "the theory or study of values, primarily of intrinsic values (as those in ethics, aesthetics, and religion) but also of instrumental values (as those in economics) particularly with reference to the manner in which they can be known or experienced, their nature and kinds, and their ontological status."

Van A. Harvey, in his *A Handbook of Theological Terms* (1964), gives the following definition of axiology: "Axiology is that part of philosophy having to do with the existence, nature, and criteria of value. It attempts to answer such questions as: (1) What constitutes anything as valuable? (2) What are the various types of value? (3) Are there any objective criteria by means of which values can be arranged on a scale or a conflict of value adjudicated? (4) What is the relation of value to being?"

9. See Langer 1982, chap. 7, "Life-Symbols: The Roots of Myth," esp. 171–81.

10. The word "kerygma" means "proclamation," or the essential meaningful message of the New Testament, which—unlike a teaching or a dogma that addresses the intellect—is capable of speaking to a person in such a way as to change his or her life.

11. Criticizing Bultmann's hermeneutic method of demythologization, Ricoeur makes the following strong statement: "Therefore, far from the objective and the existential being contraries—as happens when there is too exclusive an attachment to the opposition between myth and kerygma—it must be said that the meaning of the text holds these two moments closely together. It is the objectivity of the text, understood as content—bearer of meaning and demand for meaning—that begins the existential movement of appropriation. Without such a conception of meaning, of its objectivity and even of its ideality, no textual criticism is possible" (1980, 65).

12. Theology certainly does not have the reputation it once had as the queen of the sciences: "Theology, which could not possibly submit to scientific methods, has simply been crowded out of the intellectual arena and gone into retreat in the cloistered libraries of its seminaries" (Langer 1982, 16). A true science of God, I maintain, must objectively look at all statements on the nature of divinity from all traditions of the world; there should be a comparative theology of religion. The theologian, however, is too accustomed to administering knowledge of God only to those within the tradition to which he or she is committed.

13. Eliade explains six characteristics of symbolic meaning that are worth summarizing here. (1) Symbols have a power of revealing a "modality of the real or structure of the World" that is inaccessible to human experience. (2) All symbols have a religious character to them in that they always point to something real. (3) Symbolic meaning is multivalent; a symbol has the capacity to carry numerous levels of structurally coherent meanings not accessible to immediate experience. (4) The symbol has the capacity to open up a perspective through which things can be grasped and articulated into a harmonized system, into a unified conception of the World within which humans become an integral part. (5) Simultaneously, the symbol possesses the capacity for expressing paradoxical or contradictory aspects of ultimate reality or the supreme deity that would otherwise remain quite inexpressible. (6) Symbol is what brings meaning into the human realm; symbol not only reveals the meaning of existence but directly affects human existence (Eliade 1959, 98–101).

14. Translation mine.

References

Bhagavad-gita As It Is. Translation and commentary by A. C. Bhaktivedanta Swami Prabhupada. Los Angeles: Bhaktivedanta Book Trust, 1983.

Bultmann, Rudolf. *Jesus Christ and Mythology.* New York: Charles Scribner's, 1958.

————. *Theology of the New Testament.* Translated by Kendrick Grobel. New York: Charles Scribner's, 1951.

Cassirer, Ernst. *Language and Myth.* Translated by Susanne K. Langer. New York: Dover Publications, 1946.

Eliade, Mircea. "Methodological Remarks on the Study of Religious Symbolism." In *The History of Religions: Essays in Methodology,* edited by Mircea Eliade and Joseph M. Kitagawa. Chicago: University of Chicago Press, 1959.

Freud, Sigmund. *The Future of an Illusion* (1927). *The Standard Edition of the Complete Psychological Works of Sigmund Freud,* vol. 21. Edited and translated by James Strachey. London: Hogarth Press, 1961.

Gadamer, Hans-Georg. *Truth and Method.* New York: Seabury Press, 1976.

Geertz, Clifford. *The Interpretation of Cultures.* New York: New American Library, 1958.

Harvey, Van A. *A Handbook of Theological Terms.* New York: Macmillan, 1964.

Ingalls, Daniel H. H. General Introduction, "Sanskrit Poetry and Sanskrit Poetics." In *Sanskrit Poetry from Vidyakara's 'Treasury'.* Translated by Daniel H. H. Ingalls. Cambridge, Mass.: Harvard University Press, 1965.

Langer, Susanne K. *Philosophy in a New Key: A Study in the Symbolism of Reason, Rite, and Art.* 3d ed. Cambridge, Mass.: Harvard University Press, 1982.

Macquarrie, John. *Principles of Christian Theology.* 2d ed. New York: Charles Scribner's, 1966.

Ricoeur, Paul. "The Hermeneutics of Symbol and Philosophical Reflection." In *The Philosophy of Paul Ricoeur: An Anthology of His Work,* edited by Charles E. Reagan and David Stewart. Boston: Beacon Press, 1978.

———. "Preface to Bultmann." In *Essays on Biblical Interpretation,* edited with an introduction by Lewis S. Mudge. Philadelphia: Fortress Press, 1980.

Schweig, Graham M. "Axiological Analysis in Phenomenological Method: A Study of the Hermeneutic Task in Comparative Religion." Unpublished Th.M. thesis. The Divinity School, Harvard University, 1984.

Smart, Ninian. *Worldviews: Crosscultural Explorations of Human Beliefs.* New York: Charles Scribner's, 1983.

Smith, Wilfred Cantwell. *Religious Diversity: Essays by Wilfred Cantwell Smith.* Edited by Willard G. Oxtoby. New York: Harper and Row, 1976.

11 Psychiatry and Religion: Toward a Dialogue and Public Philosophy

Edwin R. Wallace IV

T his essay aims to heighten awareness of religious issues and their relevance both to psychiatric theory and practice and to the development of a public philosophy of psychiatry. By the latter I mean, after Browning (1987, 2), "a broad intellectual understanding of both its proper focus, as well as how it should relate to the wider aspects of social and cultural action." Careful consideration of the interface between religion and psychiatry, those two immensely powerful shapers of modern experience and self-understanding, can contribute to: the self-comprehension of each, psychiatric awareness of perennially overlooked moral and metaphysical dimensions of psychiatric theory and practice, a clearer dialogue between religionists and psychiatric physicians, and less dogmatically reductionist attitudes in both.

After a brief sketch of the relationship prior to 1909, which I call "Prehistory," I move to the clerical response to psychiatry, which for many years was virtually synonymous with the Protestant reaction. Then I turn to the specifically psychiatric and psychoanalytic response to religion and theology, including first its metaphysical dimensions and then its ethical ones. Because of space limitations, ethics and morals are treated but briefly; the interested reader is referred to Rieff (1959, 1966), Wallwork (1982), Bellah et al. (1985), Wallace (1986 a,b), and especially Browning (1987) for detailed consideration of these issues. Finally, I recapitulate the key contributions of each side of the dialogue to the other.

Prehistory

Anthropologists and medical historians acknowledge that priest and physician were originally one and the same, that this continued to be so throughout much of Europe until the secular medical schools of the late Middle Ages, and that it is still true of many nonliterate cultures (e.g., Sigerist 1951; Ackerknecht 1968, 1971).

Prior to 1800 most of the European mentally ill who received care and treatment at all received it at the hands of the church. Freud (Meng and E. Freud 1963, 21) himself deemed the Catholic confession and the Protestant "cure of souls" the psychotherapeutic forerunners of psychoanalysis; he (*S.E.* 20:255) termed the analyst a "secular pastoral worker [*Seelsorge*]." Indeed, 41 percent of Americans report that they would continue to first seek out their minister for a mental or emotional problem (McCann 1962). Holifield (1983), in a history of pastoral care ironically subtitled *From Salvation to Self Realization,* offers an excellent overview of the American cure-of-souls movement, from its inception in Puritan Massachusetts through its growing eighteenth- and nineteenth-century psychological and philosophical sophistication at the hands of those like Jonathan Edwards, James Dana, Samuel West, and Horace Bushnell.

It is probably not accidental that psychiatry, as a distinct medical specialty, was born in the Enlightenment, a time when traditional religion was under attack. Many prominent nineteenth- and early-twentieth-century psychiatrists—such as Pinel, Freud, Bleuler, and Meyer—were apostates from religious backgrounds. Certainly many psychiatrists and psychoanalysts continue to abandon the faiths of their families of origin (Henry et al. 1971), a point to which I return later.

Nevertheless, many of the leaders of Anglo-American moral treatment were pious men. Quakers figured prominently in the establishment of optimistic, humane, and psychosocially oriented mental hospitals in both countries. The rest were mainly Protestants of one cast or another. Moral and religious tenets were important in their theories and treatments. Curiously, the same was true of the more biologically minded psychiatrists of the middle and late nineteenth century—their organic theories actually protecting their religious beliefs: since soul or mind was allegedly immaterial and immortal, its finite medium, the brain alone, could become diseased.

From the religious side, the mid to late nineteenth century saw a swelling wave of religio-medical psychotherapies, such as Seventh Day Adventism, Christian Science, New Thought, and Mind Cure. Such approaches, however questionable their assumptions and hypotheses, were serious attempts to treat troubled individuals, to fill a psychotherapeutic vacuum left by both the mainline churches and the organic psychiatry of the day. Moreover, in stressing the integral relationship of "mind" and "body," and in accenting the impact of attitudes, ideas, and beliefs on total state of well being, they were significant forerunners of the psychobiological, holistic approach; they also paved the way for public acceptance of turn-of-the-century secular therapies, such as Freud's psychoanalysis.

An important early clergyman-psychiatrist collaboration was that between the Episcopal priests Elwood Worcester and Samuel Mc-Comb and the Jewish psychiatrist-psychoanalyst Isador Coriat (see their book, *Religion and Medicine,* 1908). J. J. Putnam and Richard Cabot, famous internist-psychiatrists, would also become involved. The Emmanuel Movement, as this alliance was called, begun in 1906, inaugurated the modern-day interface between psychiatry and pastoral theology; it was a key precursor of the clinical pastoral movement. Well-educated Episcopalian liberals with Ph.D.'s, Worcester and McComb viewed the Gospel accounts of Christ's healing miracles as descriptively correct but as actually mediated by psychobiological factors. The ministry of Luke and Paul was taken as paradigmatic for physician-clergyman cooperation.

The Emmanuel Clinic lasted only a few years, but its offshoots became widespread, and Worcester and McComb continued to write, counsel, and collaborate with doctors. Two of their early physician collaborators, Putnam and Cabot, eventually departed because they felt the priests were encroaching on the psychiatrist's therapeutic domain. Cabot, throughout his long subsequent association with the clinical pastoral movement, continued to favor a more limited place for the clergy with the mentally ill—that of "consoling and steadying," with the psychotherapy itself left to the doctor—a stance that led to another famous split in 1930, that between Richard Cabot and Anton Boisen. Other physicians were even more adamant about this, eschewing any clerical role whatsoever.

The Pastoral-Theological Response to Psychiatry

In 1909 an event of great significance to both psychiatry and pastoral theology occurred—Freud's visit to America. Freud's lectures stimulated interest that received considerable reinforcement from the first wave (pre-World War I) of emigré analysts and from Americans analyzed abroad. Allison Stokes (1985) argues, correctly in my opinion, that pastoral counseling and the clinical pastoral movement were born of the union between psychoanalysis, with its emphasis on the "inner," psychical life, and liberal Protestant theology, with its accent on God as immanent, its optimistic-progressivist view of human nature, and its accommodation to science and secular modernism. Prior to Freud's Clark University lectures, dynamic theory had already been used by a nondenominationally theistic American physician and psychologist, the great William James (1902), to throw light on religion; James theorized that God operated through man's "subconscious" mental life.

Although rank-and-file fundamentalist and conservative Protestants, and most Jewish and Catholic clergy as well, remained suspicious of Freud, liberal Protestants overlooked his personal antipathy to religion and his metaphysical bias in order to grasp his genuine psychological insights into religious and other human behavior. Eventually mainstream Protestants, including "progressive evangelicals," would become increasingly receptive to dynamic psychiatry—although fundamentalist and conservative churches are still often chary of, and even antagonistic toward, both psychiatry and psychoanalysis. I shall briefly describe the ideas of four of the most prominent of the many liberal Protestant clerics who engaged in dialogue with psychiatry and psychoanalysis: Anton Boisen, Seward Hiltner, Paul Tillich, and Reinhold Niebuhr.

Anton Boisen is a splendid example of a liberal pastor's capacity to separate Freud's personal attitudes from his psychiatric contributions. Reading Freud's *Introductory Lectures on Psycho-Analysis,* while an inpatient after his 1920 psychotic break, Boisen found many of his own insights into his condition independently confirmed—particularly by Freud's emphasis on sexual conflicts and on psychopathology as motivated and meaningful. Bolstered by his personal opinions and by psychoanalysis, Boisen consistently opposed his young attending psychiatrist's contention that his problems were all "organic." When Boisen insisted that there was a meaningful, purposive, and constructive side to his illness—particularly his (1960, 91) "delusion" that his life's mission was to "[break] an opening in the wall which separated medicine and religion"—his discharge was delayed, under the pressure of which he briefly relapsed (Boisen 1960, 109–15).

Boisen (1936) averred that psychoses are, at least partly, responses to a person's sense of failure and the breakdown of his or her relationship to the social environment. In emphasizing the meaningful and interpersonal aspects of psychosis and its attempts at adaptation, Boisen was akin to Jung, Meyer, Sullivan, and Fromm-Reichman, and hence a true psychiatric pioneer; consider also his image of the patient as a "living human document," to be studied historically and interpretively. In *Religion in Crisis and Custom,* an important sociopsychological-theological work, Boisen (1945) demonstrated how conversion and other religious experiences can play key adaptive roles within normal populations in times of severe socioeconomic stress and dislocation.

Psychoses, as purposive phenomena, can represent constructive attempts to reevaluate and reconstruct inadequate and incoherent personal philosophies and value systems. In this sense, Boisen not only emphasized the idea that a human phenomenon can be both pathological *and* a constructive religious-moral experience, but also offered psychiatry a more optimistic view of schizophrenia and the affective psychoses. Moreover, as Browning (1987) stresses—with his suggestion that psychiatry look not merely at the *origins* of faith, which might well include psychopathological elements, but at its *phenomenology* and its *functional-adaptational consequences*—Boisen was proposing a psychiatric public philosophy that allows religious *experience* and *behavior* to be taken seriously and nonreductively.

But Boisen also had an important message for his pastoral colleagues: that they not resist the psychiatric orientation toward the determination and consequences of religious belief and practice. From the theological perspective, one evaluates an individual's religion by how it orients him toward matters of ultimacy and obligation—that is, worldview and morality. From the psychiatric standpoint, one asks how the individual's religion contributes to identity, integration, personal agency, and biopsychosocial adaptation: "The worth of any religion or of any ethical system would thus be the extent to which it enabled its adherents to survive in the struggle for existence *and* to attain to the abundant life" (Boisen 1936, 212; my italics).[1]

The recently deceased Seward Hiltner was another prime mover in the religious response to psychiatry. Like Boisen, he embraced William James's (1902) phenomenological and adaptational approach to religion and emphasized a theological-psychiatric perspectivalism. A liberal Protestant, he chided literalist believers who confuse theological-existential biblical statements with scientific ones. For example, the liberal regards the Genesis creation story not as a *scientific* cosmology, but as a time- and culture-bound form of expression of a universal theological truth regarding man's relationship to the Deity—his creation by and continued radical contingency upon God.

I suspect that the intellectual antipathy of many psychiatrists to religion rests, as it did with Freud, on the wholesale equation of theology with its fundamentalist and conservative varieties. Such religionists do not limit themselves to metaphysical statements but indeed make ostensibly empirical declarations that conflict sharply with natural and social science. By contrast, a key tenet of liberal Protestantism is that theological statements about man and the universe cannot conflict with veridical science; assertions regarding the existence and nature of God are considered to be *meta*physical—throwing indispensable light on certain spiritual and moral experiences but understood as axioms that are not themselves empirically confirmable or refutable. This is why faith is deemed "prior to belief."

In 1956 Hiltner delineated five areas of Freud's contribution to religion: (1) his emphasis on unconscious dynamics, (2) the accent on truth and honest self-awareness, (3) the idea that human freedom comes through the consciousness of determinism, (4) the developmental approach to the psychical life, and (5) the idea that "neither conscience, impulse, nor reason can give adequate clues to what is the good for man. But if brought together into the right relationship, such clues may appear" (Hiltner 1956, 15). Hiltner saw the emphasis on experiential knowledge and on healing as common to both religion and psychoanalysis.

As a liberal theologian, Hiltner was comfortable asserting that "religion (unlike God) is a human enterprise subject to all the fallibilities that flesh is heir to" (19). By accenting the powerful and perennial psychical roots of religion and the way in which the spiritual quest may become distorted by personal history and psychopathology, by breaking the false, magical, projective idols that interfere with mature religious faith, and by furnishing psychological parallels to and justifications for religious insights (such as the importance of "letting go" in both psychotherapy and the reception of grace), Hiltner pointed out how dynamic psychiatry had much to offer religion.

Hence, each endeavor has its particular *perspective* on religious belief, experience, and behavior. The psychiatrist is concerned with the role of religion in the patient's overall adaptation, integration, and self-determination. The pastor is occupied with how the patient orients his or her capacities toward matters of spiritual ultimacy and moral obligation. Quarrels arise only when each becomes dogmatic and univocally reductionist (see Hiltner and Colston 1961; Hiltner 1971).

The famous German-American theologian Paul Tillich displayed a similar receptiveness to dynamic psychiatry. In a widely circulated manuscript entitled "Psychiatry and Theology" (1956, obtained at the Yale University Divinity School), Tillich deemed psychoanalysis a "powerful ally of Christian theology" in filling out the categories of "human creatureliness" (or "finitude"), "estrangement" (or "sin"), and "reunion" (or "salvation"). Psychoanalysis, with its principles of historical and psychical determinism, confirms the Pauline-Augustinian-Lutheran insights on the "bondage of the will" and, like Protestantism, preaches that "acceptance precedes transformation." Tillich (1957) did not regard spirituality as something enacted apart from man's psychobiology and sociality. A spiritual act is a cognitive, conative, affective, visceral act—a "bloody truth," as Nietzsche called it. God is taken to act through man's psychobiology, through his incarnateness, rather than via some immaterial soul or spirit. What characterizes numinous experience is its particular patterning and the surprising universality, across time and space, of its core aspects, rather than some alleged radically different seat of its operation (Wallace 1985).

Nevertheless, for Tillich it was crucial that psychoanalysts recognize that they speak to neurotic and not existential anxiety. The latter is related to man's *conscious* awareness of his brokenness and mortality and of the ambiguity and potential meaninglessness of life and the universe. Psychoanalysis becomes a threat to religion only if it "negates the gap between man's essential and his existential nature and if it misses the distinction between medical healing and salvation in the religious sense." This seems a useful differentiation for psychiatrists, whether or not they believe that such salvation exists, for they can readily assent that religion aims at it while psychiatry does not.

Mental healing, declared Tillich, can liberate one from compulsions and pathological tensions, but it cannot tell one what to do with the freedom thereby acquired. The latter is a function of religion and morality, and psychoanalysis subsumes it only by becoming itself a quasi-religion. Like Boisen, Tillich (in the manuscript cited above) emphasized the distinction between the empirical-clinical concerns proper to psychology and psychiatry and the metaphysical ones of religion. Statements of ultimate concern "lie in a dimension in which psychoanalysis as a scientific method can neither refute nor confirm [them]." But at the same time, he warned the theologian against entering the realms of scientific analysis or of ignoring that the "psychological and social context in which a religious experience occurs largely determines the symbols and images in which it is expressed."

Reinhold Niebuhr's (1941) response to depth psychology is more ambiguous and ambivalent than Boisen's, Hiltner's, or Tillich's. Nevertheless, it is in some respects a more integrative move to recast psychoanalytic insights into theological language and to incorporate them into an explicitly Judeo-Christian anthropology.

Niebuhr welcomed Freud's determinism and psychosocial pessimism-realism as important antidotes to the facile optimism of many theological liberals about human nature; nor did he deny the psychoanalytic contributions to understanding religious behavior. Nevertheless, he charged that Freud too sharply separated the "vitality" of "nature" (i.e., id) from the "form" of "spirit" (i.e., ego-superego). The self-seeking and impulsive tendencies in man are not confined to the "instincts," but permeate all aspects of psyche or "spirit." Moreover, in "anticipation" of the charges of Harry Guntrip, Heinz Kohut, and others, Niebuhr criticized Freud's structural theory for lacking a concept of self.

With his concept of "spirit," or "self," as Niebuhr variously called it, he employed a notion of anxiety radically different from Freud's. As Browning notes (1987, 85), for Niebuhr "it is the self . . . and its tendencies to yield to the terrors of anxiety, and not our natural impulses as such, which is the source of the inordinate self-concern that is so fundamental to human social and political destructiveness."

But this anxiety is secondary not only to man's awareness of his finitude but also to his "not know[ing] of his limitations. . . . the limitations of his possibilities" (Niebuhr 1941, 183). The "Fall" was Niebuhr's term for man's proclivity to secure himself against the anxiety of finitude and possibility with inordinate self-regard. Such anxieties and self-centered responses are present even if one has received the best child rearing, or if all adult psychopathological issues have been resolved. At times Niebuhr (1957) feared that psychiatry's predominant focus on the individual and his or her determinisms might undermine the sort of personal and collective responsibility required for social action (see also Lasch 1979 and Bellah et al. 1985).

Niebuhr (1941, 3) integrated Freud's insights on the bondage of the will with his own concept of self-transcendence. "The obvious fact is that man is a child of nature, subject to its vicissitudes, driven by its impulses, and confined within the brevity of years which nature permits its varied organic forms, allowing them some, but not too much, latitude. The other less obvious fact is that man is a spirit who stands outside of nature, life, himself, his reason, and the world."

Corresponding to the flourishing of clinically informed pastoral theology was the burgeoning development of the clinical pastoral movement (see Stokes 1985; Holifield 1983). In 1924 Boisen became chaplain at the Worcester State Hospital (Massachusetts), and a year later began accepting theological students as psychiatric attendants. From 1930, when the Council for Clinical Training of Theological Students was organized in New York by Boisen and the psychosomaticist Helen Flanders Dunbar, a growing number of such associations appeared— the Association of Mental Hospital Chaplains in 1948, the American Association of Pastoral Counselors in 1964, and the American Association of Clinical Pastoral Education in 1967. A number of psychiatric-pastoral collaborations resulted—such as the huge Religio-Psychiatric Clinic of analyst Smiley Blanton and clergyman Norman Vincent Peale. Relevant periodicals were established, such as the *Journal of Pastoral Care and Counseling* (1947) and *Pastoral Psychology* (1950), and important texts were published, such as those by David Roberts (1950), Alvin Outler (1954), and Earl Loomis (1960).

Pope Pius XII made cautiously receptive pronouncements upon psychotherapy and psychoanalysis in 1952 and 1953 (in VanderVeldt and Odenwald 1957, 149–52). Despite the antipathy of some, such as Catholic psychiatrist-philosopher Rudolph Allers (1940) and Bishop Fulton Sheen (1949), an enlarging coterie of Catholics became interested in psychoanalysis. Though lagging behind their Christian counterparts, Jewish clergy-clinicians, such as Moshe Spero (1980), see little incompatibility between psychoanalysis and Judaism; the *Journal of Psychology and Judaism* is an important development in this area.

In sum, many of the greatest contemporary Protestant theologians have been overwhelmingly receptive to Freud, some of them even detecting the hand of God in psychoanalysis and believing it can purge religious belief and practice of its infantile, neurotic, and magical idols (e.g., Pfister 1928; Ricoeur 1970; Lee 1948; White 1960; DeLuca 1977). Indeed, many Protestant clerics have been so fascinated with psychiatry that pastoral fears that members of the American Association of Pastoral Counselors and the American Association of Clinical Pastoral Education are coming to resemble secular clinicians (especially psychodynamicists and Rogerians) more than ministers are not unfounded (Houck and Moss 1977; Oates 1962; Stokes 1985, 149–50).

Psychiatry and psychoanalysis were opposed by theologians only when their theories became dogmatically reductive (e.g., religious experience and belief as exhaustively explained by beta endorphins, temporal lobe, right hemisphere, neurophysiology, projection, oedipal compromise formation, infantile dependent strivings, transitional object relations, and so forth) (see Wallace 1983, 1984 for psychoanalytic and social-science criticisms of such reductions). For example, in declaring God a projection and infantile wish-fulfillment Freud was saying, in effect, not merely that such mechanisms contribute to understanding religionists' attitudes toward the posited object of their devotion, but also that they fully account for the alleged object itself. He did not appreciate that he had slipped into transempirical and metaphysical statements. To claim to have penetrated behind the "screen" of projection and know that there is no God is quite as much a faith statement as to assert that there is. If Freud had wished to be consistently scientific he would had to have remained agnostic on this question. Indeed, liberal Protestant theologians themselves would not generally claim that God can be "known," in any directly empirical sense; belief is taken to be a matter of *faith,* although certain human experiences may then be invoked that appear indirectly to justify or make such faith reasonable. Moreover, many pastors and theologians opposed to Freudian reductionism are equally against religionists who practice a univocal theological reductionism, denying the role of psychosocial factors in shaping the form and content of the religious experience and belief of any particular culture and individual.

Examining the sophisticated twentieth-century theological response to psychiatry and psychoanalysis should disabuse psychiatrists of any notion that all clerics and religionists are single-mindedly opposed to their specialty. Let us now examine the psychiatric response to religion.

The Psychiatric Response to Religion

While the popular conception of psychiatry as antipathetic or indifferent to religion is not wholly unfounded, matters are far from as simple as this. As we have seen, mental-hospital physicians not only permitted pastors to enter their facilities but often actively collaborated with them. In fact, Boisen's clinical theological preceptorships were antedated by those begun in 1923 by an M.D., William S. Keller, at Bexley Hall in Ohio. For enumeration and discussion of the many prominent psychiatrists and psychoanalysts actively collaborating with clinical pastors and theologians, see Stokes (1985).

In 1956 the Group for the Advancement of Psychiatry formed a Committee on Psychiatry and Religion, noting that "matters of religious faith and practice play a tremendous role in the patterning of emotional life, the thinking, and the behavior of man," and hence figure in the understanding and treatment of mental illness as well (G.A.P. 1960, 317–18). Freud himself, though probably more responsible than anyone else for psychiatric antagonisms to religion, wrote Pfister that the opinions in *Future of an Illusion* "form no part of analytic theory," being merely his "personal views" (Meng and E. Freud 1963, 117). In that book Freud penned:

> In point of fact psycho-analysis is a method of research, an impartial instrument, like the infinitesimal calculus, as it were. . . . If the application of the psycho-analytic method makes it possible to find a new argument against the truths of religion, *tant pis* for religion; but defenders of re-

ligion will by the same right make use of psycho-analysis in order to give full value to the affective significance of religious doctrines. [*S.E.* 21:36–37]

This view of analysis as instrument or methodology, rather than worldview, was endorsed by Zilboorg (1962), Linn and Schwarz (1958), and the preeminent ego psychologist Heinz Hartmann (1960).

It is significant that the Menninger Clinic, a bastion of psychoanalysis and colonizer of most of the analytic institutes in the Western United States, began clinical pastoral fellowships in 1959. A psychoanalytic psychologist there, the late Paul Pruyser, wrote several extensive interdisciplinary works (e.g., 1968, 1974, 1976), as has Karl Menninger (1973) himself. An American Psychiatric Association Task Force Report (Franzblau, 1975) disclosed that 43 percent of psychiatrists believe in God or are personally religious, with about half of these regularly attending religious services, and a surprising 12.5 percent serving as consultants to religious organizations. This is in striking contrast to figures of 1.1 percent (Malony 1972) for theists in the American Psychological Association.

Finally, one cannot overlook the host of secular-religio-moral psychotherapeutic syncretisms—including Alcoholics Anonymous, arguably the most theoretically and therapeutically successful of them all. Armando Favazza (1982) summarizes many of these from the Christian side, including the more orthodox faith-healing movements, as well as more idiosyncratic manifestations such as the late Ruth Carter Stapleton's mélange of evangelical Protestantism and psychoanalysis (Christ as "Lord of the repressed memory"). A number of psychiatrists themselves attempt to meld secular psychiatry with broadly religious or spiritual orientations as well. Consider Tournier's (1958) inspirational approach, Frankl's (1955) logotherapy, Deikman's (1982) frankly mystical psychiatry, Jung's (1938) psychologizing of metaphysics and sacralizing of psychology, and Peck's (1978) religio-psychodynamic books and audiotapes, which are gaining an astonishingly large popular following. Anthropologist Atwood Gaines (1985) writes about the Christian psychiatry movement, whose adherents, recently active at such prominent medical centers as Duke University, combine prayer and religious counseling with pharmacologic and psychodynamic approaches. While such orientations are often problematic on theoretical, therapeutic, and even theological grounds, they nonetheless represent an important interface between psychiatry and religion. Academic psychiatry at the Medical College of Georgia (Augusta), while not promoting religio-medical therapies, has a cadre of clinicians and social scientists studying the interface from a variety of perspectives.

For the most part, however, psychiatry and psychoanalysis have lagged behind religious willingness—especially that of liberal Protestant and "progressive" Protestant evangelical churches—to enter dialogue. By and large, they have not returned the compliment of those like Boisen, Hiltner, and Tillich. Larson and Pattison and their colleagues (1986) document the paucity and poor scientific methodology of articles dealing with religious dimensions in the major American, Canadian, and British psychiatric journals. Significantly, a substantial number deal with cults, even though their adherents constitute less than 1 percent of the population. The fourth edition of *The Comprehensive Textbook of Psychiatry* (Kaplan and Sadock 1985), the bible of the specialty, contains *no* entries on overlapping issues with religion, ethics, or even philosophy.

Moreover, although it may be surprising that as many as 43 percent of psychiatrists are theistic, this pales when compared with Gallup Poll (1985) documentation that over 95 percent of Americans currently believe in God, that most retain formal religious affiliations, and that some 40 percent regularly attend religious services. This, coupled with the fact that the majority of nontheistic psychiatrists and psychoanalysts come from religious backgrounds and are hence apostates (Henry et al. 1971), suggests a considerable discrepancy between psychiatrists and the population they serve. And the analytic subspecialty of psychiatry contains a far, far smaller percentage of theists than does psychiatry as a whole (Henry et al.). Although it is rarer to find out-and-out antipathy toward religion in the analytic literature or among analysts (such as Earl Loomis [personal communication] encountered because of his Union Theological Seminary professorship when he sought to transfer his membership from the Philadelphia to the New York Psychoanalytic Institute and Society in the late 1950s), indifference or amused and patronizing acceptance often replaces it: religion is simply the best that the great infantile, dependent, and projecting unwashed can do. Might such attitudes result, in part, from projective identification—derogation of religionists for dogmatic elements that psychiatrists cannot acknowledge in themselves?

Pattison (1965) documented the astonishingly low rate of referrals by ministers to mental-health facilities and their feeling that psychiatrists ignored or patronized the clergy. When one considers that 30 percent of Americans first resort to prayer in times of distress, that 41 percent state that if they had a mental or emotional problem they would first turn to a pastor (McCann 1962), that normal controls are much more likely than psychiatric patients to attend services and be active in their denominations (Lindenthal 1970; Stark 1971; Hadaway and Roof 1971; Bergin 1983; McCready and Greeley 1976), and that Freud (Meng and E. Freud 1963, 16; *S.E.* 11:146; *S.E.* 18:142) himself felt that religious adherence protects against psychopathology, then it is foolish for psychiatrists to ignore the tremendous role that organized mainstream religion plays in treatment and preventive psychiatry. Fortunately, some community mental-health centers (such as the Connecticut Mental Health Center, affiliated with Yale University, in New Haven) are realizing the key role of churches and church-based social groups in the care, prevention, and follow-up of major mental illness (Anderson 1979).

Pattison (1978, 122) may well be correct that "bioethics" institutes (such as those in Houston, Galveston, Washington, and Hastings, N.Y.) are replacing earlier institutionalized interest in religion and health. While medical ethics is crucial, surely it would be cant to ignore the worldviews from which these ethics derive and the socioeconomic-political structures that they may come to subserve. Recently the Park Ridge Center for the Study of Health, Faith, and Ethics (Chicago), with its journal, *Second Opinion,* is attempting to fill this vacuum.

Finally, I am struck by the absence or paucity of religious histories in the workups of my colleagues and of residents I supervise—even when these clinicians are themselves personally religious. This suggests a considerable psychiatric denial of religious issues. Do psychiatric patients have no religious life? Or is it that psychiatrists have theoretical, methodological, and metaphysical commitments that blind them to their patients' religious experience and preoccupations, as well as a public image that discourages patients from discussing their faith? If so, then clinicians are engaging in an endlessly self-fulfilling prophecy: that patients do not present religious themes becomes further "evidence" that such issues are unimportant to them. This is unfortunate indeed for, as Chicago philosopher Marilyn Nissim-Sabat (personal communication) suggests, the clinician's experience of his or her patient's religious phenomenology and its place in the latter's overall psychical life would be an ideal empirical place for psychiatry to begin building a public philosophy that permits conversation with religion. In addition, by not attending to religious history, psychiatrists miss valuable psychodynamic and social information about their patients—in terms of the way in which culture, socioeconomic ambience, personal history, personality structure, interpretive style, defenses, compromise formations, and self-image and self-esteem reveal themselves in aspects of religious life and belief (see Draper 1965).

Such concerns were addressed by the controversial Catholic theologian Hans Küng, in a brilliant 1986 Pfister Address, "Religion: The Last Taboo?," to an overflowing audience at the Annual Meeting of the American Psychiatric Association. He declared religion "the last taboo": in the face of an explosion of all manner of popular religiosity, psychiatry continues to "repress" the religious dimension of human existence. Its preoccupation with obviously distorted and pathological varieties of religion, such as those in many cults, allows it to continue to pay short shrift to mainstream religion and to the general human dimension of religiousness.

If in fact Freud was correct that gropings for belief constitute man's deepest and oldest strivings, and if they are repressed, then does this not allow for the possibility of all manner of compromise formations and substitutes—such as fanatical devotion to secular ideas, movements, and individuals (Küng ms., p. 12)? Might, by contrast, a preferable alternative be for clinicians to facilitate the conscious recognition of any such conflicts—both those present in themselves and those in their patients—so that they can be "relieved" by means of "decision—acceptance or rejection" (p. 13)? This would foster the "reciprocal challenge of religion and psychiatry" and help clinicians to take religion seriously, as "one of the specifically human forms of expression" (p. 22).

With repression of recognition of the religious dimension in patients' lives may go the denial of how psychiatric systems themselves can assume dimensions of overarching meaning and self-transcendence for clinicians—and their patients; in many ways, Freud can be cited as a case in point (Roazen 1971; Fromm 1972; Wallace 1984). Probably, as Browning (1987) suggests, psychiatric theoretical-therapeutic systems always subtend horizons of ultimacy, though this does not preclude there being *degrees* of cosmology inherent in the different approaches. For example, there may be little in the core theoretical, investigative, and therapeutic structure of psychoanalysis that compels the practitioner to take up a metaphysic similar to Freud's. Recall that the most vociferous critics of the mechanistic face of Freud's metapsychology are analysts themselves; moreover, the various orientations within dynamic psychiatry—ego psychology, object-relations theory, self psychology, dynamic culturalism, and classical psychoanalysis—probably imply differing cosmologies.

A cosmology and ethic (of the goodness of self-actualization and of its inherent harmony with the needs of society) are much more clearly and narrowly entailed by the "humanistic" than by the dynamic psychologies. Religion, as an overarching metaphysical-moral system, has less to fear from psychiatric approaches that can be characterized more as empirical subdisciplines and therapeutic "technologies" than as *Weltanschauungen* and ethics. By contrast, when psychiatry assumes overriding cosmological pretensions and theology scientific ones, each needs to be wary of the other.

But it is not simply a matter of the clinician's personal attitude or of cosmological positions necessitated by psychiatric orientations themselves. We must also consider the patient's needs. Chafing at the lack of Philip Rieff's (1966) "positive communities" with their compelling symbolisms and commitment cures, many wittingly-unwittingly enter analysis looking for the *Weltanschauung* their history and society deny them. For these individuals psychoanalysis, with its premium on insight and enhanced self-determination, may no longer be simply a means to increase integration and broaden the range of choice; rather, it may become an end in itself—a commitment therapy with doctrines, ethic, community, and cult. Do we have any reason to believe that meaningfulness issues are less deeply rooted than the self-esteem problems and sexual, aggressive, and dependent conflicts with which psychiatrists are more familiar? While the former may in part reflect or derive from the latter, they may have their own feet as well—at least they can be *experienced* as pressing issues in their own right. It may even be, as Browning (1987) suggests, that optimal resolution of such quandaries is necessary to the mental health of many patients.

What are psychiatrists to do when patients raise such queries to which we obviously have no answers? Surely most would pause before encouraging them, like Jung, to seek out the religious conversion of their choice or before providing them with our own "solutions" to these questions. Equally hazardous would be interpreting them away. Here psychiatrists should probably do what they do in all but the more supportive therapies—be sufficiently nonconflicted to: first, encourage the patient to unfold the issues and their history, interpersonal nexus, and motivational contexts; then, interpret any dynamic conflicts that appear to be fueling these questions; and, finally, to leave the patient to make his or her own choices.

Ethics

Although I am not here exploring the moral dimensions of psychiatry, Browning (1987) is indeed correct that the various psychiatric-psychotherapeutic theories and therapies have normative as well as descriptive, explanatory, and technological aspects. Freud himself was both supportive and antipathetic to Judeo-Christian morality; though he waffled between permissive and interdictory motifs, he generally favored the latter, combined with the reality principle and ego (Rieff 1959, 1966; Wallace 1983, 1986a).

The variegated history of psychiatry, in its mutually shaping interaction with culture, drives home that the specialty is not a value-free enterprise. Psychiatry rests, like the rest of modern medicine, on a current encomium of "health values" that, Temkin (1977) notes, has hardly been universal—contrasting sharply, for example, with the medieval emphasis on preparation for the eternal life, and even ascetic mortification of the flesh, as the *supremum bonum.* "Health" in psychiatry, while overlapping with that supreme good in the rest of medicine, is even vaguer, broader, and, in its nexus with moral and religious categories of the good life and person, more problematic than its general medical sister. In dynamic psychiatry, for instance, the premiums on adaptation, autonomy, self-awareness, self-expression, and nonjudgmental views of sexual and aggressive fantasies and feelings clearly constitute moral, and not merely therapeutic, values. Doctrines such as psychic determinism conflict with popular moral and religious conceptions of freedom of the will (although, interestingly enough, some of the hardest determinisms are theological—e.g., those of Augustine, Luther, Calvin, Edwards) (Wallace, 1986b).

Moreover, the domain of dynamic psychiatry—motivation and behavior—is that of ethics as well. The possibility of contradiction enters immediately. To reinterpret fantasies, attitudes, intentions, interpretations, and actions as manifestations of history, defense, compromise formation, and unconscious wish and mentation is not thereby to remove them from the moral sphere—which embraces, preeminently, the impact of one's behavior on others. Of all psychologists, William James (1890, 1902) most fastidiously appreciated the simultaneously physiological, psychological, and moral dimensions of the human being.

Although psychoanalysis may entail certain cosmological and moral positions, it seems that the objective of self-discovery is more a *means* to an *end*—the enhancement of integration and range of choice. Thus it is in some measure a "metaethic," as Engelhardt (1973) terms it—not necessarily dictating the content of decisions or the manner in which augmented capacities will be used. Furthermore, to collapse everything into the "moral," as William James was wont to do, robs the concept of its meaning. It overlooks that certain aspects of psychiatric mental health, such as enhanced personal integration and self-determination, are to some degree nonmoral or premoral goods—which may themselves further moral or immoral pursuits.

In any event, the contribution of dynamic psychiatry to ethics lies not in its functioning as a substitute morality but in its instruction upon the fundamental psychobiological tendencies with which ethics must deal. Although, as Heinz Hartmann and Sigmund Freud emphasize, morality and mental health do not necessarily go hand in hand, and although one cannot necessarily deduce moral values from psychological facts, there is yet much that psychoanalysis proffers to ethics. If moral inadequacy is due to neurotic causes, then successful dynamic treatment might remedy it. The strengthening of the ego, diminution of the harsh and archaic qualities of the superego, and heightened awareness of one's moral values and their dynamic significance—which can result from analysis—can make for a more consistent and integrated moral code. Deepened insight can lead to a more realistic sense of self- and other-responsibility, the avoidance of easy rationalizations, and more subtle forms of self-control. The current demand to base moral evaluations on more complete psychological knowledge is, moreover, as Hartmann (1960) asserts, a legacy of Freud. And the ethic of honesty, the awareness that there are egoistic and antisocial motives in all of us, that our moral capacities are largely molded by early constitutional-environmental factors beyond our control, and that conscious moral positions are often functions of (and rationalizations for) unconscious defensive or expressive (including aggressive) trends helps attenuate one species of what many consider immorality: intolerance and self-righteousness. Indeed, although psychodynamic therapy is often accused of promoting immorality and egoism (see La Piere 1960 and Mowrer 1961), it is my impression that successfully treated people are generally more invested in others and more morally responsible than before.

Conclusion

The history of the interaction between psychiatry and religion is long and complicated in this country. Although the bulk of the interest has been from the pastoral-theological side, there have always been psychiatrists willing—at times even eager—to collaborate. While Freud's personal antipathy to religion remains all too characteristic of psychiatric attitudes, I believe they are softening somewhat—that an eighth of all psychiatrists regularly consult at religious institutions is a promising sign. Nevertheless, antagonism is often replaced by indifference, and psychiatrists still have far to go before learning the moral and metaphysical lessons religion has to teach about psychiatry and before realizing the preventive and health-care potential inherent in effective and respectful relations with the clergy.

Religion and theology remind psychiatry that, however much it might wish to, it does not practice in a moral and metaphysical vacuum or without a social ethic and public philosophy. By becoming aware of its values and *Weltanschauungen* psychiatry can evaluate them rather than be thoughtlessly subservient to them. By teaching the key role of systems of overarching meaning and morality in maintaining the mental health of many, religion confronts psychiatry with decisions regarding the proper stance of a secular therapeutic discipline vis-à-vis the human search for self-transcendence. I believe a common cause of psychiatric antipathy to religion is psychiatrists' own conflicts about the place of such systems in their own lives. They may retreat from psychotherapy to biochemistry and the purely pharmacologic treatment of neuropsychiatric disorders and psychoses to escape moral-metaphysical issues, but the latter will surely follow them there. While psychiatry need not—and certainly should not— wed itself to a specific religious or cosmological creed, it must at least have a public philosophy that permits it to take its patients' experiences and beliefs respectfully.

On the other hand, psychiatry—especially psychodynamics—has much to contribute to the religionist's understanding of his or her belief and experience. Psychoanalysis can clarify the relationship and degree of integration between an individual's religious beliefs and his or her basic dynamics and personality structure. It can disclose conflicts for which religious convictions serve as the vehicle of expression or defense or in which these convictions contribute force to one side or the other. It can illumine the history of each individual's religious beliefs, the childhood object cathexes and identifications that are associated with and help determine the final form of these beliefs—that is, the transferential aspects of one's attitude toward the object of his devotion. Finally, it can comment upon the role of one's religion in one's overall adaptation (or maladaptation) to the internal and external environments.

In fine, psychoanalysis is on most solid ground when it is investigating the *psychological* meaning and motivation of the religious beliefs of *any given practitioner*—that is, the more or less idiosyncratic (because of personal history and constitution) contribution of each religionist to what is otherwise a cultural affair. Only from the cumulative results of such laborious, *clinically based* studies can dynamic psychiatry make meaningful statements about religion and religionists *in general.* What psychoanalysis can never do, again, is comment upon whether, after all the psychodynamic factors are removed, there is an ultimate truth justification for religious faith; for "God" is, logically speaking, an axiom and not an empirically testable scientific hypothesis—albeit an "axiom" that many feel throws incomparable light on their deepest human experience.

Nevertheless, I do not imply that theoretical and practical integration among religious philosophy and ethics and psychiatry is a facile task. Despite common concerns, parallel ideas, and areas of functional overlap, it remains that pastoral theology and clinical psychiatry have vitally different legacies and oftentimes widely divergent approaches to similar phenomena.

Productive dialogue must honestly address the differences, as well as the similarities, between the two. Among the former I shall tersely cite but five, elaborating on the first only.

(1) The psychiatric commitment to mental health and adaptation ostensibly poses problems on pastoral-theological grounds, where the primary emphasis, presumably, is metaphysical and salvific; it is hardly difficult to conceive of instances where implementing the two goals could make them counter each other. Nevertheless, the possibility for antipathy here has been overemphasized and frequently founded, as Joseph Smith (personal communication) suggests, on misequation of the psychoanalytic concept of "adaptation" with vulgar conformity or political subservience. Close reading of Hartmann (1964, 59–60) shows that by "adaptation" he meant neither the above, nor simple biological survival or sheer dominance of self-interest and rationality (recall, for example, his praise for Kris's "regression in the service of the ego"). Adaptation, in its psychoanalytic sense, might best be comprehended as creative and productive engagement with reality (akin to Freud's *Arbeiten und Lieben*)—one optimally suitable for the deeply rooted needs, desires, and aims of self, and cognizant of beloved and loving others and the human and nonhuman environments. Surely this blunts the edge of Michel Foucault's (1965, 1970, 1976a,b, 1977, 1978, 1986) charge that psychoanalysis is primarily a secular heir to the power-hungry and conformity-compelling medieval Catholic church, with its confessional and moral theology the ancestors of allegedly "adjustment"-promoting free association and analytic interpretation.

If one wishes to relate psychoanalytic "adaptation" to its neo-Darwinian version—although it is doubtful that the two can be mapped wholly onto one another—Darwin's inclusion of sexual, alongside natural, selection may be a starting place. In fine, I suggest that sexual selection, as an important source of (proto) aesthetic variety in the animal kingdom, is the *ur*-mechanism of the abundant living (arts, religion, and at least one dimension of the cultural and intellectual life in general) that Boisen places in the purview of human "adaptation." Here Freud and Darwin would join hands—with their respective principles of sublimation and sexual selection.

Moreover, the concepts "autoplastic" and "alloplastic" convey that psychoanalytic "adaptation" means not simple "adjustment" to self and world as they actually are, but active attempts at self- and environmental-transformation. Adaptation permits not only creative action and altruism but also, in extreme sociopolitical situations, imprisonment or the sacrifice of life itself (e.g., Dietrich Bonhoeffer's courageous martyrdom in Nazi Germany and Martin Luther's refusal to recant in the face of Charles V's Catholic tribunal). Even biological evolutionists do not generally mean only "survival of the individual" by "survival of the fittest." And the most committed of them (e.g., Stephen J. Gould 1982) seldom argue that natural selection correctly explains *all* human activity.

Most, if not all, human beings appear to have powerful and pervasive needs for meaning and are necessitated, Freud's (E. Freud 1975, 436) assertions notwithstanding, to ask the "big questions" for which there are no sure empirical answers.[2] Hence the search for symbolic self- and group-transcendence, whether explicitly religious or not, can hardly be declared prima facie illusory or maladaptive (either from an individual or biological-sociocultural standpoint). The person's and a society's "answers," albeit tentative, can profoundly influence their living of life. Freud himself believed religion promoted social cohesion, contributed to the self-restraints necessary for civilization, and protected against the development of individual psychopathology. Whether religious beliefs are wholly illusory cannot be determined by psychoanalysis or any other empirical science; whether they are adaptive must be decided by their functions and consequences.

(2) Historically, psychiatry's strongest currents are Enlightenment ones. It is a fundamentally secular, human-centered discipline, while religion is God-centered. The latter could well consider psychiatric *human*ism as yet another species of the Fall, hubris, or pridefulness.

(3) By elucidating the developmental-psychopathological roots of religious experience and behavior, psychiatry has not, as previously mentioned, proved that these are its only determinants or ruled on its truth value. Nonetheless, like other social- and biological-science explanations of religion, psychiatric explanations potentially oppose religion on grounds of parsimony. They provide yet other secular explanations for religion, bypassing the need to postulate an irreducible "drive" to religion or a fundamental human awareness of a super-

natural reality. Moreover, psychiatry, like all sciences, aims at empirically supportable or sappable laws and hypotheses; propositions beyond such test, like religio-theological ones, are ipso facto scientifically suspect.

(4) Psychiatric determinism presents serious problems to most theological images of man and morality (Wallace 1986a,b).

(5) Finally, there is no easy place in psychiatry for a concept of sin.[3]

In sum, this essay has three messages for psychiatrists.

(1) Whether the psychiatrist deems religious belief and experience illusory or not, it *is* reality that most patients have religious histories (however ambivalent) and believe in God, and that many continue to attend regular services. While this has no bearing whatsoever on the question of truth value or on the psychiatrist's personal beliefs about the matter, it alerts the clinician that there is no a priori reason to assume that religious experience and history will figure any less in the patient's well-being, illness, and total psychosocial fabric than do other areas of life. With their suggestion that psychiatry adopt a phenomenological, perspectival, and functional-adaptational approach to the individual patient's religious behavior, Boisen, Hiltner, and Tillich have emphasized the appropriateness of psychiatric acknowledgment of religious issues and of clerical-psychiatric dialogue.

(2) It is also reality that 41 percent of Americans say they would first seek out their pastor in times of mental and emotional distress and that ministers are exceptionally remiss in failing to refer their parishioners to psychiatric services. Surely, we cannot lay all responsibility at the door of public and pastoral attitudes. Should psychiatrists not consider that part of the problem may lie with their stance, however subtle, toward ministers and religionists? In any event, lack of psychiatrist-clergy collaboration seriously affects the preventive, therapeutic, and after-care services received by a large segment of the mentally ill population. Tremendous potential resources for the care of the psychiatrically distressed are left fallow. *It is the duty of psychiatrists to the public to utilize all available resources in the promotion of mental health and the treatment of mental disorder.* This is a matter not of crass adjustment—"adaptation" in the vulgar sense—to forms of belief with which psychiatrists may not agree, but rather of a dialogue with such institutions in the interests of patients' biopsychosocial well-being, or "adaptation" correctly understood.

(3) Serious reflection upon religious and mental-health issues disabuses psychiatrists of the hypocrisy that there are no moral and meta-

physical dimensions and implications in psychiatric theory and practice. Moreover, since such issues are social issues, they alert psychiatry
to its general failure to evolve a viable social ethic. Nor have psychiatrists articulated a self-conscious public philosophy—although they almost certainly implicitly practice any number of them—that guides
them in relationships with professions such as the law, education, the
ministry, general medicine, the other mental-health disciplines, and to
wider socioeconomic and political forces by which they are unwit-
tingly shaped and which, again, they may come to subserve. Whether
or not it would be feasible or even desirable for psychiatry to enunciate
any integrated and unitary public philosophy, it is socially irresponsible
to ignore psychiatry's powerful role in actually molding private and
public consciousness, the individual's and society's understanding of
themselves, and social mores. This third message is perhaps the most
important of all from the area of common concerns of psychiatry and
religion.

Notes

Gratefully dedicated to E. Mansell Pattison, M.D., profound student of psychiatry and religion.

This essay was a Plenary Presentation at the Twenty-fifth Birthday Annual
Meeting of the American Association of Pastoral Counselors in St. Louis on
April 8, 1989.

1. From the Washington School of Psychiatry, Joseph H. Smith, editor, and
Gloria Parloff, assistant editor, supply (personal communication) interesting
data on the relationship between Anton Boisen and the home-grown dean of
American psychiatry Harry Stack Sullivan. Boisen published eight articles and
several reviews in *Psychiatry* (which Sullivan launched and edited) from 1938
to 1952. When Sullivan's foster son, Jimmie, died, among his adopting father's
books was an inscribed copy of Boisen's 1936 groundbreaking interpersonal
religio-psychiatric study, *The Exploration of the Inner World;* the affinity
(perhaps mutually determinative) with Sullivan's interpersonal psychiatry and
perspective on schizophrenia is patent. Smith adds that Lewis Hill, well-known
Baltimore-Washington analyst and author of one of the first texts on psychotherapy with schizophrenics, was an admirer of Boisen's.

2. Elsewhere (Wallace 1984) I have argued that Freud's personal "repression" of the "big questions" failed, resulting in a number of highly conjectural,
even eccentric and fanciful compromise formations—e.g., his lifelong fascination with the occult and parapsychology; his "fate neurosis" and preoccupation with numbers and death dates; his occasional performance of magical, apo-
tropaic actions (such as smashing a cherished statue as a "health offering"

when his daughter was near death); his friendship with "mystical" physicians such as Fliess and Jung; his attitude toward German mechanistic science and toward even his own psychoanalysis; his ambivalent, lifelong preoccupation with religion; and, preeminently, metaphysical tracts such as *Beyond the Pleasure Principle,* fancied "history" such as *Totem and Taboo* and *Moses and Monotheism;* and "god-terms" such as "Eros," "Thanatos," the "Nirvana Principle," "repetition compulsion," and so forth.

3. When asked, shortly before he was incapacitated through coma following a tragic automobile accident in October 1987, where thirty years' reflection on the psychiatry-religion-ethics interface had led him on the relationship of sin to psychiatric disorder, distinguished social psychiatrist E. Mansell Pattison, until recently chairman of Psychiatry and Health Behavior at the Medical College of Georgia, replied, half jokingly, half seriously: "Sin is something we do constantly, psychopathological is something we are only part of the time" (personal communication, 1987). One is reminded of that splendidly ironic Genesis text: "The thoughts of the heart are only evil continuously." Dr. Pattison died, without regaining consciousness, on September 9, 1989.

References

Ackerknecht, Erwin. *A Short History of Medicine.* Rev. ed. Baltimore: John Hopkins University Press, 1982.

———. *Medicine and Ethnology.* Baltimore: Johns Hopkins Press, 1971.

Allers, Rudolph. *The Successful Error.* New York: Sheed and Ward, 1940.

Anderson, Robert. "The Role of the Church in the Community Based Care of the Chronically Mentally Disabled: Reclaiming an Historic Ministry." *Pastoral Psychology* 28 (1979): 38–52.

Bellah, Robert N., Madsen, Richard, Sullivan, William M., Swindler, Ann, and Tipton, Steven, M. *Habits of the Heart: Individualism and Commitment in American Life.* New York: Harper and Row, 1985.

Bergin, Allan E. "Religiosity and Mental Health: A Critical Re-Evaluation and Meta-Analysis." *Professional Psychology: Research and Practice* 14 (1983): 170–84.

Boisen, Anton. *The Exploration of the Inner World.* New York: Harper, 1936.

———. *Religion in Crisis and Custom: A Sociological and Psychological Study.* New York: Harper, 1945.

———. *Out of the Depths: An Autobiographical Study of Mental Disorder and Religious Experience.* New York: Harper, 1960.

Browning, Don S. *Religious Thought and the Modern Psychologies.* Philadelphia: Fortress, 1987.

Deikman, Arthur. *The Observing Self: Mysticism and Psychotherapy.* Boston: Beacon Press, 1982.

DeLuca, Anthony. *Freud and Future Religious Experience.* Totawa, N.J.: Littlefield, Adams, 1977.

Draper, Edgar. "On the Diagnostic Value of Religious Ideation." *Archives of General Psychiatry* 13 (1965):202–7.

Engelhardt, H. Tristram, Jr. "Psychotherapy as Meta-Ethics." *Psychiatry* 36 (1973):440–45.

Favazza, Armando. "Modern Christian Healing of Mental Illness." *American Journal of Psychiatry* 139 (1982):728–35.

Foucault, Michel. *Madness and Civilization.* New York: Meridian, 1965.

———. *The Order of Things.* New York: Harper and Row, 1970.

——— *The Birth of the Clinic.* New York: Vintage, 1975.

———. *Mental Illness and Psychology.* New York: Harper and Row, 1976a.

———. *The Archaeology of Knowledge.* New York: Harper and Row, 1976b.

———. *Discipline and Punish: The Birth of the Prison.* New York: Pantheon, 1977.

———. *The History of Sexuality.* 2 vols. New York: Pantheon, 1978, 1986.

Frankl, Viktor. *The Doctor and the Soul: From Psychotherapy to Logotherapy.* New York: A. Knopf, 1955.

Franzblau, Abraham. *Psychiatrists' Viewpoints of Religion and Their Services to Religious Institutions and the Ministry.* APA Task Force Report, Washington, D.C.: American Psychiatric Association, 1975.

Freud, Ernest, editor. *The Letters of Sigmund Freud, 1873–1939.* New York: Basic Books, 1975.

Freud, Sigmund. *The Standard Edition of the Complete Psychological Works of Sigmund Freud.* Edited and translated by James Strachey. 24 vols. London: Hogarth, 1953–74.

    Leonardo Da Vinci and a Memory of His Childhood (1910), vol. 11.

    "The Future Prospects of Psycho-Analytic Therapy" (1910), vol. 11.

    Introductory Lectures on Psycho-Analysis (1915–17), vols. 15, 16.

    Group Psychology and the Analysis of the Ego (1921), vol. 18.

    "Postscript to *The Question of Lay Analysis*" (1927), vol. 20.

    The Future of an Illusion (1927), vol. 21.

Fromm, Erich. *Sigmund Freud's Mission.* New York: Harper and Row, 1972.

Gaines, Atwood. "The Once- and the Twice-Born: Self and Practice among Psychiatrists and Christians." In *Physicians of Western Medicine,* edited by Robert Hahn and Atwood Gaines. Boston: D. Reidel, 1985.

Gallup, George. *Religion in America—50 Years: 1935–1985.* The Gallup Report. Princeton: Princeton Religious Research Center, 1985.

Gould, Stephen J. *The Panda's Thumb: More Reflections on Natural History.* New York: W. W. Norton, 1982.

Group for the Advancement of Psychiatry. *Psychiatry and Religion: Some Steps Toward Mutual Understanding and Usefulness.* Report Number 48. New York: G.A.P. Publications, 1960.

Hadaway, Charles, and Roof, Wayne. "Religious Commitment and the Quality of Life in American Society." *Review of Religious Research* 12 (1971):165–76.

Hartmann, Heinz. *Psychoanalysis and Moral Values.* New York: International Universities Press, 1960.

————. *Essays on Ego Psychology.* New York: International Universities Press, 1964.

Henry, William, Sims, John, and Spray, S. Lee. *The Fifth Profession: Becoming a Psychotherapist.* San Francisco: Jossey-Bass, 1971.

Hiltner, Seward. *Religion and Health.* New York: Macmillan, 1943.

————. "Freud, Psychoanalysis, and Religion." *Pastoral Psychology* 6 (1956): 9–21.

————. *Theological Dynamics.* Nashville, Tenn.: Abingdon Press, 1971.

Hiltner, Seward, and Colston, Lowell. *The Context of Pastoral Counseling.* Nashville, Tenn.: Abingdon Press, 1961.

Holifield, Brooks. *A History of Pastoral Care in America: From Salvation to Self-Realization.* Nashville, Tenn.: Abingdon Press, 1983.

Houck, John, and Moss, Daniel. "Pastoral Psychotherapy, the Fee-for-Service Model, and Professional Identity." *Journal of Religion and Health* 16 (1977):172–82.

Jackson, S. *Melancholia and Depression: From Hippocratic Times to Modern Concerns.* New Haven: Yale University Press, 1986.

James, William. *Principles of Psychology,* 2 vols. New York: Henry Holt, 1890.

————. *Varieties of Religious Experience.* New York: Henry Holt, 1902.

Jung, Carl G. *Psychology and Religion.* New Haven: Yale University Press, 1938.

Kadushin, Charles. *Why People Go to Psychiatrists.* New York: Atherton, 1969.

Kaplan, Harold, and Sadock, Benjamin, eds. *Comprehensive Textbook of Psychiatry,* 4th ed. Baltimore: Williams & Wilkins, 1985.

La Piere, Richard. *The Freudian Ethic.* London: Allen and Unwin, 1960.

Larson, David B., Pattison, E. Mansell, Blazer, Dan G., Omran, Abdul R., Kaplan, Berton H. "Systematic Analysis of Research on Religious Variables in Four Major Psychiatric Journals, 1978–1982." *American Journal of Psychiatry* 143 (1986):329–34.

Lasch, Christopher. *The Culture of Narcissism: American Life in an Age of Diminishing Expectations.* New York: W. W. Norton, 1979.

Lee, Robert. *Freud and Christianity.* London: James Daake, 1948.

Lindenthal, John. "Mental Status and Religious Behavior." *Journal for the Scientific Study of Religion* 9 (1970):143–49.

Linn, Louis, and Schwarz, Leo. *Psychiatry and Religious Experience.* New York: Random House, 1958.

Loomis, Earl A. *The Self in Pilgrimage.* New York: Harper, 1960.

Malony, H. Newton. "The Psychologist-Christian." *Journal of the American Scientific Affiliation* 24 (1972):135–44.

McCann, Richard. *The Churches and Mental Health.* New York: Basic Books, 1962.

McCready, W., and Greeley, A. *The Ultimate Value of the American Population.* Beverly Hills, Calif.: Sage, 1976.

Meng, Heinrich, and Freud, Ernest. *Psychoanalysis and Faith: The Letters of Sigmund Freud and Oskar Pfister.* New York: Basic Books, 1963.

Menninger, Karl. *Whatever Became of Sin?* New York: Hawthorne, 1973.

Mora, George. "History of Psychiatry." In *Comprehensive Textbook of Psychiatry,* 4th ed., edited by Harold Kaplan and Benjamin Sadock. Baltimore: Williams & Wilkins, 1985.

Mowrer, O. Hobart. *The Crisis in Psychiatry and Religion.* New York: Van Nostrand, 1961.

Niebuhr, Reinhold. *The Nature and Destiny of Man,* vol. 1. New York: Scribner's, 1941.

———. "Human Creativity and Self-Concern in Freud's Thought." In *Freud and the 20th Century,* edited by B. Nelson. New York: World, 1957.

Oates, Wayne. *Protestant Pastoral Counseling.* Philadelphia: Westminster, 1962.

Outler, Alvin. *Psychotherapy and the Christian Message.* New York: Harper, 1954.

Pattison, E. Mansell. "Functions of the Clergy in the Community Mental Health Center." *Pastoral Psychology* 16 (1965):21–26.

———. *Pastor and Parish: A Systems Approach.* Philadelphia: Fortress, 1977.

———. "Psychiatry and Religion Circa 1978: Analysis of a Decade," Parts I and II. *Pastoral Psychology* 27 (1978):8–25, 119–47.

Peck, M. Scott. *The Road Less Traveled.* New York: Touchstone, 1978.

Pfister, Oskar. *Psychoanalyse und Weltanschauung.* Vienna: Internationaler Psychoanalytische Verlag, 1928.

Pruyser, Paul W. *A Dynamic Psychology of Religion.* New York: Harper & Row, 1968.

———. *Between Belief and Unbelief.* New York: Harper & Row, 1974.

———. *The Minister as Diagnostician.* Philadelphia: Westminster, 1976.

Ricoeur, Paul. *Freud and Philosophy.* New Haven: Yale University Press, 1970.

Rieff, Philip. *Freud: The Mind of the Moralist.* New York: Viking, 1959.

———. *The Triumph of the Therapeutic: Uses of Faith After Freud.* New York: Harper, 1966.

Roazen, Paul. *Freud and His Followers.* New York: Meridian, 1971.

Roberts, David. *Psychotherapy and a Christian View of Man.* New York: Scribner's, 1950.

Sheen, Fulton. *Peace of Soul.* New York: McGraw-Hill, 1949.

Sigerist, Henry. *A History of Medicine,* vol. 1. Oxford: Oxford University Press, 1951.

Spero, Moshe H. *Judaism and Psychology: Halakhic Perspectives.* New York: Yeshiva University Press, 1980.

Stark, Richard. "Psychopathology and Religious Commitment." *Review of Religious Research* 12 (1971):165–76.

Stokes, Allison. *Ministry after Freud.* New York: Pilgrim Press, 1985.

Temkin, Oswei. *The Double Face of Janus and Other Essays in the History of Medicine.* Baltimore: Johns Hopkins University Press, 1977.

Tillich, Paul. *Dynamics of Faith.* New York: Harper, 1957.

Tournier, Paul. *Guilt and Grace.* New York: Harper, 1958.

VanderVeldt, John, and Odenwald, Richard. *Psychiatry and Catholicism.* New York: McGraw-Hill, 1957.

Wallace, Edwin R., IV. *Freud and Anthropology: A History and Reappraisal.* New York: International Universities Press, 1983.

———. "Freud and Religion: A History and Reappraisal." In *The Psychoanalytic Study of Society,* vol. 10, edited by W. Muensterberger, L. B. Boyer, and S. Grolnick. Hillsdale, N.J.: Analytic Press, 1984.

———. "Further Reflections on Psychoanalysis and Religion." *Listening: The Journal for Religion and Culture* 20 (1985):175–94.

———. "Freud as Ethicist." In *Freud: Appraisals and Reappraisals,* edited by P. Stepansky. Hillsdale, N.J.: Analytic Press, 1986a.

———. "Determinism, Possibility, and Ethics." *Journal of the American Psychoanalytic Association* 34 (1986b):933–74.

Wallwork, Ernest. "Thou Shalt Love Thy Neighbor as Thyself: A Freudian Critique." *Journal of Religious Ethics* 10 (1982):269–84.

White, Victor. *Soul and Psyche: An Inquiry into the Relationship of Psychotherapy and Religion.* New York: Harper, 1960.

Worcester, Elwood, McComb, Samuel, and Coriat, I. *Religion and Medicine: The Moral Control of Nervous Disorders.* New York: Moffat, Yard, 1908.

Zilboorg, Gregory. *Psychoanalysis and Religion.* New York: Farrar, Straus, and Cudahy, 1962.

12 De-authorization of the Law: Paul and the Oedipal Model

José Faur

Christianity is a unique system within the history of religions insofar as it comes to substitute a new religion for another that it recognizes as authoritative. Paradoxically, the religion for which it claims to substitute is the ultimate justification for its own being and authority. The Christian Scripture, that is, comes not only to displace the Torah but also to fulfill it. Similarly, the Christian faithful displaces, and thereby becomes, *Verus Israel*—the "true Israel."

This act of displacement and substitution is subject to two alternatives: it can lead either to insight into the similarities between the old and the new, or to an emphasis on the differences. Over the centuries, there have been various negative modes—ranging from the merely defensive to the demonic—of emphasizing the differences, modes that have transformed the people of Israel into a stateless mass void of rights and virtues, wherein both the Hebrew Scripture and the Hebrew people are regarded as dead and deadly. Although much recent work in the psychoanalytic study of religion has concentrated on the relation of religion to the stages of preoedipal development, the oedipal stage might best help us understand some of these defensive dimensions of the Christian posture toward Judaism.

I

In classic psychoanalytic theory, of course, "God" is thought of as the projection of the father's image, and therefore, as Freud writes, our "personal relation to God depends on [our] relation to [our] father in the flesh" (*S.E.* 13:147).[1] Freud also made the very important observa-

222

nt. The accusation of deicide against the Jews displaces the guilt
n the son by projecting it onto the Jewish people. Put differently: a
's symbolic murder of the Father could be redeemed only when
mother accepts the son as her rightful consort. By refusing to ac-
t the son in place of the Father, the Jews or symbolic wife of the
-Father rendered the son no longer a Savior but a deicide—the
rper of the Father.[11]

The oedipal symbolism of this doctrine is strikingly clear, but it
ld escape those who are culturally immersed in it. The Hebrew
pture representing Law and paternal authority is to be substituted
by the Son who replaces authority with Love. The Son might be
ified if the mother would accept him in matrimony. Were the
ple of Israel to have accepted the Son as their rightful husband and
, the demise of the Father would have been justified. As in the
lipus complex, there is a need simultaneously to murder, identify
h, and replace the Father. As it stands, the refusal of the Jews to
ept the Son in place of the Father must then be explained as an act
etrayal, as an expression of their own wretchedness. Accordingly,
ipal guilt must be displaced—theologically speaking, *imputed*—
hem.

n a sense, the symbolic elimination of the father-role is already ex-
it in the denial of the physical paternity of Jesus. It has been ob-
ed that "the father-denial ideology" is oedipal in its motive: "He is
killed, he is defined out of existence as far as his children are con-
ned." According to this belief, the "mother is impregnated by a
it of the totem." Socially, the father is "castrated, rendered ineffec-
, defined away" (Fox 1980, 70–71). Anthropologically, this repre-
ts an "act of symbolic patricide" (Jones 1925). It is an expression of
p hostility on the part of the son, and "is directed against the father
is role not as a pater, but as a progenitor" (Spiro 1982, 65). Con-
ing a son's rejection of the role of his father as genitor, Melford
o writes:

> That a son should wish to reject knowledge of the fact that his father is
> his genitor is not, of course, a strange notion in the annals of child devel-
> opment. One explanation for this frequently found wish is based on the
> assumption—derived from psycho-analytic theory, and supported by a
> great deal of empirical evidence—that fathers are both loved and hated,
> and that the latter emotion derives from one or both of the following
> conditions: resentment over their punitive authority, and/or jealous ri-
> valry for the love (sexual and/or affectionate) of the mother. But hatred
> of the father leads to a typical Oedipal conflict. On the one hand, the
> child, motivated by resentment or by rivalry, wishes to harm, to be rid,

tion in *Moses and Monotheism* that Christianity is a "son" religion,
whereas Judaism is a "father" religion:

> [T]he Christian ceremony of Holy Communion, in which the believer
> incorporates the Saviour's blood and flesh, repeats the content of the
> old totem meal. . . . The ambivalence that dominates the relation to the
> father was clearly shown, however, in the final outcome of the religious
> novelty. Ostensibly aimed at propitiating the father god, it ended in his
> being dethroned and got rid of. Judaism had been a religion of the fa-
> ther; Christianity became a religion of the son. The old God the Father
> fell back behind Christ; Christ, the Son, took his place, just as every son
> had hoped to do in primaeval times. [*S.E.* 23:87–88]

Paul's doctrines, especially, lend themselves to the interpretation
that in Christianity the God-Father not only was "dethroned" but also
was dead, and replaced by the Son. For the Passion can symbolize not
only the God-Father sacrificing his son but also his yielding to the
oedipal instincts to kill the Son. Similarly, the Son can be seen as fulfilling his wishes and replacing the Father. Referring to this pivotal point
in Christianity, Freud writes in *Totem and Taboo* that the son also attains the goal of "his wishes *against* the father. He himself became
God, beside, or, more correctly, in place of the father. A son-religion
displaced the father-religion" (*S.E.* 13:154).

The Freudian interpretation of Jesus' death thus involves two distinct scenarios: one in which the father kills the son, and a second
where the father dies and the son is enthroned. Both scenarios are inti-
mately related: the second is the result of the first, the first is the outer
layer of the second. In the first scenario, the God-Father kills his son as
an expiatory sacrifice. In the second scenario, introduced by Paul, it is
the God-Father who finally dies. And in classical psychoanalysis, both
these scenarios are closely interrelated.

Child sacrifice and infanticide were common religious practices
throughout the heathen world but fiercely opposed by the prophets of
Israel. "The increasing resistance to killing one's own child," explains
Wellisch, "created the wish that another child should die in his place."
Eventually, "This led to the widespread ancient custom that the King's
son should be sacrificed as a *vicarious sacrifice* for the community
(1954, 27).[2] In Christian Scripture, this model was adopted and God
was depicted as killing his own son in a sacrificial atonement. A variation of the same oedipal motif, foreshadowing the actual Passion, is the
story of King Herod's attempt to murder the infant Jesus. As a man,
Herod represents the father yielding to the oedipal impulse to kill his
son; as a king he foreshadows the final Passion, where God sacrifices

his only son: the miraculous event of the Passion requires a genuine *death* (thus making resurrection real) (see Paul 1980, 292). The second scenario is the effect of Paul's interpretation of the Passion: as a result of the resurrection of the son, the God-Father dies and is replaced by Jesus.

The code-term encapsulating the legal theory underlying the entire edifice of the Pauline doctrine is *daitake*. Originally this term stood for "agreement" or "covenant," as in Aristophanes' *The Birds* (439). It is used in this specific sense in the *Septuagint* (the Greek translation of Hebrew Scripture) to translate the Hebrew word *berit*, "covenant."[3] Similarly, in 1 Maccabees (1:57, 63) it stands for "Torah" or "Law." Later, in Hellenistic literature, *daitake* underwent a semantic change and came to mean "last will" or "testament." Christian Scripture and rabbinic literature used the word exclusively in this particular sense.[4]

Paul's doctrine of the abrogation of the Torah and definition of the Christian Scripture as a "New Testament" thus applied to the early *daitake*-covenant of the Septuagint, the later meaning of "last will" or "testament" current in Hellenistic literature.[5] Alluding to the legal rights of a testator to annul his last will and issue a new one, Paul argued that the Christian Scripture is the "New Testament" or new *daitake* issued by the Father, annulling thereby the Torah or "Old Testament." And Paul himself becomes "the minister of this new *daitake*" (2 Cor. 3:6).[6]

The Torah or now "Old Testament" becomes, then, a kind of divine "last will." For a *daitake* in the sense of a "last will" is operative only upon the death of the testator. Before the new *daitake* could take effect, God, so to speak (or more precisely the Jewish God-father), would have to die.[7] For example, in a key passage in Hebrews (9:15–17), Paul explains how upon the death of the testator the beneficiaries of the new *daitake* were called to take hold of their eternal inheritance:

> And because of this, he [Jesus] is a negotiator [*mesites*] of a new *daitake*, so that death having occurred for redemption of transgressions under the first *daitake*, those having called out might receive the promise of the everlasting inheritance. For where a *daitake* is, death must take place of him who willed [*diathemenon*] a *daitake*, since it never has force when the testator is living.

In Christian commentary, the testator's death is now accomplished vicariously through Jesus' death, and Jesus becomes the "mediator" in a "sacramental" sense. This interpretation, a "strong misreading," altered what had been the original function of *mesites* as "negotiator" or

"arbitrator." The *mesites* or arbitrator was to be
perimeter of both the testator and the beneficiari
Jesus must be regarded as the one *negotiating*
will and *arbitrating* on behalf of the two parties
heirs. Originally, this responsibility of *mesites* v
while he was alive: if Jesus as *mesites* had died *in*
the *daitake* legally would have been invalid and
would have remained unfulfilled. Now, however,
testator—the God-Father—Jesus became "the
daitake" (Heb. 8:6).

Another variation involving the "death of God
in Romans (7:2–4). When attempting to explain
longer bound to observe the Torah, Paul compar
to a widow; because her husband has died, she i
bound to him.[8]

> For the married woman was bound by law to t
> the husband dies she is set free from the law of
> the husband is living she will be called an adult
> other man's. But if the husband dies she is free fr
> not to be an adulteress by becoming another
> brothers, you also were made dead to the La
> Christ, for you to become another's to the one
> that we may bear fruit to God.

Paul contends that Israel, who is bound to Gc
nantal ties as a wife to her husband, is now wido
the Son, who had been raised from the dead. In
argument is introduced, namely, that the *peopl*
in Jesus, and thus they are now free from the La

There are two implications: as a widow, Isra
ture with no rights of her own. At the same tin
marry the son and "bear the fruit to God." It i
point: Israel's means of salvation is by marrying
do so, Israel is beyond salvation, but more impc
son's designs: his mission remains unfulfilled.[10]
possible sources for depicting Israel as deject
therefore legitimating violence against her, a poi
tragic consequences in Western history.

In classical counteroedipal fashion, the crucif
terpreted as the murdering of Jesus—the Messi
the Jews—by his own children, the people of Is
the primeval oedipal guilt, beyond redemptio

of the father. On the other hand, whether from a *talion* fear ("I want to harm him, therefore he wants to harm me") or from guilt ("Since he loves me and/or since I love him, how can I wish to harm him?") this wish is extremely painful. In the absence of institutional or cultural assistance in dealing with this conflict, the child must cope with it by his own internal resources, of which I shall mention only two. He can *repress* his hatred, which is the typical (and normal) technique found in Western society, or he can express it symbolically by *denying* in fantasy that his father is genitor. (The latter is often accomplished, both in private fantasy as well as in hero myths, by the substitution of grandiose fathers—gods, kings, and so on—for the real father.) Sometimes, it should be added, rather than denying that his father is genitor, the child denies that he had any genitor. [1968, 256]

The Oedipus myth had nuclear importance in the formation of the religious life and ideas of the pagan world, a point extensively examined by Theodor Reik. Christianity, of all the major religions, succeeded best in synthesizing the psychic constellations of impulses and conflicts of the Greek and Roman societies—a source of its great appeal. Cautiously hinting at the impact of the Oedipus myth on Christianity, Reik writes:

> I do not know how far I have succeeded in giving the reader of the foregoing pages a notion of the great importance of the Oedipus myth in the religious life of the Greeks, and of the close and cryptic relation of the performance of the *Oedipus* to the religious ritual of Hellas. The profound and lasting influence of the Oedipus legend in antiquity must, I believe, be ascribed to the religious motive which revealed the instinctual life of men in conflict with the laws of the gods. For here, as in the Dionysian games, and the ritual of Attis, Adonis, and Osiris, a young revolutionary savior was represented, rebelling against the old and powerful father-god and suffering a terrible punishment for his offense. I believe the influence of these performances may be compared with that of the ecclesiastical Passion play on the faithful of the Middle Ages, for it depended on the same psychic precedents. The prehistory of Christ is not unlike that of Oedipus. It should be emphasized that in the Oedipus myth, as we now have it, the profoundest psychic motives, which led to the formation of religion, though unrecognized by the auditors, were nonetheless plastically represented, and that here an unconcious sense of guilt was evoked. [1988, 61; see esp. 21–65]

II

The oedipal complex, although universal in structure, is subject to cross-cultural variability.[12] I would also argue here that Judaism is one

of the variants wherein the possibility of oedipal resolution is augmented in favor of renunciation, sublimation, and the acceptance of a
supreme Law representing the will of the Father (see Zeligs 1988,
xviii, xxiii, 311–14). Various cultural factors could have contributed
to this outcome. To begin with, the Jewish Law was not imposed but
was the result of an *accord* negotiated by the people of Israel and God;
a mutual *berit* or "covenant" (the *daitake* of the Septuagint) was established. The people of Israel "choose" God, and God "chooses" the
people of Israel. By "choice" (*behira*), a free, spontaneous act is meant,
unconditioned by either an outside force or an inner compulsion. The
Law-*berit* embraces all—God the Father, the biological father and his
offspring, as well as all social, political and ecclesiastical authorities
and institutions (see Faur 1968, 33–55).

Freud writes that "the authority of the father or the parents is introjected into the ego, and there it forms the nucleus of the super-ego,
which takes over the severity of the father and perpetuates his prohibition against incest" (*S.E.* 19:176). In Jewish thought, though, because
authority rests in the Jewish Law and not in the *person* of the father,
hostility can be significantly reduced. In exercising his authority, the
father is merely an instrument of the Law: were he to order his son to
break the Law, he should not be obeyed (*Mishne Tora, Mamrim*
6:14). Moreover, in Judaism, the father's authority is not categorically
superior to that of the mother. The child must honor his father first
simply because—*as a consequence of the matrimonial bonds*—the
mother, too, owes him respect. If the parents divorce, it is up to the
son to choose whom he wants to honor first.[13]

Unlike the Oedipus and other ancient myths dealing with father-son
hostility, in the biblical story of the ʿ*Aqeda* or "Binding"—where Abraham binds his son Isaac as a sacrifice to be offered to God (Gen.
22:1–9)—neither father nor son is killed.[14] Rather, the ʿ*Aqeda* shows
how the discovery of the Law leads to conscience formation and a successful resolution of oedipal hostility. Abraham is restrained by a Law
that stands above father and child. From "the delusion of parental omnipotence," the child passes into the discovery of a moral father and a
supreme Law. In Richard Kaufman's interpretation:

> The wishes to displace, succeed, or imitate the father can be superseded
> by an acceptance, respect, and cultivation of the father's values, stan
> dards, goals, morals, and those of the parental generation. Father's val
> ues, the child can recognize, have existence apart from father. There is a
> change of function of father image from regulator to exemplar. The
> child can see the parent demonstrate the positive implications of plac

ing morality and justice superordinate to power and brute strength. The
father who acts becomes the father who is acted on and, ultimately, the
father who acts upon himself. Finally, to the image of the ideal father is
added the image of the father as a man *with* ideas. The dreaded oedipal
father becomes the postoedipal father and his heritage. [1982, 253]

It also seems that Abraham succeeded in attaining a measure of reconciliation with his own father, Terah.[15] By contrast, Oedipus, ban-
ished by his father, eventually became his father, and inflicted on himself the wrath of the father. As Kaufman puts it:

> There is a salient distinction between Abraham and Oedipus. Abraham
> dealt with his father. At the crossroads, Oedipus *became* his father, a
> vengeful, hateful, impulsive man. There was no atonement, repentance,
> or reconciliation. When caught for his crime, Oedipus turned on him-
> self in an outburst of rage with the same unforgiving wrath that de-
> stroyed Laius, a wrath that now typified his own superego. Through
> Oedipus's own superego, Laius achieved a posthumous victory. What fa-
> ther inflicted on the son was repeated by the son upon himself: mutila-
> tion and exile. [1982, 250][16]

In Jewish tradition, however, by accepting the Law-*berit,* the son
secures his own sacred and inviolable rights. Parental authority as
a source of rivalry is mitigated. (One could also argue that in Jewish
culture, it is indeed the very rejection of the Law and covenantal
ground between Father and Son that intensifies oedipal resentment
and hostility.)

In this context, it is highly significant that in developing Christian
doctrine, Paul transfigured *daitake,* the term standing for "Law" and
"covenant" (and the grounds for father-son reconciliation), into a
term standing for "testament" and the death of the father. In doing so,
Paul transformed the Scriptural concept of sin into oedipal guilt. In
order to explain the need for Jesus' expiatory death, Paul argued that
God cannot freely forgive the repentant. Hence, Jesus' death must be
the sole means of salvation. And yet a fundamental premise of the Hebrew Scripture is that sin is redeemable: through *Teshuba,* "repen-
tance," the sinner totally erases his transgressions (see Fromm 1969,
193–94). In fact, according to the Rabbis, sins and transgressions can
be transformed into something positive. "At the rank where the repentant stand," taught the Rabbis, "the perfect righteous cannot stand"
(*Berakhot* 34b; see *Mishne Tora, Teshuba* 7:4). George Foot Moore,
the greatest rabbinic scholar to have come from the Christian world,
noted in amazement:

> How a Jew of Paul's antecedents could ignore, and by implication deny, the great prophetic doctrine of repentance, which, individualized and interiorized, was a cardinal doctrine of Judaism, namely, that God, out of love, freely forgives the sincerely penitent sinner and restores him to his favor—that seems from the Jewish point of view inexplicable. [1967, 151]

Paul's position becomes comprehensible when we realize that he had abandoned Scriptural sin (*ḥeṭ,* "error," or *'abera,* "transgression") for oedipal, that is, Greek guilt. For the Hebrews, sin was never final and categoric: it never carried the overwhelming sense of helplessness and foreboding. As Mordechai Rotenberg writes, psychologically the Jews treated their past as an "open book," subject to *hermeneutics,* and thereby revision and change. The relation of the sinner to the past is not a schizophrenic disconnection with his former transgression but a *confrontation* and new representation of the sin (Rotenberg 1986).[17] By contrast, oedipal guilt, like Paul's original sin, is *hermetically* sealed, a "closed book" and beyond correction. It is hereditary, and it demands *catharsis,* "guilt cleansing," or a schizophrenic "death-rebirth" resulting in an absolute rupture of the sinner with his past (see Dodds 1968, 33–37; Rotenberg 1986, 51–54).

This type of guilt is implacable and unremitting, haunting the offender and his descendants until the end of time. When effective, atonement must involve the symbolic death of the offender. Put in different words: whereas according to the Torah a son could always return to the God-Father, Oedipus can never return to Laius. And by opting for the Greek *guilt* in place of the Hebrew *Teshuba,* Paul in effect transfigured the God-Father of the Hebrews into the oedipal father of the Greeks.[18] The consequence was an absolute and irreconcilable break with the Jewish Scripture.

III

There is an important aspect of the translation—both literal and figurative—of Hebrew Scripture into Greek. According to Jewish tradition the Torah was translated by Jews into Greek under the patronage of Ptolemy II Philadelphus (285–246 BCE). Written in the colloquial language of the time and in an uncomplicated, flowing style, this translation (the Septuagint) made a great impact among the general Greek-speaking public (Bickerman 1976a, 175–77).[19] The existence of proselytism among the Greek-speaking population further corroborates this point. (Perhaps the spread of Christianity was partly dependent on this knowledge of the Torah by the masses.)

And yet it was ignored by the Greek intelligentsia. Although the ancient Greeks were the first to study the peculiarities of other people and had ample contacts with the Jews, they failed to make any mention of them. When Greek philosophers and historians mentioned the Jews after the destruction of the Persian Empire, they refrained from describing them *objectively,* as *they really were;* rather, the Jews were depicted in quasi-mythological terms, as a race of philosophers and priestly sages. As the historian Arnaldo Momigliano writes:

> About 300 B.C. Greek intellectuals presented the Jews to the Greek world as philosophers, legislators and wise men. A few decades later, the alleged philosophers and legislators made public in Greek their own philosophy and legislation. The Gentile world remained indifferent. . . . The failure of the LXX [Septuagint] to arouse the interest of the pagan intelligentsia of the third century B.C. was the end of the myth of the Jewish philosopher. [1975, 92; see also 74–78, 82–87][20]

From that moment on, any mention by Greek writers of the Jews and the Law would be of an anti-Semitic character. And only what *others* said about the origin and beliefs of the Jews (Manetho, Apion, Apollonius, Molon, and so forth) mattered, whereas Jewish accounts of themselves were systematically ignored. What was the reason for this change of heart? More specifically, why did Greek thinkers refuse to look at the Scripture and come to grips with its ideas and institutions?

An even more disturbing aspect of this situation was that the Torah was not simply *ignored.* Antiochus IV Epiphanes, the Seleucid king, aimed at the total eradication of the Torah. About December 167 B.C.E. he undertook the systematic destruction of Jewish life in Judea, making the observance of the Torah a capital offense. The population of Judea was subjected to torture, martyrdom, and wholesale massacre. This type of religious warfare had no precedent. It violated the standards of the time: Hellenization never involved forcible abolishment of an existing cult or the imposition of a new one. Moreover, it ran contrary to the king's own ideology: as a follower of the Epicurean school he should have condoned the observance of traditional rites (Bickerman 1976b, 72, 68).

The Law was to be abrogated not simply by forcing the Hebrews to *abstain* from practicing its commandments but by imposing on them a new cult. Referring to this basic issue, Elias Bickerman writes: "The persecution meant not only the suspension of the previous law, but also the introduction of a new one. This is the point at which any attempt fails to explain the measures of Epiphanes on the basis of his own ideology or on the conditions of the age" (1979, 78).

Furthermore, such a "cult" consisted of *transgressing* the laws of the Torah. It was a carefully thought-out system aiming at abolishing a religion by forbidding what it had prescribed and prescribing what it had forbidden. The scrolls of the Law were ordered destroyed, and their possession was punishable by death. The sanctity of the Temple and the priesthood was abolished. The most important laws regulating the spiritual life of the Jews were prohibited under the penalty of death. Those who persisted in the practice of the Sabbath, circumcision, and other commandments were massacred or martyred. What the Law had forbidden was now imposed on the Jews as a *religious duty.*[21]

There is evidence that these activities were not motivated by antipathy to the Jewish laws themselves, for the Samaritans were free to observe the Sabbath, circumcision, and all the other laws that were forbidden to the Jews under the penalty of death (Hengel 1974, 1:293–94). Anti-Semitic writers, from Diodorus to Tacitus to modern apologists, defended Antiochus on the grounds that he was only attempting to bring civilization and enlightenment to the Jews. Bickerman, though, has shown that contemporary documentation, both Jewish and Greek, fails to mention that he ever had such a mission in mind: "We do not find a single reference to the civilizing mission of Epiphanes or the barbarism of the Jews" (1979, 12–14, 81).[22] It has also been argued that enlightened Hellenized Jews, advocating some sort of "rational natural religion," had persuaded the king to take these measures in order to save their brethren from "Jewish particularism" (Bickerman 1979, 83–88; Hengel 1974, 1:292–303). There is no doubt, as contemporary Jewish sources clearly show, that there were those who had "abandoned the holy covenant" (1 Mac. 1:15) and collaborated with the Greeks. At the same time, it is hardly conceivable that Jewish reformers would have sanctioned the massacres and atrocities committed against the people of Judea—that they would approve, for example, of murdering newborn infants, simply because they were circumcised, by tieing them around their mothers' necks and smashing them down the wall of the city (1 Mac. 1:60–61).

Granted that *at some level* Jewish apostates participated in the abolition of the Law; granted, too, that there may have been ideological and political reasons on the part of the king; yet the crux of the problem remains unsolved: How can one explain the brutality and ruthlessness with which this cultic reform was implemented? Why was there such an intense hatred against the Law and the people who observed it? And why did the same attitude continue to thrive in the West throughout the ages, through the Hadrian persecution (117–138 C.E.) to the Spanish and Portuguese Inquisitions, to countless similar atrocities punctuating Jewish history until modern times?

Since the problem pertains to the ethos of a people, the answer must be sought in the realm of the psychological and the anthropological, along with the strictly historical.

IV

Again, the oedipal model can help us understand the Greek mind and its attitude toward the Law. It is especially interesting at this juncture to recall that *Oedipus Rex,* in contradistinction to the full trilogy by Sophocles, and to the oedipal complex, deals almost exclusively with rebellion against authority (Fromm 1959, 424–26, 445–48). Jewish contemporary sources, and Josephus later, offered a psychological reason for the Greek attitude toward the Law and persecution of the Jews: "the arrogance of the Gentiles." [23] Simply put, it meant that the Greek conquerors could not conceive of a moral Law, absolute and categoric, standing above *all* types of authority, including their own. That was perceived as a challenge to heroic thinking.

Using an expression similar to that used by the Jewish authors, the great Italian thinker Giambattista Vico also referred to "the supreme arrogance characteristic of barbarous times, which formed their heroic nature," and to "the conceit of nations." [24] An important element of "heroic thinking" was the attitude of the Greeks toward their wives and children. "Wives were maintained as a necessity of nature for the procreation of children. In other respects they were treated as slaves" (Vico, #671, 254).[25] A consequence of this attitude was the harsh, brutal authority exercised by the father. The heroic ideal of education involved what Vico describes as "cyclopean paternal authority":

> the [heroic] education of the young was severe, harsh, and cruel, as in the case of the unlettered Lacadaemonians, who were the heroes of Greece. These people, in order to teach their sons to fear neither pain nor death, would beat them within an inch of their lives in the temple of Diana, so that they often fell dead in agonies of pain beneath their father's blows. This cyclopean paternal authority survived among both the Greeks and Romans, permitting them to kill their innocent born babes. [Vico, #670, 254; cf. #256, 80–81]

The structure of the Greek family, in other words, served as the grounds for the archaic religious feelings of guilt. Accordingly, Dodds characterizes Greek culture as "guilt culture" and describes the Greek family as follows:

> Its organization, as in all Indo-European societies, was patriarchal; its law was *patria potestas.* The head of a household is its king . . . and his

position is still described by Aristotle as analogous to that of a king. Over his children his authority is in early times unlimited: he is free to expose them in infancy, and in manhood to expel an erring or rebellious son from the community, as Theseus expelled Hyppolytus, as Oeneus expelled Tydeus, as Strophios expelled Pylades, as Zeus himself cast out Hephaestos from Olympus for siding with his mother. In relation to his father, the son had duties but no rights; while his father lived, he was a perpetual minor—a state of affairs which lasted at Athens down to the sixth century, when Solon introduced certain safeguards. And indeed more than two centuries after Solon the tradition of family jurisdiction was still so strong that even Plato—who was certainly no admirer of the family—had to give it a place in his legislation. [1968, 45–46; see also chap. 2]

This family structure resulted in an unshakable feeling of dread and anxiety, symptomatic of strong repression:

The peculiar horror with which the Greeks viewed offenses against the father, and the peculiar religious sanctions to which the offender was thought to be exposed, are in themselves suggestive of strong repressions. So are the many stories in which a father's curse produces terrible consequences—stories like those of Phoenix, of Hyppolytus, of Pelops and his sons, of Oedipus and his sons—all of them, it would seem, products of a relatively late period, when the position of the father was not entirely secure. [Dodds 1968, 46]

This situation gave rise to strong feelings of hostility and aggression against the father:

The family situation in ancient Greece, like the family situation today, gave rise to infantile conflicts whose echoes lingered in the unconscious mind of the adult. With the rise of the Sophistic Movement, the conflict became in many households a fully conscious one: young men began to claim that they had a "natural right" to disobey their fathers. But it is a fair guess that such conflicts already existed at the unconscious level from a very much earlier date—that in fact they go back to the earliest unconfessed stirrings of individualism in a society where family solidarity was still universally taken for granted. [Dodds 1968, 47]

A similar situation prevailed in Roman society, where the power of the fathers over the sons was total and absolute. Sons belonged to the "have-not" group and constituted a rebellious class striving to usurp parental authority. Concerning the status of the son in Roman society, Otto Rank noted:

The right of every citizen to social fatherhood meant no right for the son except the one to become a father in his turn, that is, a social type prescribed by this first totalitarian state. Since the legal power of the father over his sons was equivalent to his power over his slaves (the word "family" is derived from "famulus"—servant, slave) we can justly say that the sons dominated by legal fatherhood actually were the first "have-nots." Not that the slaves had more, but they had no hope and hence no real desire to demand or take what the "haves" possessed. It was different with the sons, who, despite their lack of legal rights, were brought up with the idea of promotion—provided they behaved—from the "have-not" into the "have" group. Hence, they could easily form the nucleus of a rebellious class striving to overthrow the ruling class of fathers. [1958, 126]

The Roman father had invested himself with the same attributes of the hero and best exemplified the primeval tyrannical dominance over the "herd of brothers":

At the height of the patriarchal rule in ancient Rome, the father had become invested with a power derived from the magic self of the hero in whose image civic fatherhood was created as a social type. Paradoxically enough, it seems that Freud's "primitive dominance of the father" who ruled tyrannically over the "herd of brothers" only existed politically in the highly organized Roman state at the peak of its power. [126]

In Western tradition, the father continued to exercise "heroic authority" until relatively recent times. (Rank writes that this patriarchal ideology collapsed with the end of imperialism in World War I.)

Malinowski has described this kind of father as the "absolute ruler of the family," "the source of authority," and "the origin of punishment." In families of lower economic income, the father is brutal and sadistic:

When a father returns home tired from work, or drunk from the inn, he naturally vents his ill-temper on the family, and bullies mother and children. There is no village, no poor quarter in a modern town, where cases could not be found of sheer, patriarchal cruelty. From my own memory, I could quote numerous cases where peasant fathers would, on returning home drunk, beat the children for sheer pleasure, or drag them out of bed and send them into the cold night. [Malinowski 1953, 29, cf. 43–44]

One could well argue that this behavior is less than typical and does not exemplify the Western father, particularly in our times. Furthermore, the father's brutality need not be the grounds for filial hostility. The father's harsh treatment of the son may be motivated by his own oedipal rivalry (see Malinowski 1953, 27, n. 1, and Spiro 1982, 36–37). Be that as it may, the absolute authority exercised by the father in

Western tradition resulted in profound resentment harbored by sons against their fathers, as well as the augmented sympathy and love toward their mothers—two essential elements of the oedipal model. It also resulted in a "guilt culture"—that is, a society obsessed with obtaining atonement for an archaic sense of guilt. And short of atonement, guilt feeling as anger turning inward can be temporarily alleviated by finding a scapegoat upon which to vent anger outwardly. Anti-Semitism, both military and theological, often served this purpose.

V

The oedipal complex, of course, can undergo structural transformations, and this is particularly true in societies in which it is not successfully resolved, so that there is a need for constant repression. As Spiro notes:

> in societies in which unconscious Oedipal conflicts require persistent repression for their containment, the Oedipus complex may undergo structural transformations as a result of defensively motivated projections and displacements which importantly affect other social relationships and institutions. [Spiro 1982, 172–73]

Persecution of the Jews may indeed be regarded as one of those cultural displacement mechanisms designed to drain off hostile emotions.[26] The fact that in the persecutions, the Jew would be burned wrapped in the scroll of the Torah shows the intimate relation between Jew and Law in the eyes of the gentiles (see Faur 1986, 4–6). That is, the Greek, Roman, and other subsequent conquerors perceived the Jew as the embodiment of the Law and the "representative of the God-Father" on earth, the personification of God's authority. The gentile hated and murdered the Jew for the same reason that Brutus raged against Caesar and killed him.

Thus anti-Semitism may be perceived as a culturally constituted defense, designed to gratify the oedipal impulses of society and thereby protect it from disruptive, antisocial behavior.[27] As with all culturally sanctioned myths, the individual does not feel any moral or psychological responsibility for acting out those fantasies. With the advent of Christianity came the possibility, as in any religion, for the defensive or demonic deployment of its tenets. Such deployment became the basis for a culturally constituted "religious" behavior.

In summary, then, Paul's doctrines lent themselves to interpretations that were recurrently the basis of efforts to effect theologically what the Greeks and Romans attempted to do militarily. According to those interpretations, the abrogation of the Law marked not only the end of the Father; by eliminating God's authority on earth Paul was eliminating the Jewish people as *Verus Israel.* Several basic differences, however, separate the theological and military approaches. Strategically, the military aims at the abrogation of the Law by eliminating the people of Israel; at the theological level, the Law is to be eliminated by eliminating the Father, transforming the Torah into an old *daitake.* Furthermore, in the theological approach, oedipal *ambivalence* is a necessary element: the victim must be simultaneously loved, murdered, and substituted by the slayer. According to this model, the role of the slayer must be performed by the son. Only someone like Paul, presenting himself as a bona fide Jew, could simultaneously slay, identify with, and replace God-Father and the Law.

Maimonides noted that in its attempt to vanquish Israel, Christianity simultaneously used the military and theological options: it would massacre the Jews with one hand and offer the Gospel with the other (see 1952, 10–11). By the seventeenth century, when the military option was no longer practical and the theological method appeared a bit awkward in an age of enlightenment and skepticism, Uriel da Costa, a heretical Jew, offered a new alternative by reenacting the oedipal model. In the same fashion as Jesus of the Gospel, da Costa had a program that would "spiritually uplift" his brethren and "quicken" their ultimate salvation. Like Jesus, he, too, sought to "emancipate" his brethren from the "burden of the Law" and superstition, and to substitute "Love" for the "yoke of the Pharisees." Like Jesus, he, too, was "betrayed and martyred" by his "ingrate brethren."

Although da Costa technically was killed by his own hands, the guilt was displaced and imputed to the Jews: the responsibility was laid on the Jewish community in Amsterdam—and, indeed, on *all* those Jews who persisted in the same kind of folly. By rejecting da Costa in favor of the Law, the Jews once again murdered the son, proving to be wretched and beyond redemption.[28] Uriel da Costa, however, initiated a role that would serve as a paradigm for alienated Jews in generations to come. By attacking and subverting Jewish authority, they could now gain recognition and access to Western society; there was no need to convert. On the contrary, *ties* with Judaism are of the *essence.* In this manner, oedipal ambivalence is maintained. Without such ambivalence, the de-authorization process of murdering the Father and guilt deplacement could not be effected. The undisputed master of Jewish de-authorization and guilt displacement was Spinoza, who played da

Costa's role to the hilt. Hence his exceptional success. But this role has been followed by many in recent times as well, and perhaps Freud's "last testament," *Moses and Monotheism,* is another example.[29]

Notes

1. Dodds has also noted how the Greek gods were modeled on the image of the paterfamilias (1968, 47–48).

2. Italics in original. See also pp. 9–30.

3. Moulton and Milligan (1952, 148); cf. Arndt and Gingrich (1957, 183). Since Christian theologians assume that the Hebrew covenant was unilaterally imposed by God, the lexicographers lost this sense of "agreement" or "accord" in this term in the Septuagint. On the precise meaning of "covenant" in Hebrew thought, see my "Understanding the Covenant" (1968).

4. This is the *only* sense of this term in the Christian Scripture. See also Sperber (1984, 84–86).

5. Conversely, translators and commentators shocked by the implications of the concept *daitake*-testament were forced in many situations to interpret it as "alliance," although the context involves "inheritance," "testator," and other similar notions pertaining to "last will" rather than to "covenant." Lexicographers were unable to distinguish between the *Septuagint,* which uses it *exclusively* in the sense of "covenant," and Paul, who uses it *exclusively* in the sense of "last will."

6. On this fundamental point see the brilliant analysis by Boaz Cohen (1966, 33–35). The rabbis noted and answered this argument; see Cohen (34–35).

7. On the death of gods in general anthropology, see Frazer, *The Golden Bough* (1951). The death of the God-Father is also a fundamental doctrine of Marcion, the second-century Christian thinker. For him, the God of the Hebrew Scripture is a mere demiurge and the enemy of mankind, who died with Jesus' resurrection. For a summary of his views, see Moore (1920, 155). For a detailed discussion of his principal doctrines, see Heschel (1962, 299–306) and Jonas (163, 130–46).

8. To counter this position, the rabbis, *Midrash 'Ekha* commenting on the verse "she was like a widow" (Lam. 1:1), declared: "She was *like* a widow— but not a widow!"

9. See Faur (1968, 50–52). This argument presupposes the rabbinic doctrine that the dead are free from all obligations. This is valid, however, as long as the individual persists in a state of death—not if he came to life again. The implications of Israel's formally becoming a widow were also bewildering and not properly defined by Christian theologians and commentators. See Kasemann (1973, 176–81).

10. Those who detect in *Don Quixote* occasional references and allusions to Jewish situations may find an excellent metaphor for the unrequited love of Christianity for Israel, in 1.14.

11. Unresolved libidinal attachment to the mother is expressed in the cult of Mary, which perhaps comes to fill the vacuum left by Israel-wife. As the mother in the Western family, Mary, too, is an "intermediary" and "intercessor" with the father. This role is particularly important among southern Italian families and similar societies exhibiting the "typical Mediterranean pattern," where sons are unable to transfer their libidinal attachments from their mothers. See Anne Parsons (1969, 135–50). This is also related to the Madonna cult (Parsons, 95–96, 274–75).

12. See Bronislaw Malinowski, *Sex and Repression in Savage Society* (1953). On the famous Jones-Malinowski debate, see Parsons (1969, 3–63). For a devastating critique of Malinowski, see Spiro's *Oedipus in the Trobriands,* particularly chap. 2.

13. See *Qiddushin* 31a; *Mishne Tora, Mamrim* 6:14, and Radbaz ad loc. Although my thesis here is that the Judaic religion of the Father is more in accord with the ideal of oedipal resolution, it is likely that in either a Jewish or Christian family—or perhaps any religious family—there would be an emphasis on what Lacan calls the "law" or "Name of the Father" that would tend to mitigate the father-son hostility. However, such a context would be but one of multiple factors influencing the oedipal crisis and its outcome. There is abundant evidence that no religion alone can prevent mental illness associated with failure of the oedipal resolution.

14. This basic point was overlooked by Christian commentators who interpreted the ʿAqeda in Christological terms. See Wellisch (1954, 70–71). This applies to many modern writers as well; cf. Paul (1980, 290).

15. According to the rabbis, Terah repented. See Gen. 15:15, where God assures Abraham, "You shall come to your fathers in peace," i.e., that he shall die peacefully. Furthermore, when it comes time to find a wife for his son Isaac he tells his servant to search for one "from my family" (Gen. 24:4).

16. The blinding is a symbolic castration; Devereux (1973).

17. On the Greek concept of guilt, see Dodds, *The Greeks and the Irrational,* chap. 2. Rotenberg discusses at length the difference between sin in the Torah and oedipal guilt, and the relation of hermeneutics and interpretation to rehabilitation. Cf. Ps. 51:15; *Mishne Tora, Teshuba* 2:1.

18. Freud, in *Totem and Taboo,* writes:

> In the Christian myth the original sin was one against God the Father. If, however, Christ redeemed mankind from the burden of original sin by the sacrifice of his own life, we are driven to conclude that the sin was a murder. The law of talion, which is so deeply rooted in human feeling, lays it down that a murder can only be expiated by the sacrifice of another life: self-sacrifice points back to blood-guilt. And if this sacrifice of a life brought about atonement with God the Father, the crime to be expiated can only have been the murder of the father. [*S.E.* 13:154]

19. On the historical veracity of this tradition, see Bickerman, 1976a, 167–200. There is no thorough study on the proselytizing of Greek-speaking gentiles during that period. For some interesting remarks, see the doctoral dis-

sertation of Uriel Rapaport, *Jewish Religious Propaganda and Proselytism in the Period of the Second Commonwealth* [Heb.], submitted to the Senate of the Hebrew University, April 1965.

20. This was consistent with Greek intellectual tradition, whereby other people and cultures are described, exclusively, in terms of Greek ethnography and cultural patterns. See my book *Golden Doves with Silver Dots* (1986, 7–8). Momigliano adds: "No Hellenistic poet or philosopher quoted it, although modern scholars have sometimes deluded themselves on this subject. The first certain quotation of the Bible in a Greek philosopher is to be found in the treatise *On the Sublime* attributed to Longinus, which is usually dated in the first century A.D. (98)" (1975, 91).

21. See Martin Hengel, *Judaism and Hellenism* (1974, 1:293–94). I disagree with Hengel, who ascribes this "zeal against the law" exclusively to "Jewish reformers" and not the Greeks themselves. Unknowingly, Hengel is pursuing the old tradition of exonerating the enemies of the Jews and blaming the Jews for everything, including anti-Semitism.

22. A few questions raised by Bickerman help us evaluate the merits of that defense: "Why was the circumcision of a Hellenized Jew forbidden, but not that of a Hellenized Arab? Why did Epiphanes consider it a crime that an inhabitant of Jerusalem should serve Zeus and, at the same time, abstain from pork? After all, the pig was considered unclean by all Syrians, and they were allowed to continue holding this view" (1979, 77).

23. See Bickerman (1979, 19–20; cf. 16, 23). Cf. Dan 7:8; 1:20; 1 Mac. 1:21, 24; 2:47; 3:20; 6:34, 38, 42. This is also Maimonides' position; see his *Epistle to Yemen* (1952, 8–9).

24. When the philosophers first appeared, "the Greeks were still in a crude state of barbarism" (*The New Science of Giambattista Vico*, 1968, #38, p. 24.; #3, 125, p. 61; #21, 158, p. 66). As Dodds also argued so brilliantly in *The Greeks and the Irrational*, classical scholars have systematically stressed the rationality of the Greeks and disregarded the decisive role in Greek culture and character played by irrationality and orgiastic ecstasy.

25. One cannot dissociate this attitude from the heroic habit of abandoning the wives that they had taken from the *hostis* (see Vico, #611, 225–26). Heroic thinking, where *might is right*, is the *arche* of Greek culture and Western civilization. Vico wrote of the ways in which the strong men caused themselves to be worshiped as gods (#449, 151; cf. #437, 143–44). The heroic "man was so arrogant that, as we would say nowadays, he [would] not let a fly pass the end of his nose." A hero would avenge a personal offense, even at the cost of "the ruin of his entire nation" (#667, 252–53). The plebs, of lower status, were sworn enemies, an attitude held also by the Romans. Anyone attempting to relieve their lot with some legislation, "was accused of treason and sent to his death" (#668, 253).

Another consequence of heroic thinking was heroic enslavement of the vanquished, who "were regarded as godless men, so that along with civil liberty they lost natural liberty" (#676, 255). For the Greeks and Romans, slaves were nonpersons and had no right even to bear a name. Moreover, it was believed that "among gods as among mortals the king can do no wrong and the conquered no right" (Harrison 1922, 339). The *right of the sword,* the *merum imperium* or absolute dominion over the vanquished, underlay the right for civil and criminal administration of justice.

In Hebrew thought, however, the Law—a covenant made with God, and therefore requiring no promulgation and admitting no abrogation—established the principle that *right is might.* This idea constituted a direct challenge to heroic thinking. It is particularly keen in the Hebrew concept of *Galut* or "Exile." Although militarily vanquished, the Jewish people have regarded themselves as *an autonomous* Nation in Exile, that is, with the right to their own administration of civil and criminal law. Accordingly, national and individual rights were to be neither effaced nor affected by military might: heroic thinking is groundless and unlawful. Of course, the tendency to think *might is right* may also characterize ruling classes, and *right is might* minorities. Power, no doubt, provides a strong temptation for the enactment of oedipal hatred against a scapegoat, particularly a group that directly challenges the philosophy and ethics of the mighty.

26. On this type of defense mechanism, see Spiro (1961, 486–87).

27. In a different context Spiro writes: "In societies in which religious behavior is appropriate to, rather than disruptive of, the behavioral environment of the actors, and in which a religious world view is consistent with, rather than a distortion of, 'reality,' religion serves as a highly constituted defense mechanism" (1965, 113).

28. I have developed this subject in my book *In the Shadow of History: Iberian Jews and* Conversos *at the Dawn of Modernity* (in preparation), chaps. 6–8.

29. See the brilliant analysis by Susan A. Handelman, *The Slayers of Moses: The Emergence of Rabbinic Interpretation in Modern Literary Theory* (1982, 129–52). On this topic, there is also an excellent monograph by Marthe Robert, *From Oedipus to Moses* (1976). See also the valuable remarks of Immanuel Velikovsky, *Oedipus and Akhnaton* (1960, 196–202).

References

Arndt, W. F., and Gingrich, F. W. *A Greek-English Lexicon of the New Testament and Other Early Christian Literature.* Chicago: University of Chicago Press, 1957.

Bickerman, Elias. *Studies in Jewish and Christian History,* vol. 1. Leiden: E. J. Brill, 1976a.

———. "The Maccabean Uprising: An Interpretation." In *The Jewish Expression,* edited by Judah Goldin. New Haven: Yale University Press, 1976b.

———. *The God of the Maccabees.* Leiden: E. J. Brill, 1979.

Cohen, Boaz. *Jewish and Roman Law,* vol. 1. New York: Jewish Theological Seminary of America, 1966.

Devereux, George. "The Self-Blinding of Oidipous in Sophokles: *Oidipus Tyrannos.*" *Journal of Hellenic Studies* 93 (1973):36–49.

Dodds, E. R. *The Greeks and the Irrational.* Berkeley: University of California Press, 1968.

Faur, José. "Understanding the Covenant." *Tradition* 9 (1968):33–55.

————. *Golden Doves with Silver Dots.* Bloomington: Indiana University Press, 1986.

Fox, Robin. *The Red Lamp of Incest.* New York: E. P. Dutton, 1980.

Frazer, James George. *The Golden Bough,* part IV. 2 vols. New York: Macmillan, 1951.

Freud, Sigmund. *The Standard Edition of the Complete Psychological Works of Sigmund Freud.* Edited and translated by James Strachey. 24 vols. London: Hogarth Press, 1953–74.
Totem and Taboo (1913), vol. 13.
"The Dissolution of the Oedipus Complex" (1924), vol. 19.
Moses and Monotheism (1939), vol. 23.

Fromm, Erich. *Escape from Freedom.* New York: Avon, 1969.

————. "The Oedipus Complex and the Oedipus Myth." In *The Family: Its Function and Destiny,* edited by Ruth Nanda Ashen. New York: Harper, 1959.

Handelman, Susan A. *The Slayers of Moses: The Emergence of Rabbinic Interpretation in Modern Literary Theory.* Albany: State University of New York Press, 1982.

Harrison, Jane Ellen. *Prolegomena to the Study of Greek Religion.* New York: Cambridge University Press, 1922.

Hengel, Martin. *Judaism and Hellenism.* 2 vols. Translated by John Bowden. Philadelphia: Fortress Press, 1974.

Heschel, Abraham J. *The Prophets.* New York: Burning Bush Press, 1962.

Jonas, Hans. *The Gnostic Religion.* Boston: Beacon Press, 1963.

Jones, Ernest. "Mother-Right and the Sexual Ignorance of Savages." *International Journal of Psycho-Analysis* 6 (1925):109–30.

Kasemann, Ernst. *Handbuch zum Neuen Testament,* 8a, *An die Romer.* Tubingen: J. C. B. Mohr (Paul Siebeck), 1973.

Kaufman, Richard V. "Oedipal Object Relations and Morality." *Annual of Psychoanalysis* 11 (1982):245–56.

Maimonides. *Epistle to Yemen.* Edited by Abraham S. Halkin. New York: American Academy for Jewish Research, 1952.

Malinowski, Bronislaw. *Sex and Repression in Savage Society.* London: Routledge & Kegan Paul, 1953.

Momigliano, Arnaldo. *Alien Wisdom.* New York: Cambridge University Press, 1975.

Moore, George Foot. *History of Religions,* vol. 2. Edinburgh: T. & T. Clark, 1920.

————. *Judaism,* vol. 3. Cambridge, Mass.: Harvard University Press, 1967.

Moulton, James H., and Milligan, George. *The Vocabulary of the Greek Testament.* London: Eerdmans, 1952.

Parsons, Anne. *Belief, Magic, and Anomie.* New York: Free Press, 1969.

Paul, Robert A. "Symbolic Interpretation in Psychoanalysis and Anthropology." *Ethos* 8 (1980):286–94.

Rank, Otto. *Beyond Psychology.* New York: Dover, 1958.

Reik, Theodor. "Oedipus and the Sphinx." In *The Oedipus Paper,* edited by George H. Pollock and John Munder Ross. Madison, Conn.: International Universities Press, 1988.

Robert, Marthe. *From Oedipus to Moses.* Translated by Ralph Mannheim. Garden City: Anchor Books, 1976.

Rotenberg, Mordechai. "The 'Midrash' and Biographic Rehabilitation." *Journal for the Scientific Study of Religion* 25 (1986):41–55.

Sperber, Daniel. *A Dictionary of Greek & Latin Terms in Rabbinic Literature.* Ramat Gan: Bar-Ilan University Press, 1984.

Spiro, Melford E. "Religious Systems as Culturally Constituted Defense Mechanisms." In *Context and Meaning in Cultural Anthropology,* edited by Melford E. Spiro. New York: Free Press, 1965.

———. "Virgin Birth, Parthenogenesis and Physiological Paternity: An Essay in Cultural Interpretation." *Man* 3 (1968):242–61.

———. *Oedipus in the Trobriands.* Chicago: University of Chicago Press, 1982.

———. "An Overview and a Suggested Reorientation" In *Psychological Anthropology,* edited by Francis L. K. Hsu. Homewood, Ill.: Dorsey Press, 1961.

Velikovsky, Immanuel. *Oedipus and Akhnaton.* Garden City: Doubleday, 1960.

Vico, Giambattista. *The New Science of Giambattista Vico.* Translated by Thomas Goddard Bergin and Max Harold Fisch. Ithaca: Cornell University Press, 1968.

Wellisch, Erich. *Isaac and Oedipus.* London: Routledge & Kegan Paul, 1954.

Zeligs, Dorothy F. *Psychoanalysis and the Bible.* New York: Human Sciences Press, 1988.

Index